Dedication

To Sharon,
Christian, precious wife, mother of three,
and elementary school coach,
who lets the Lord put wind in her sails
and helps put wind in mine

Contents

Acknowledgments

Deceiving Winds has represented a treasure hunt – a look at the clash of Asian cults and Christian faith and worship in ancient Ephesus and the lessons for our time. Similar to any treasure hunt, I have received help from numerous people along the way – first from the writings of archaeologists, historians, teachers, and preachers of the Word. Further, family and spiritual family in the Lord have asked important questions, commented on the writing, and helped correct grammar and spelling.

First and foremost I am thankful to the Lord for my wife, my daughter, and my sons. Sharon, Lauren, Aaron, and Stephen have applied their own curiosity, faith, and reading of the Word to the book. My children's questions, comments, and kind counsel (e.g. "Dad, please break away from Ephesus for awhile!") have helped along the way. In addition to reading chapters and appendices, my wife also gently pulled me away from ancient history from time to time.

I am also thankful to the Lord for my sister and brother-in-law, Janet and Ron Riley. I appreciate both their navigating through a chapter in order to provide input and as well for their examples of people willing to face the spiritual storms that come in this world.

Spiritual family at the East Fifth Street Church of Christ in Katy, Texas has added another layer of critique and help. First, I am thankful for the English language and editing skills of Laura Winckler. Handing a manuscript to someone who knows English well represents a sobering moment in life; it is best to forget about the research, writing, and revision and try to pretend that someone else wrote the book. Elders and their wives, Wendell and Pat Autrey, Mac and Beth Brockman, Woodrow and Leanna Coleman, Tom and Kathy Gillson, Cecil and Joyce Hutson, Larry and Marilyn Russell, Douglas and Mary Sheppard, and Joe and AnnieJo Simmons read and commented on portions of the book. John and Fernanda Cannon, Bill and Gayle Smithson, and Cynthia Williams read and commented on the appendices about religious feminism and present-day mysticism. Additionally, I appreciate the input from a next generation of Christian women, as well as the comments by their husbands. Leslee Bond, Sheila Cain, Suzanne Gillson, Christine Gonzalez, Carrie LeBouf, Kristy Lewis, Kelly Overman, Shawna Powell, Daena Shelton, Alison Sublett, Paula Taylor, and Laura Winckler read the chapters having to do with marriage and with the church as the bride of Christ.

Other knowledgeable followers of Christ have also made important contributions to my growth in the Lord, directed me to helpful sources, and provided other counsel. Everett Ferguson, Abilene Christian University (Professor of Church History Emeritus), Neil Lightfoot, Abilene Christian University, and Edward Wharton, Sunset International Bible Institute, saw an early version of the manuscript and provided important input and challenging questions. I am also grateful for F. LaGard Smith urging an international perspective regarding neopaganism, feminism, etc. I am certain I did not always avoid a provincial American view, but I made the attempt. Additionally, I continue to appreciate the counsel of Richard Oster, Harding University Graduate School of Religion, to a generation of students to keep in sight inscriptions and coins as sources of information for studying the world of the New Testament.

Further, I am thankful to the Lord for Tom Tignor's guidance toward making the book more readable and as well the work of the staff of *21st Century Christian*. I am also thankful for the assistance of Mrs. Hope Shull and use of the Loden-Daniel Library at Freed-Hardeman University. Additionally, I am grateful for use of the Brackett Library at Harding University and the Fondren Library at Rice University.

Finally, I am thankful for the labors of those who have spent months and years excavating at the sites of ancient Ephesus and Aphrodisias. The Austrian Archaeological Institute and the Crisler Library at Ephesos continue to surface important findings about the metropolis of Roman Asia. Further, I appreciate the work of the Ancient Borderlands Research Focus Group at the Interdisciplinary Humanities Center of the University of California, Santa Barbara and specifically the contributions of Christine Thomas. Additionally, I appreciate the detective work in ancient Aphrodisias by Joyce Reynolds, Cambridge University and Charlotte Roueché, King's College London. I also appreciate Joyce Reynolds' time given to comment on occurrences and use in Asia Minor of the Greek word *kosmeteira* (female magistrate). The above individuals and institutions have helped shed light on the Roman province of Asia and its capital city – which in turn has helped students of the New Testament gain a better view of the region and of the earliest churches within its borders.

I give thanks to the Lord for relationships with people who have chosen to believe the Word and follow the Lord. They have helped me grow in the Lord. As for this book, misinterpretation of Scripture, history, and other corruption and errors remain my property. I pray this work honors the Lord.

Introduction

Twenty-first century American religious culture and that of ancient Ephesus in the time of the apostle Paul have had much in common. This book is about both where we live and also a city 2000 years removed. It is about religious beliefs and expressions that impacted Ephesian Christians' spiritual voyage that is now history. It is also about the religious voyage of people following Christ today. The book focuses on three of the apostle Paul's letters: Ephesians, 1 Timothy, and 2 Timothy. Each was written to Christians in Ephesus (and the first perhaps to the entire Roman province of Asia).

Deceiving Winds looks at Paul's letters, not chapter-by-chapter, but instead by key religious questions that had surfaced in Ephesus and Asia. However, a complete reading of the letters helps set the context of the questions. Interestingly, the same questions have surfaced in our day. For example, will following Christ lead to financial success? Is apostolic teaching from God? What does it mean to be a Christian? What should we make of sensational worship and instrumental music as part of Christian assemblies? What are the characteristics of the roles of husband and wife in a marriage? What role should women have in the worship, work, and leadership of the church? Similarly, what is the role of a church elder/pastor and who should staff the role? How can Christian adults talk to children, teens, and young adults about religious matters without frustrating them? How should Christians reach out to people of other religions and how much should they embrace their beliefs and practices? What about goddess worship and religious mysticism?

Some of the questions have carried prominence for decades (and longer) in a society filled with images and news of the feminine. Newsstands, television broadcasts, and Internet websites abound with images of female politicians, entertainers, journalists, cooks, lawyers, models, athletes, medical professionals, and police officers. More closely related to New Testament teaching, of late female religious leadership has influenced millions of people and assembled a treasury that probably exceeds a billion dollars. The news, while positive in addressing inequities in the workplace, has also placed pressure on apostolic teaching and the language of Scripture. The pressure urges us to spend a little time better understanding the setting of apostolic teaching and how it compares to today.

The Deceiving Winds of Ephesus

The winds of religion that blew in the first century Roman province of Asia had been blowing with gale force for centuries. Ephesus, the religion, trade,[1] and education center of the region, woke up each morning to a goddess image believed to have fallen from heaven (Acts 19:35). Surrounding the image was a massive marble building accented with gold. An opening in the roof allowed light to fall on and accent the complex statue covered with carvings of various creatures. The supposed goddess was perceived as a protector; the diverse symbols may have illustrated belief in her authority over both the natural and supernatural realms.

The temple to the supposed goddess Artemis (Roman Diana)[2] had no rival in the ancient world (see Illustration 1 for an example of the temple portrayed on a coin of Ephesus). Situated about two miles northeast of downtown Ephesus, the marble structure represented a powerful expression of civic pride. It was also a prominent part of the capital city's economic security. As large as a football field and adorned with famous sculptures[3] and rich, colorful mosaics, the temple was known as "the common bank of Asia."[4] The gleaming white and gold structure, as tall as a mature pine, had been built with vaults for securing large caches of coins.[5] Guarding the vaults was the role of a dedicated security force.[6] To further protect the deposits, the foundation of the temple had been carefully built with layers of stone, charcoal, fleece, and wool to absorb the shock of earthquakes.[7] Ephesus saw its financial and spiritual fortress as a place where heaven touched earth.

Tending the Artemis cult's legendary resources was the influential council of priest/bankers.[8] The priests and priestesses[9] offered sacrifices and blessings. They loaned money and likely assisted people walking in to make a payment on their loan or to pay taxes to the supposed goddess.[10] The cult leaders even managed the ancient equivalent of fishing leases around the capital city.[11]

Further, the priestly council performed important social functions. It reviewed requests for asylum from people experiencing difficult financial and social circumstances. The priests and priestesses also managed the child slaves that owners consigned or dedicated to the supposed goddess.[12] Two inscriptions from Ephesus and the city of Aphrodisias, 100 miles east, link the office of High Priestess with the title "Magistrate of Artemis Ephesia."[13] Religious leader; banker; supervisor; social worker; game warden. The priests and priestesses of Artemis fused together numerous important roles, reinforcing the power of the goddess cult.

Belief in the patron goddess was deeply rooted in centuries of stories, gifts, and family heritage and powered a far-reaching cult (see Illustration 4 for an image of the supposed goddess). Ephesians and others visited her temple even when it meant wading through low areas flooded during heavy rains.[14] They trusted her to guard them from evil spirits and illness.[15] Ancient novels and histories from the Roman period have revealed just how much Artemis, her temple, and other religions mingled into the daily thought of the city.[16] The Asian cults flexed a strength that extended far beyond the boundaries of a given public sanctuary.[17]

The visual trappings of Artemis Ephesia's magnificent temple and her cult priests and priestesses fueled the belief that her power was immense. Waves of veneration and worship to the supposed goddess spread throughout the Mediterranean world. Acts 19:27 records no idle boast.[18] The powerful cult captured the attention of trade unions as well as individuals and couples seeking a spiritual blessing. It also enticed a younger group as well. One Ephesian coin prominently featured boys playing a fortune-telling game at the temple foundation (see

Illustration 3).[19] Other evidence indicates that cult priestesses often were chosen from the young virgins of aristocratic Ephesian families.[20]

The Artemis cult's popular cohort, the Dionysus (Roman Bacchus)[21] cult, was known for its sensational religious celebrations. Weaving through the streets, holding symbols as visible and sexually charged as newsstand pornography, Dionysus worshipers were not easily ignored. The city of Ephesus knew well the feminine dominance and leadership,[22] sense of freedom, and emotional draw of the religion. It was familiar with seeing waves of women leaving the city for all-night celebrations to the god of wine.

Female worshipers of Dionysus believed that intoxication from wine and frenzied worship helped usher them into an intimate relationship with the supposed god, perhaps strengthening them for childbirth.[23] Both women and men were captivated by the religion, believing that people experienced the presence of Dionysus. Under the supposed god's influence, women even believed that they received supernatural knowledge for a time.[24] The religious group represented a powerful, broad-based example of ancient mysticism.

Similar to the religious sights of the city, the sounds of Ephesus often ushered in thoughts of religion as well. Marketplace bartering enlivened the sale of silver shrines of the goddess (Acts 19:24).[25] Applause from theaters and gymnasiums accented religious festivals. The shouts of children playing at the temple and prophecies by the young priestesses of Artemis announced to the city a next generation of faith. The famous display of prophecy may have been associated with priestesses' drinking sacred honey wine.[26] Perhaps related to honey wine (mead), the bee represented the long-standing symbol of the city. The ancient symbol was stamped on city coins dating back more than 500 years before Paul's arrival (see Illustration 2).

Additionally, the first century metropolis of Asia heard the sound of music to the patron goddess of the city and to the god of wine (and other supposed deities). Artemis was called the "Queen of Clamor;"[27] Dionysus was renown for his supposed entrance to the sound of shrill, bellowing instruments.[28] In light of the prominence the two religions enjoyed within the city, it would have been no surprise to see and hear festivals and religious rituals erupt frequently.

Ephesian and Asian evenings probably heard even more music than the daylight hours. Dionysus worship, especially prominent at night, declared itself with music from flutes, tambourines, cymbals, and frame drums (kettledrums).[29] The religion was famous for its instrumental music – laced with lots of wine. Music and wine were joined at the hip – or the vine – in celebration of the supposed mountain god. Dionysus worship rituals and celebrations fed off people's desire for sensual events, connection with the supernatural realm, and the blessing of the god. (See Appendix C for more information.)

The two religions, together with others such as the worship of the supposed goddess Isis, likely penetrated deeply into every path of life. Fathers and mothers; silversmiths; dock workers; ranchers; leather workers; cooks; fishermen; physicians; shipbuilders; merchants; city administrators; accountants; soldiers; blacksmiths; teachers; slave housekeepers; midwives; professional athletes; jailers; stonecutters; entertainers; students; wine growers.[30] The people of the capital city and metropolis looked to the Asian religions and their priests and priestesses for social and religious camaraderie, economic security, and medical counsel. As such the familiar cults influenced much of the city, province, and Mediterranean world – and served as a very capable religious wrecking crew of Christian faith. The squalls of ancient religion confronted the benevolent wind of the Gospel of Christ with force. So, it is no surprise that the city of Ephesus, along with all of Roman Asia, had the distinction of receiving the largest number of letters from the risen Lord and his apostles. The Spirit guided the writing of the letters to the seven churches of Asia, Ephesians, and 1 and 2 Timothy (and 1 Peter, along with the rest of Asia Minor).[31]

Where We Live

The ancient cults promoted thought and practices that have trickled into (or flooded) our time and place 2000 years later. Our nation

15

has experienced teaching about Jesus and worship in the name of Christ that have been sheared by the strong winds of mysticism, sensational religion, and even the idea of the "inner goddess." Spiritual events drenched with inviting sights, sounds, and stories have permeated our society.

Influential religious mediators and leaders – both real and imaginary – have made their mark on our time. Numerous Internet websites link the supposed ancient goddesses Artemis and Isis with present examples of religious renewal. Strong currents of religious feminism and equal rights continue to shape Christian understanding of the role of women in worship assemblies and church leadership. The powerful currents challenge the application of Paul's teachings regarding female submission in the family and in the church (Eph. 5:24, 1 Ti. 2:11).

Equally important, at the beginning of the twenty-first century we have begun to witness the broad distribution of gender-neutral and feminist Bible translations. Further, many people have asked what we should make of phrases such as "heavenly Father" that have described a being who is spirit. These and other similar questions have raised the suggestion by some that parts of Scripture represent no more than an outdated perspective. They have suggested that God wants us to sift and discard what is obsolete in his Word as we grow an equal rights society. Questions about male headship, submission, and God as Father have developed into a strong tension between people (see, for example, *www.cbmw.com, www.cbeinternational.org, www.gal328.org,* and *www.herchurch.org*).

Adding to the religious melting pot, an increasing number of worship groups, seminars, and university curriculums have urged people toward various forms of religious mysticism as a means to experience God and feel/see the supernatural. Wiccan and New Age Spiritualism, religious feminism, and some "emerging church" voices have begun to harmoniously blend together in their message of mysticism. Significant change has penetrated even religious groups long known for a strong commitment to Scripture and to apostolic authority. Christians today have begun to feel more acutely the deep struggles Ephesian Christians felt when they realized that following Jesus pressed so strongly against much of Asian society.

At the same time, western Turkey has grown in importance for archaeologists, feminist scholars, and students of earliest Christianity.[32] As a land of deeply-rooted goddess religion, many have explored it in order to better understand the ancient cults. The surge of goddess religion in our day has itself helped urge the well-crewed exploration. The excavations at ancient Ephesus and other ruins in western Turkey have also led to a better understanding of the people who received Paul's letters.[33] They have revealed inscriptions, coins, and architecture that tell us more about the thriving metropolis of the Roman period.

Conclusion

Owing to the cultural, financial, and historical importance of Ephesus and Roman Asia, apostolic teaching in the region has had far-reaching significance. Asia Minor was a land bridge. As the Gospel took root in the capital city, it quickly spread into one of the most important regions in the ancient world. Not surprisingly, potent spiritual dangers stalked the region. Perhaps for both reasons the Spirit's guidance through an apostle of Christ has provided counsel for some of the most challenging spiritual times and issues – both then and now.

It is the strength of the letters that they reveal far more than Asian, Greek, or Jewish religion and thought. Ultimately, they show us the eternal, immortal, invisible King (1 Ti. 1:17) and what it means to submit to his care and guidance as children of light (Eph. 5:8). In the middle of one of the greatest challenges early Christian faith faced, the apostle Paul addresses the real spiritual needs of the young Christian congregation in Ephesus.

For Christians seeking to navigate turbulent religious winds in our day, Paul's letters to Ephesus help us steer through a stormy sea as well. They show us how to unfurl our sailcloth and trim the mainsail. They help us get our bearings, adjust the jib and keep our head when the ocean swells become huge. They guide us to Jesus Christ.

Chapter One

Adopted by God and the Blessing of Hope, Wealth, and Power

(Acts 18:24-19:41; Ephesians 1:3-23; 1 Timothy 6:3-10)

The three words hope, wealth, and power captivate people. Whether a better job, hope tied to a specific stock investment, a lottery ticket, or an Internet scam, many frequently search for ways to build a stronger bank account. Indeed, the last quarter century has seen the nation buy heavily into the concept of a global economy and NAFTA. We have been sold the belief that progress and hope are bound up largely with economics.

Perhaps for that reason it is common to hear messages about Christ that attempt to weave Jesus' teachings together with the goal of financial or social strength. *The Gospel of Good Success*;[1] truth measured by a group's size or wealth; charitable giving as the key to financial success. All point to a gospel of economic power. So, what is our portrait of God when following Christ holds economic trials? Equally challenging, what happens to our faith when feelings, imagination, or family heritage becomes our source of religious strength?

The people of Ephesus faced precisely those temptations – as have many Christians today. Paul made clear that some of the Christians in Ephesus had bought into religion centered on financial profit (1 Ti. 6:3-10). The Lord knew their spiritual needs and provided help through Paul's preaching and through his letters. The same apostolic teaching continues to fill a similar need in our day.

The Gospel Spreads to Ephesus

We are introduced to Ephesus, the "metropolis of Asia,"[2] in Acts 18:24-19:41. Luke's narrative reveals a capital city interested in the Gospel and also stunned by images of genuine power. Paul describes the spiritual interest in the city as being "a wide door for effective service" (1 Cor. 16:9, NASB). However, he also sees opposition, as the later riot in the city makes clear (Acts 19:23-41). Despite the opposition, many of the Ephesians – both Jews and Gentiles – are attentive to Paul's teaching and discussion in the lecture hall of Tyrannus (Acts 19:9-10).[3] A city is also captivated by the supernatural healing acts of God. Indeed, in one of the ancient world's most famous medical centers, many burn their magic books![4] (Acts 19:19)

Many of the Ephesians had been firm believers in the power embedded in their religions – to secure their health, social standing, finances, and afterlife. The temple-bank, priestly blessings, and border stones of the supposed patron goddess's cattle and grain estates announced long-standing security. The cult spoke of power built by many generations of time, taxation, loans, gifts, and human thought and emotion. Still, the power of God that the Ephesians saw caused them to be "seized with fear, and the name of the Lord Jesus was held in high honor." (Acts 19:17, NIV)

Similarly, the stories about Dionysus told how the supposed god had been born during a lightning strike.[5] They described how his presence caused nature to erupt with milk, wine, and honey[6] or become barren at his whim.[7] The drum music of his worshipers recalled an army on the move.[8] Sensational Dionysus worship ritual expressed freedom. Even in Paul's day the religion's rituals probably were considered ancient; the rituals may have represented a corrupt, distorted look at the very beginning of humanity.

In unique ways the worship of Artemis, Dionysus, and other supposed deities breathed of ancient, long-standing power, wealth, and security. The deeply rooted religions captured the hope and imagination of many of the people of Ephesus and Roman Asia. It is therefore no surprise that Paul uses a triad of words familiar to Ephesus. While Paul talks about faith, hope, and love in his first letter to the Corinthian church, he writes to the Ephesians emphasizing hope, wealth, and power (Eph. 1:18 19). The apostle wants people to see adoption by God for the wondrous blessings it bestows. So, what did the Ephesians hear in apostolic teaching about adoption by a King and Father? What is its importance for our day?

Adopted by God and Marked With a Seal

When Paul writes to the Christians in Ephesus, he begins his teaching with a sentence composed of numerous powerful phrases. The text reads like a ship unfurling sail after sail, with each moment gaining speed. Both Paul's remarkably long sentence in Ephesians 1:3-14 and his concluding emphasis speak volumes about the work of God and the blessings to his people. In Ephesians 1:3-14 we hear a description of God's powerful and loving work. Ephesians 1:13b-14 completes the securing image begun in 1:5. Our adoption (1:5);[9] our status as chosen (1:11); our position as being "included in Christ" (1:13, NIV). Each successive phrase leads us to the climaxing statement in verses 13b-14 (NIV):

> Having believed, you were marked in him with a seal, the promised Holy Spirit, who is a deposit guaranteeing our inheritance until the redemption of those who are God's possession – to the praise of his glory.

Christians have received a "deposit" guaranteeing their inheritance: the Spirit of God. In Ephesians 1:3-14, Paul turns Ephesian religious thought upside down. He uses the economic and religious security structure that is familiar to the Ephesians, but provides a striking revision. Instead of making a deposit in the temple-bank, Paul writes that Christians have received a deposit from the true God. In contrast to striving for Artemis' attention, Christians have already received the Lord's attention and affection as adopted children.[10] We have been adopted by a heavenly Father and King who acts out of his compassion, wealth, and strength. The Ephesian Christians, together with all of God's people, are the beneficiaries of a remarkable inheritance; the guarantee is seen in the seal they have received.

Seals (tattoos, skin cuts, or brands) having to do with religion were common in Paul's day.[11] They declared ownership by a supposed deity; they also indicated that a person was under the supposed deity's protection.[12] Based on what we know of prominent religion in Ephesus, it is likely that many people walked the streets of the metropolis with the ivy-leaf symbol of Dionysus cut or seared into their skin.[13] Indeed, similar to people in our day who try to remove a tattoo, many early Christians may have tried to cover up or remove a "seal" which indicated their former allegiance.

So, is Paul using language and imagery familiar to the ancient cults to describe spiritual truth? Yes, it appears he is doing exactly that in Ephesians 1:13 and 4:30 (cf. 2 Cor. 1:22). Instead of being marked with the seal of Dionysus or another supposed deity, Paul urges the Christians in Asia to see that they have received the mark of the true God.

One important aspect of being "marked" was its character as a visible event at a specific moment in time. As G. R. Beasley-Murray, for one, suggests from Ephesians 1:13 and 2 Corinthians 1:22, being sealed with the Spirit occurs as a visible event, as a person is baptized into Christ (by means of immersion in water). "The seal is given when a man is washed, sanctified, justified, in the Name of the Lord Jesus and in the Spirit of our God, even as he is baptized to the one Body in the one Spirit."[14] The nineteenth century preacher T. W. Brents made the observation that "if we are now sealed with the Holy Spirit, as these Ephesians were, it takes place after, and is something more than hearing, believing, and receiving the Word."[15] The apostle to the Gentiles was declaring the reality of a supernatural event in our baptism (see also Titus 3:4-7).

Marcus Barth takes the point further by suggesting that Ephesians 1:3-14 and being sealed with the Spirit represents the very heart of Paul's letter. Indeed, Ephesians may represent a baptismal manual of sorts.[16] The apostle describes exactly when Christians have become the possession of God (Eph. 1:14). As such Ephesians 1:13-14 represents an echo of Matthew 28:19.

Paul is describing, not an invisible spiritual event alone, but one that is visible and dramatic – a moment similar to ancient "sealing." He is talking about people's belief in and submission to Jesus Christ that is coupled with a supernatural event; the Spirit is sealing them as they take part in Christ's death and resurrection (see Ro. 6:1-7). The apostle reminds his readers how and when they have been "sealed" by the living God – outwardly and inwardly. Our adoption by God has included our being marked with the seal of the King. Baptism into the name of the Father, Son, and Spirit makes us God's possession.[17]

Hope and Riches in the Lord

The hope Paul talks about in 1:18 becomes the hope the Ephesian Christians were called to in 4:4, a hope that is part of their unity. Rudolf Bultmann has summarized that the word "hope" in the New Testament "embraces at once the three elements of expectation of the future, trust, and the patience of waiting."[18] The Ephesian Christians are to live for the Lord in the present by holding on to their hope for the future. Paul challenges them to keep in mind "the riches of the glory of His inheritance" (Eph. 1:18, NASB).

Beyond this initial emphasis on hope, Paul gives the majority of attention to the other blessings. The word "riches" (Gk. *ploutos*) is found more times in the Ephesian letter than in any other letter Paul wrote:

Ephesians 1:7, 18; 2:7; 3:8, 16. The focus on the riches of God's grace served to announce what Paul saw to be a great need in Ephesus. The Christians in the capital city were reminded daily where the wealth of their metropolis was located. Some may even have become wealthy as a result of the capital city's commercial and religious status (1 Ti. 6:17). They had a need to look beneath the surface of the supposed goddess's seemingly vast sea of wealth and perhaps their own.

Ephesus and the religion of Artemis Ephesia embraced a wealth-bond where each supposedly strengthened the other. The Artemis cult had funded numerous public works. In turn the city was seen as the supposed goddess's temple guardian (Acts 19:35). The action of the silversmith guild (Acts 19:24-25) illustrated the strong chains securing the relationship. Both rich and poor were held in tow by the supposed goddess. However, the native religions at work in Ephesus were no mere systems of banking or social welfare. They were deceptive spiritual inventions – morally decadent and religiously destructive. At the same time as their priestly sponsors and councils proclaimed them to be sources of wealth, safety, and camaraderie – a fit ship – they were in truth a leaky hull with a broken keel.

In contrast the apostle of the Lord emphasizes that the Ephesian Christians know true wealth; they have received the grace of God. Paul says nothing to indicate that Christian identity is determined by deposits in the "common bank of Asia." He also provides no encouragement to perform public expressions of honor toward others as a means to gain status. His letters contain no counsel toward competitive consumerism. Instead, in Ephesians 3:16-17a he writes, "I pray that out of his glorious riches he may strengthen you with power through his Spirit in your inner being, so that Christ may dwell in your hearts through faith." (NIV) Christians have received wealth that is secure – that is not of this earth (1 Ti. 6:17).

Two thousand years later Christians have the same need to see spiritually. In a time and place where appreciation can get tied to the right running shoes, fashionable clothes, the latest electronics, or an automobile with panache, Paul is describing the spiritual wealth of God's grace. It is a grace that reclaims and that spiritually renews us to do good works (Eph. 2:7-10). In contrast to a faith and economic perspective that mimics the Artemis cult, Paul is urging Christians to see (spiritual) wealth that will not vanish in the howling winds of a recession, a failed business, or a stock market plunge.

The Power of God, Christ's Resurrection, and Our Spiritual Security

As the Lord's ambassador talks about God's power, he does not point to cult magic. Ephesians were ready to hear about evil spirits and powers.[19] They believed in such and believed that magic incantations (cf. Acts 19:19) summoned the protection of Artemis or other supposed deities.[20] The symbolism that covered her temple image announced her supposed sovereignty over the spirits. But the apostle was upending their view of the supernatural world. It is Christ who commands sovereignty over an evil ruler and its minions. All other powers are, in actuality, the subjects and tools of the dark lord he calls "the ruler of the kingdom of the air." (Eph. 2:2, NIV)

In place of power they believed was real, Paul called them to believe in a true blessing. He urged them to believe in God's power seen in the event that announced the Lord of Lords and freed creation from darkness. The apostle announced he was praying that the Ephesian Christians may know,

> his incomparably great power for us who believe. That power is like the working of his mighty strength, which he exerted in Christ when he raised him from the dead and seated him at his right hand in the heavenly realms, far above all rule and authority, power and dominion, and every title that can be given, not only in the present age but also in the one to come. (Eph. 1:19-21, NIV)

Further, he emphasizes that the power that raised Christ from the dead is the power that has raised Christians up with Him. (Eph. 2:6)

Paul does not write about the Christian's resurrection that is future, he writes about the spiritual one that has already happened! The Christians in Ephesus (and beyond) have been raised with the head over all creation. They too are seated at the right hand of the Father; they need not depend on the wealth or incantations of an Asian cult. If they look by faith, they will see the spiritual poverty of religion built on little more than marble, gold, deposits of coins and deceptive speech by cult priestesses.[21] Similar illusions exist today, urging people to ride out spiritual storms on nothing but driftwood. Paul calls Christians to sail at speed on an unsinkable vessel.

The apostle pens his message of the power of God as the means for followers of Jesus "to grasp how wide and long and high and deep is the love of Christ, and to know this love that surpasses knowledge – that you may be filled to the measure of all the fullness of God." (Eph. 3:18-19, NIV) This power is not at a distance; it is at work within Christians in every place and age. Surrounded by the Asian cults and language of supernatural possession, teaching about the Spirit at work in the inner being (Eph. 3:16) announced true power. But it also described a power different from any "feeling" Gentiles (and perhaps Jews) had experienced. Paul announces that God's Spirit in the inner being helps people see the love of God. It is a love announced by the cross and the empty tomb. But can people dismiss the power of Christ's love? Yes. Can they remain blind to it? Yes. The power of God does not pour into our lives – our inner being – as an overpowering trance. Gentiles (and Jews) can remain caught up in deception. And for that reason Paul prays for them. He provides exactly the counsel they need to follow the Lord. He points to the love of Christ.

Paul's message about the power of God weaves throughout the various teachings in the letter, reaching its conclusion in Ephesians 6:10-18.[22] By closely relating the power of God with the armor of God, Paul calls the attention of the Christians in Ephesus to a typical sight in the Roman world: the Roman military. Arrayed in crafted metal and leather, the Roman military's strength and discipline provided an impressive image of security. However, in Ephesians 6:12 Paul emphasizes that the struggle Christians experience is far different from what Roman Legions face. The Christian's conflict is against "the powers of this dark world and against the spiritual forces of evil in the heavenly realms." (Eph. 6:12, NIV)[23]

Perhaps no challenge is greater for people – both then and now. We, like the Ephesians, can find ourselves deceived by wealth and power in the hands of those who proclaim a religious illusion that captures broad attention. It is likely that the Artemis cult could fill a huge amphitheater during a religious festival. Similarly, we can be caught up in the belief that who/what can fill a large auditorium or treasury must hold truth. Sailing close to a rocky coast, the surface of a sea can hide danger to a ship and its crew. Paul reminds Christians of their unseen spiritual danger and urges them to "be alert and always keep on praying for all the saints." (Eph. 6:18, NIV) As the Lord taught his disciples, "I tell you, my friends, do not be afraid of those who kill the body and after that can do no more. But I will show you whom you should fear: Fear him who, after the killing of the body, has power to throw you into Hell." (Lk. 12:4-5, NIV)

The Danger of a Form of Godliness Without Power – and the Apostle's Counsel

In his second letter to Timothy, Paul summarizes for the missionary what to expect in the work ahead. People will begin to lose their focus on the unseen, replacing it with selfishness, a desire for wealth, and a longing for sensuality. They will have a form of godliness, but will deny its power (2 Ti. 3:5). Paul uses the word "godliness" frequently in his letters to Timothy (1 Ti. 2:2; 3:16; 4,7, 8; 6:3, 5, 6, 11; 2 Ti. 3:5). The word (Gk. *eusebeia*) carries with it the idea of religious conduct.[24] But following Christ demands more than ritual. The apostle warns that some Christians will take to sea, but neglect to set the sails and adjust their heading to catch the wind. They will loose sight of true spiritual power. As a result the boat will do no more than flounder dangerously on the swells.

In 1 Timothy 5:15 Paul may have been talking about Christians who had strayed back under the influence of the native Asian religions.[25] Indeed, Paul's use of the word typically translated as "busybodies" in 1 Timothy 5:13 (ESV, KJV, NASB, NIV; Gk. *periergos*) may have carried a religious as well as social sense in a city drenched in medical lore and magic arts. Luke uses the same word in Acts 19:19 to indicate "sorcery" (NIV). In a city the size of Ephesus (est. population of 200,000 in the first century),[26] people existed who believed in a supposed goddess or god and who also practiced civil living – but were blind to the true spiritual dangers. A dark lord used the religious melting pot of Ephesus to confuse spiritual reality and truth and urge people to shift their eyes away from the risen Lord. The early Christians in Ephesus and Asia faced a daunting task. They had to unravel themselves from a culture that wove together civics, religion, medical arts, relationships, financial matters, and entertainment into a single piece of cloth.

Similar to the Christians in Ephesus, we need to keep in sight our Father's power that raised his Son. Jesus' resurrection announced his deity and sovereignty – and our hope. Just as Paul's message challenged the raging confusion of Ephesus, it has met an equally desperate need in our day. Western society is battered by rapid change. However, change and danger are hardly new in the West. For example during the 1940's and 50's (and after), theologians such as Rudolf Bultmann urged believers in Christ to accept a "closed" universe. He was convinced that the ancient world-view was obsolete and that the supernatural did not penetrate our world.[27] He believed scientific observation had correctly rendered miracles as nothing more than fiction. As such Jesus' resurrection was no more than myth.[28] Given the (supposedly superior) perspective of his day, Bultmann concluded that Christian belief must change. But by change he did not mean vanish; he believed that people could believe that the cross of Jesus saved even if the resurrection did not happen![29] Time has judged his view naïve and empty; even science (courtesy of Quantum Physics) has recognized the limitations of observation. However, the danger has not passed.

More important than Rudolf Bultmann's conclusion about Jesus' resurrection is what he illustrates. We see in his notion a portrait of temptation. A dark lord desires to strip Christian faith and teaching of power and cast it adrift. Jesus, Scripture, the church, and the work of the Spirit get pressured by the social and religious culture of a given time and place. Similar to Bultmann's time and to Roman Ephesus, spiritual reality and truth are under siege in our day as well. Paul revealed to Ephesus the expression of true supernatural power and ethical and spiritual truth's "true north": the resurrection of Christ (Eph. 1:19-22). The empty tomb declared the victor in an epic spiritual war. It announced that Jesus had been given all authority over every supposed god or goddess, religious thought, ritual, incantation, hymn, or prayer – for all time and all places. Each either has honored the King or dishonored him.

Conclusion

Earliest Christian faith needed far more than mere myth, sheer numbers of believers, or family tradition to give it substance. The Asian religions, built on centuries of belief, powerful priests, captivating ritual, and financial investment, held far deeper roots in the Ephesian soil. In his letter to Christians in the capital city and beyond, Paul talks of the hope, wealth, and power found in the risen Jesus Christ. He is revealing to the Ephesians who can unite them, put wind in their sails, and guide them out of the dark, raging storm of the surrounding cults – the work of a dark lord. He is showing them a hope that will endure day after day. In the face of cold, bitter financial trials, pain from corrupted relationships, job pressures and oppression, illness and even death, the risen Lord will be with them. He has raised them to heaven and to His care. They need to trust Him, listen to His Word, and follow and obey Him as the risen King.

Our day carries similar spiritual dangers – and like needs. We too can be deceived into letting our faith and understanding lean on no more than friendship, personal experience, family beliefs, centuries of religious history, a religious group's size, or the influence of a religious leader. We are urged to trade following the risen Lord for what seems real and close at hand. A dark lord offers a narrow ship with a shallow draft.

In contrast, Paul announces the Father's power seen in his "mighty strength, which he exerted in Christ when he raised him from the dead and seated him at his right hand in the heavenly realms...." (Eph. 1:19-20, NIV) The event of the risen Christ lays at the foundation of Christianity then and now. Every mission effort by Christ's ambassadors. Every miracle. Every apostolic action to pen a letter or a Gospel. Each depends on the risen King or offers nothing more than dark deception. Even humanity's supposed crown jewels of experience are shown to be valueless next to a first century tomb stripped of death.[30] It is telling that Paul's letters to Ephesus begin with a look at the blessing of hope, wealth, and power – the power that raised Jesus and gave to him all authority.

Our setting course with sails trimmed requires that our hearts and minds take hold of the event that changed the world: the resurrection of Jesus. Singing Anna Barbauld's beautiful eighteenth century song *Again the Lord of Light and Life* provides one helpful way to focus on the event that proclaimed Jesus' identity and authority. The risen Lord stands as the sovereign ruler over every religious and spiritual thought and expression (2 Cor. 10:5). He commands that our faith stay focused on the power of God to recreate us and equip us to do good – helping others (Eph. 2:8-10).

Chapter Two

Our Glorious Father, the Eternal, Immortal, Invisible King

(Ephesians 1:15-17; 2:11-22; 1 Timothy 1:17; 6:15; John 14:9)

Few would have difficulty describing why the word "father" has lost some (or much) of its luster in our day. Beyond the issue of children who have rarely seen their father, many in our nation have felt the impact of scofflaw fathers.[1] The realities have torn the nation's sails and threatened the voyage of childhood for many children. The strength of many women has been worn down in their efforts to undo some of the emotional and economic damage in their relationships and families. Perhaps as one reaction, television advertisements in the past several years have consistently portrayed husbands and fathers as uncaring, bumbling, dull-minded, or at best unwise family leaders or members.[2]

The feminist Sue Monk Kidd passionately describes and personally illustrates much of the nation's pain. She tells how two men – complete strangers – belittled her teenage daughter's femininity – and emotionally hurt her.[3] As I read how two men laughed about Ann Kidd being "on her knees" (in a servile posture) as she worked, I wondered if the men were husbands and fathers. If they were I wondered if they loved their daughters and encouraged them (and their wives and sons as well). In the face of such cruelty and absence of love – which I have seen as well – husbands and fathers should not be mystified when the girls and women in their lives want to put distance between themselves and a dark, belittling family leader.

The social pain our nation experiences from evil assaults on gender ripples into the religious realm as well. Belittling speech influences how many speak of deity. The Scriptures are clear that both men and women are created in the image of the Creator (Gen. 1:27). Neither is superior to the other. However, many people have bound gender struggles and "God-language" together tightly (see Appendix B).[4] All of this pushes against what Paul wrote to the Ephesian and Asian churches regarding God. So, what should we make of Paul's references to a heavenly Father? Are we seeing only the residue of a patriarchal society, or something more? And how can we hear Scripture against the rumble of evil, loveless male leadership in many of the nation's families?

God, the Father Who Loves His Family

In his letter to the Ephesian church, Paul refers to God as "Father" more often than in any other letter he wrote – eight times (Eph. 1:2, 3, 17; 2:18; 3:14; 4:6; 5:20; 6:23). Beyond his use of the word in titles (e.g. God our Father), Paul describes God as a glorious Father (1:17), the Father "from whom his whole family in heaven and on earth derives its name" (3:14, NIV),[5] and "Father of all" (4:6, NIV). Further, the ambassador of Christ talks of God as having a household (2:19). God is the Father of all fathers. He is the one who has adopted even the Gentiles into his household (Eph. 2:11-22). A divine mystery has been revealed: "through the Gospel the Gentiles are heirs together with Israel, members together of one body, and sharers together in the promise in Christ Jesus." (Eph. 3:6, NIV)

Additionally, in 1 Timothy 1:17 and 6:15 Paul refers to God as King. The two texts are the only references to God as King in the apostles' letters. Paul's words sound like an echo of the word so often found in Jesus' speech, the word that announces the King's domain: kingdom (e.g. Lk. 6:20; 11:2; 13:18-21; 22:14-18).

For Christians in Ephesus, the message from the King's ambassador was understandable. Living within the shadow of a supposed goddess and her spiritual fortress, the Spirit breathed a message Ephesus could grasp and one they needed to hear. Indeed, it is interesting, on seeing the similarities between Ephesus and our day to observe Paul's emphasis on God's Fatherhood. Some in our day who hold tightly to Scripture's authority urge that Christians not dwell on God's Fatherhood; they urge that we speak without gender about the Creator.[6] Influenced by the religious feminism they seek to counsel, some miss a key apostolic message in the Ephesian letter. Paul spoke of God as the Father to a society familiar with speech about a supposed mother goddess.

The apostle to the Gentiles speaks in certain and clear language about the Father. God is Father, with every father so named after the heavenly Father.[7] But God the Father is no mere male alternative to supposed goddesses – which archaeology has shown were widespread in the ancient world.[8] Also, he is entirely unlike Zeus, the supposed rapist father of Greek stories. The Creator of the universe reveals himself as deity who has a family (Eph. 3:15). He has a divine Son and we are his loved offspring as well (Acts 17:28). The language is patriarchal; it is also a revelation that is unique in comparison to all that surrounds it. While countless peoples have invented both gods and goddesses, Paul announces him as "the God of our Lord Jesus Christ, the glorious Father...." (Eph. 1:17, NIV)

If the apostle Paul's message of the Father of Jesus Christ was unique in the Mediterranean world, so also was the portrait of God's selfless love. The New Testament rings with a message of such love. In contrast to myths saturated with evil sexual actions, God the Father reveals himself in scenes of genuine love. The Father selflessly gives his Son, even to the point of watching his Son die. The Son reveals the Father (Jn. 5:19) and the Spirit reveals the Son (Jn. 16:12-15). The New Testament paints the portrait of a God who, even in the form of his revelation, illustrates selfless love. He is the Father because he is the head of the heavenly family (Eph. 3:15), he has given his divine Son (Jn. 3:16), and he loves the Son and Spirit.

Similarly, the Father brings power and compassion together perfectly; both express his love. The Lord's blessings encompass "the heavens above, blessings of the deep that lies below, blessings of the breast and womb." (Gen. 49:25, NIV) Israel's mothers are blessings from the Creator, just as are the gifts of rain, sunshine, and stars. God the Father reveals his love through the image of a mother's care and comfort (Isaiah 46:3-4, 49:15, 66:13). He shouts as a warrior and cries out with care as a woman with child; Yahweh reveals himself in both earth-shaping power and in compassion for the blind (Isaiah 42:13-16). Jesus reveals the power, wisdom, and compassion of Father, Son and Spirit.

Another letter from Paul (to Asia Minor) carries an important message nestled in the Father's love as well. Galatians 3:28 has been trumpeted as an equal rights (egalitarian) statement. The irony is that it is not – not as Americans typically have constructed equal rights. The statement is framed by the Father's wisdom that works out our salvation (Gal. 3:26-4:7). He is our Father, and we each – whether male or female, Jew or Greek, bond or free – are his children. The emphasis is not on "rights," but on a heavenly Father's gift of grace that is given without preference to gender, race, or social standing.

Certainly, God is Spirit (Jn. 4:24), but the Creator's ultimate self-revelation through his Son announces that he reveals himself by his actions. The Creator is no earthly father, but he has revealed himself as the Father. As Paul writes to the Ephesians, "For this reason I kneel before the Father, from whom his whole family in heaven and on earth derives its name." (Eph. 3:14-15, NIV) Just as parents name their children, so also does the Father name his heavenly and earthly family. The revelation of God in his Son announces the Creator and Father's ultimate revelation to his creation. As Jesus announced, "Anyone who has seen me has seen the Father." (Jn. 14:9, NIV)

God the Father, Goddess Religion, and Spiritual Peril

Jesus' revelation of God as Father has left us with the message that there is more to patriarchy than sin and corruption. However, in our day we can be tempted to give corrupt patriarchy sway in shaping our view of the Word.[9] Additionally, we can get swept up in a strong current that suggests "God the Father" is a way of thinking the nation has left far behind. We are urged to think differently now. Prominent voices announce that God's Fatherhood is inseparable from (flawed) Rationalism and belief in a machine-like universe.[10] Some even suggest that worshiping God as Father represents a form of idolatry.[11]

In our day the sounds of social and religious freedom strive to drown out the Father's message of love and authority. Not only is God's power to reveal himself on trial, so also is his wisdom. Does deity exist who knows us perfectly, who can speak to us, and who can nurture and teach us to be all we were intended to be? The struggle is as old as Eden. However, in our time the blinding winds of Sociology have added pressure to the storm. The barometer is dropping. Much of the thought of Sociology's inventor, Frenchman Auguste Comte, has brought about both religious confusion and a strong shaping of Western society. His proposal that society progresses from religion to "rights" to the discarding of "religious truth" has penetrated deeply. The science of Sociology has shaped parenting, education, business analysis, government, organized sports, and the blazing power of visual entertainment. It has even influenced how companies and product marketing have viewed and manipulated our children.

Auguste Comte confidently announced that humanity could handle things just fine without the supposed counsel of God.[12] Typically, Sociology has embraced his conclusions. In our day the concept of self-reliance continues to carry prominence. Questioning (or ignoring) the authority of the risen Christ, his chosen ambassadors, and their writings is closing in on being commonplace. The feminist Mary Daly highlights the subject in her book *Beyond God the Father*. She observes that the Bible announces our dependence on God the Father, a dependence she suggests we need to dismiss. She proposes that it be replaced by a feminist surge of creativity and power (see also Appendix B).[13]

The modern goddess movement announces a similar message. It is a movement typically not about a specific female deity, but about mystical cosmic power and "the inner goddess." The idea is that individuals now "tap" power that ancients referred to with such names as Artemis, Isis, Quan Yin, Teteo Inan, White Buffalo Calf Woman and a host of other supposed goddesses (see Appendix D). The climaxing words of Merlin in the 2001 film *The Mists of Avalon* have expressed the powerful message to millions of movie-watchers: "I think the Goddess lives in our humanity and not anywhere else."

Honoring the Creator has been replaced by the deception of inner power that people believe they can draw from in time of personal need or to help others. Much of the captivating influence of goddess religion in our day is related to a genuine desire to help – abused women and children and an abused environment. The noble actions present a powerful draw in a society that can, at times, breed isolation. As Sue Monk Kidd writes, "To embrace Goddess is simply to discover the Divine in yourself as powerfully and vividly feminine."[14] She believes the world must recover the "Divine Feminine" in order to survive social and ecological crises.

Christians draw the wrong conclusion to deem goddess religion as little more than another religious fad or a movie experience. Books such as Sue Monk Kidd's *The Dance of the Dissident Daughter* have shown up in Internet forums as influential reading for women who identify themselves as Christians. Her writing has been especially popular within the "emerging church" movement. Sue Monk Kidd's memoir describes the spiritual decay of masculinity with clarity. However, her feminist reaction – filled with understandable deep hurt – mirrors the very decay she challenges.[15]

I felt great sadness as I read *The Dance of the Dissident Daughter*. It came from grasping the effect of dark, twisted masculinity that hurt Sue Monk Kidd and her daughter. It also surfaced as she described the mystical goddess religion she came to depend on. She says little about Jesus and his teachings. She never mentions the resurrection of Christ. Her journal reads as if God becoming human did not happen. She writes that eventually she turned from prayer to silent meditation for inner healing.[16]

Julie Clawson's essay about "spiritual awakening" charts a similar path and leaves confusion in its wake. Her equal rights approach to Christian teaching accents the solution she believes she has discovered in Scripture.[17] She is deceived into severing the ropes that tie together the life and teaching of Jesus of Nazareth, his death, the authority of the risen Christ, and the teaching of his chosen messengers – such as Paul.

Further evidence of the "divine feminine" in popular religion of late has come in the form of Sue Monk Kidd's 2002 novel *The Secret Life of Bees*. The story about an unloved teenager helped by a family of African-American women has soared to long-standing bestseller status – and become a major motion picture. The novel's portrait of kind, caring (African-American) matriarchy has captured the hearts of many. Its portrait of goddess religion may have received an equally warm welcome.[18] William Young, Wayne Jacobsen, and Brad Cummings's suggestion of God the Father in the image of an African-American woman in their 2007 novel *The Shack* has painted a portrait with similarities.

What is indeed ironic is that the goddess religion in *The Secret Life of Bees* (worship of the "Black Madonna") itself depends upon Scripture at some points. The book seems to assume some belief in Mary, the mother of Jesus. As such it also makes a (silent) statement about who Jesus is, but gives no attention to his identity as deity. Similarly, feminist Charlene Spretnak argues that Mary was in some way changed to become semi-divine by giving birth to Jesus. The Gospels become part of the basis for her belief. However, throughout *Missing Mary* and her other writings, she gives little attention to the resurrection of Christ – the event that declares his deity. Instead, she argues that Mary represents a goddess tradition that reaches back to a time before Christ.[19]

So, how do people who believe that Mary has special power ignore Christ? How can Charlene Spretnak have both a Mary with deep ancient roots before Jesus and a Mary made semi-divine because of

Jesus? The answer is she cannot. She does not seem to be aware of Hebrews 1:1-3 or Ephesians 1:18-23. Instead, she simply suggests that belief in Christ also needs a goddess. However, her writing undermines the very Gospels that tell her anything about Mary. Beyond the story of Mary and the Social Gospel of Jesus, she gives the Gospels little attention. As such *Missing Mary* represents one of the most revealing looks at Catholic mysticism and the deception of goddess religion associated with Jesus Christ. The reality is that eventually the Goddess replaces Christ; she stands alone.

The deception of religious independence shows up in another form as well. At the same time as it has announced freedom, religious feminism typically has also carried with it a lethal snare. It often misses one group of people among us: our children. For example, the feminist Mary Daly's recent book *Amazon Grace* talks at great length about women's rights, animal rights, and environmental protection. Certainly, she is correct that women, animals, and the earth have suffered as a result of evil (see Hosea 4:1-3). However, within her considerable collection of issues and rights, Mary Daly herself falls prey to spiritual blindness; almost no mention is made of children – an astonishing characteristic of the book.[20]

Our time might value the words "heavenly Father" more if we more highly valued the word "children." In an age when people often get measured by their revenue-bearing status, it is hard to argue convincingly that little children are highly esteemed beyond the love of their parents, teachers, doctors, and friends. Instead, frequently they are esteemed only insofar as they are the consumer of a product that people want to sell.

So, if children are not highly valued in our society, then the words "father" or "mother" run the risk of losing their luster as well. This may be the greater part of what causes the foundation of Christianity (and Western society as a whole) to fracture and crumble in our time. Childlike dependence is not a message most crave. The winds of freedom and independence represent a powerful cultural force. They are made more powerful in our day by memories of childhood confined to car seats and waiting in line.

Drawing Close to Our Heavenly Father

So, with all of the cultural winds blowing against us, how do we draw close to our heavenly Father? How close can we come? How do we assess spiritual truth about God the Father? The second question may seem strange, but it has a history thousands of years old. At the same time as people have thought about a supernatural being that cares for them, they have also thought about that being's power. How close can the Creator come to the creation? Julie Gold's 1985 song *From a Distance* expressed the sense that God is far removed from creation. Similarly, even some people committed to the authority of Scripture have urged of late that if the Creator is viewed as a heavenly Father, he becomes a distant figure. He is then "an absent, tyrannical sovereign father."[21]

By contrast, in our time those who have desired a "close God" have often leaned toward the idea that God is in everything; God (or goddess) is found embedded in all of nature – including humanity (see Appendix D). What the New Testament has announced is that God the Father has brought far and near together in Jesus of Nazareth. As Jesus announced, "Anyone who has seen me has seen the Father." (Jn. 14:9, NIV) Listening to Jesus' teaching and reflecting on his life as revealed in the four Gospels helps us draw close to both the Son and the Father.

Another part of the answer is found in allowing for opportunities to experience the wonder that surfaces from seeing things afresh. Similar to children sensing snow or the waves of the ocean for the first time, we need times of true "recreation" during a given week. Psalm 19:1 reminds us that the heavens declare the Creator's glory. However, in an age of motion picture myths of "warp speed" and "hyperspace," we have supposedly whittled the universe down to size a good bit. The mystique of the stars and the sheer size of what surrounds us have been compromised by illusion and special effects. Some numbers may help adjust the view. As one example, if a present-day spacecraft were to begin a trip to the nearest star, the astronauts aboard would arrive in the short space of about 165,000 years.

So, what should we make of such size? Deeper looks into the heavens have shown us the answer more clearly with each year. The creative work of the Father extends in size beyond the grasp of our minds – for a reason. It declares God's glory. Psalm 33:6 announces that he breathed the stars into existence. The flatness of the universe defies the science of Physics.

With each year people stand amazed, even stunned, by what surrounds them – and by what is inside of them. The wonders that take place as we breathe; human DNA; the amazing biochemistry of the human brain; the complexity of the human eye and sight; the marvel of human hearing; the astonishing design of muscles and ligaments; our body's defenses. All just as the Lord intended (Ps. 139:13-15). He intended that no matter how finely-tuned our instruments and our optics, we have a need for our minds to be renewed. We need to be captivated and refreshed by the wonder of his work and his Word – in the heavens above, in the earth that surrounds us, in the life of his Son, and in Scripture.

A third part of the answer to the question is wrapped up in the challenge we face in listening to God's Word. We live in the middle of a society that continues to be molded by an ever-growing pace of fast food, express commerce, and stories that wrap up in two hours or less. After years of conditioning, many find their inner "pace" meter seems to be acting erratically. Our ability to listen to the Word, especially for stretches, is hindered. Its message may not match what we were expecting at a point. So, we switch it off – too busy to reconsider. Then we switch it back on again when something catches our attention. On and off. On and off. After much conditioning we may discover that we really do not understand the God who speaks through Scripture.

We may try to compensate by attempting to more deeply "feel" our way to God. However, our young children (and even our animals) represent some of our best teachers. The only way we can know our children is by understanding their hearts – because we have listened to them, spent time with them. Our feelings about who they are or what they want can be as much the target missed as hit. Feelings serve as no guarantee of understanding or of relationships built – either with our children or with our heavenly Father.

Conclusion

Especially in our nation and our time, surrounded by injustices and wearied by the pace of work, we can be tempted to want closeness to God on our terms. Hurt associated with the word "father" can tempt people to ignore the power and wisdom of the Father's actions. A wise and powerful Creator knew that we would face the deception that twists divine revelation. He knew that dark, corrupt men would inflict great hurt upon many women – and children. He knew that selfish masculinity would take without regard and use strength without love. He knew that evil would twist the images behind the words "masculine" and "feminine" until it was hard to see the glory the Creator intended for man and woman. In all of this our Creator and Father planned for a fresh wind of glory and hope in this world – an expression of what he intended for his creation. He sent Jesus.

Jesus came to reveal the Father (Jn. 8:58; 14:9) and to reveal what the Creator intended in the creation of humanity – both male and female. Jesus was a man – and also God made human.[22] He understood fully the thoughts, feelings, needs, and hopes of both men and women. He captivated the hearts of both. The Gospels reveal that many women followed him; some even helped support him financially (Lk. 8:1-3). He listened to them and treated them with dignity and kindness. He expressed respect and gratitude for their spiritual actions (Lk. 10:38-42; 8:36-50). He helped them heal inwardly. Men dropped their work and followed him. Even fierce, hardened soldiers were stunned by his teaching and his presence.

It was the Creator's wisdom that Jesus came to be our brother as well as our Savior and Lord. He came, not to shore up corrupt masculinity or to build deceived feminism, but to break the self-destruction and the oppression inflicted by both. He came to reveal the Creator who is more than the god or goddess of our imaginations. He came to guide us through the dark siege of selfishness and deceptive religion. By looking to Jesus Christ we grow in strength, wisdom, and compassion as we look up and sing songs such as Twila Paris's *We Will Glorify*. With time we will heal to find that our Lord reigns over a wondrous Kingdom where the Creator wants us to soar on wings like eagles, run and not grow weary, walk and not faint (Is. 40:31).

Chapter Three

Guarding the Deposit: Hearing and Teaching the Lord's Word

(I Timothy 1:3-4; 4:1-16; 6:11-20; 2 Timothy 1:8-14; 2:1-2; 3:10-4:8)

Few religion topics have generated more writing and dialogue than has the subject of the character and authority of the New Testament. At stake is nothing less than Christian faith and whether or not a supernatural being has acted to influence human communication. Few would question that Rudyard Kipling wrote *The Jungle Book* or that Abraham Lincoln penned the *Gettysburg Address*. Further, Aristophanes' authorship of the ancient Greek play *The Frogs* typically is not challenged. However, both the authorship and authority of apostolic writing continue to be sources of vigorous debate. Why? Probably much has to do not with its age, but with its supernatural claims and with its role in Christian teaching.

Further, surrounded as we are by Bible translations that vary greatly from gender-neutral interpretations to careful translations, it is easy to feel spiritually confused. Not only do we face questions regarding authorship and spiritual authority, we also feel the ripple effect of significant social changes. Specifically, how should an equal rights society listen to a patriarchal message? Should it revise the message? Further, can people even hear the message in unison? Can they understand it alike? Paul's letters to Timothy suggest that the Christians in Ephesus and Asia knew some of the same spiritual challenges we have known – despite being historically closer to the teaching.

Apostolic Teaching as a "Deposit"

As we approach Paul's letters to Christians in the metropolis, what quickly surfaces is the apostle's use of terms familiar to the city and region. The ambassador of the Lord uses the words "guard," "entrust," and "deposit." He accents his teaching to Timothy with words associated with commerce, financial transactions, or things of enduring value (including family heirlooms, etc.). He uses imagery about things that maintain their worth over an extended period and that carry a related responsibility.[1] For example, Paul writes in the first letter, "Timothy, my son, I give you this instruction in keeping with the prophecies once made about you...." (1 Ti. 1:18a, NIV). When the apostle writes "I give you," he is using a word that describes the act of entrusting something to someone.

Similar to money changing hands within the Temple of Artemis, Paul writes that he has "deposited" the Lord's revelation with Christians in Ephesus. His teaching – a model of soundness or constant value (2 Ti. 1:13)[2] – carries a certain, non-volatile character. Paul uses the image to instill into Timothy the work of the Spirit and the character of apostolic teaching. In financial terms the idea of a "deposit" carries with it the important characteristics of understanding and agreement. People must collectively understand the language printed or stamped on the currency. For example, together they have to understand the words "one dollar," "one euro," "one pound," or "one peso." Second, they must agree as to the meaning and value as the money passes hands. Finally, a "deposit" requires that someone have responsibility for what has been entrusted.

As an example consider what happens in our day when someone deposits a sum of money with a bank teller. The bank accepts the deposit and confirms to the customer that the deposit will remain in trust at the bank (they collectively understand and agree as to the value). If a year later, the person returns for the deposit, imagine the clamor that will take place if the teller or bank questions the validity of the deposit. Instead, banking officials are keenly aware of their responsibility to guard the deposit. Paul is telling Timothy and Christians in Ephesus and beyond that they have no less of a responsibility. Why? Embedded in Paul's letters is the powerful message that apostolic teaching is from the Creator of the universe (2 Ti. 1:11).

Can We Lose the Deposit?

As a "deposit" Timothy was to secure apostolic teaching. But how? The missionary and the Ephesian church were to guard and use the deposit (1 Ti. 6:11-20; 2 Ti. 1:14). They were to teach others (2 Ti. 2:2) and they were to challenge those who had chosen corruption and counterfeit faith (2 Ti. 3:8).

Timothy faced a capital city familiar with the pull of religion strongly shaped by human experience and supposed divine-human relationships. The Dionysus cult emphasized strong emotion and the belief that the supposed god possessed a person – guiding and strengthening them. The experience of Asian cults had likely woven itself into the lives of some (or many) of the Ephesian Christians. How were they to sift through their memories and previous beliefs? How could they explain the powerful rituals they had experienced? What was real? Not easy questions for Ephesus. They are no easier for people today.

In the shadow of such religion Paul emphasizes that the experience of following the risen Christ begins with hearing apostolic teaching. People were to listen to the teaching of Christ's apostles and the Scriptures (2 Ti. 1:9b-11; 3:14-17). The apostle reminds the missionary to Ephesus that he heard God's herald (2 Ti. 1:11); he heard God speak through Paul's teaching. With Paul gone Timothy was to remember what he had been taught (2 Ti. 1:13; 2:8).

Additionally, Paul stressed that Timothy was to use the "deposit." His mission included devoting himself to public reading, preaching, and teaching the Word (1 Ti. 4:13; 2 Ti. 4:1-5). He was to press Paul's Spirit-guided teaching into service in order to draw a distinction between spiritual deception and what was true (1 Ti. 6:3-5). As such Timothy was to keep the teaching free from corruption; he was to prevent it from being mingled with false religion (1 Ti. 1:3, 4:1-2; 2 Ti. 2:14). He was to entrust it to reliable people who would then be qualified to teach others (2 Ti. 2:2).

Christians today have a similar responsibility. It is bound up with listening to the Lord as we read and/or hear his Scripture read. The deposit "is not something which the church's minister works out for himself or is entitled to add to; it is a divine revelation which has been committed to his care, and which it is his bounden duty to pass on unimpaired to others."[3] We are to tell others what we have read – even read it with them. As his breath the Lord has declared that his Word will accomplish his purposes (Isaiah 55:10-11). The Lord will see that his Word is preserved in some way in every age. However, it can also be lost at a given point in time or place – lost to an individual, a family, or a church.

Sometimes the loss is related to passing along the message. Let me share a family activity to help illustrate. Our household has a valued heirloom, a recipe for a huge batch of tasty cookies made of oatmeal, peanut butter, chocolate chips, and more (the heirloom is included in endnote four).[4] As my daughter and sons recently tackled the task of making a batch of the cookies for a Vacation Bible School, an interesting situation unfolded. While at the grocery to quickly purchase ingredients, my oldest son was distracted by a stocker who decided to discuss the "national peanut butter crisis" with him while he shopped. As he listened to the man, he glanced at the label and quickly purchased what he thought were three one-pound jars of peanut butter (recalling that peanut butter was packaged by the pound). Once home my daughter and sons then worked together, quickly emptied the three jars into a mixing bowl, and began to add the other ingredients.

While my daughter was stirring, she commented on how much peanut butter was in the mixing bowl as my wife passed by. My wife, moving quickly, was not ready for the message, trusted her children, and initially just listened. A little later she grabbed one of the jars, read the label, and began to laugh. It read "NET WT 28 OZ (1LB 12 OZ)."

I then joined the conversation and within the next few moments the five of us were hurting from the laughter. After adding all of the ingredients to match the extra peanut butter, we discovered we were now in possession of enough cookie dough to feed the whole VBS! As the laughter subsided, we thought for a few minutes about the chain of trust and moving quickly – normal human events. My oldest son trusted a distracted reading and what he had heard. My daughter and youngest son trusted my oldest son's purchase and did not give the jars a second thought. My wife trusted her daughter and sons – which typically is justified (in contrast to their dad's recollection; he also thought peanut butter was still packaged by the pound and probably was responsible for the whole mess!). Out of the work, laughter, and reflection, what surfaced was how much we depend on each other and trust each other in day-to-day events – especially when we are working quickly.

It is not difficult to see how the same thing happens relative to our religious beliefs and conclusions. We can hurriedly read, hear others, draw like conclusions, and lose track of the recipe – or more. No substitute exists for taking time to read at length, reflect, and pray about apostolic teaching.

Was the Deposit the Result of the Spirit's Power and Guidance?

The apostle's language also carries with it the unsettling possibility that the deposit can be snatched away. It can be stolen just as someone can steal valuables, misstate a company's books, or deceptively backdate stock options and steal from stockholders.[5] Our time specifically has seen a squall line of violated trusts in American business.[6]

The storm has become so serious that we have even witnessed legislation enacted at speed to help address the national issue.[7] The threats to economic trusts and apostolic deposits can have similar roots. They can grow from a selfish desire to gain control – of company assets or, more seriously, of spiritual revelation.

The violated financial trusts our time has experienced make an impression on us. It is likely they affect how we view spiritual trusts as well. So also does talk of "lost gospels" and "lost Scripture." Discussion about the New Testament Apocrypha (books not in the New Testament) abounds in our day. For example, why is the *Epistle of the Apostles* not in our New Testaments? The brief answer is that it was written well after the apostolic age. So why was it titled *Epistle of the Apostles*? Perhaps the title represented an attempt to gain credibility. A Christian history without false authorship would offer a much easier answer regarding who wrote what. However, we have not inherited that history (compliments of "the ruler of the kingdom of the air," Eph. 2:2, NIV). As a result the questions people now ask about the authorship of the New Testament documents certainly are valid. They are central to our determining if we really have a Spirit-guided "deposit" (e.g. Jn. 16:12-15; 1 Cor. 14:36-37; 1 Ti. 4:1) or instead nothing more than a lie. But the questions also have to be asked with regard for what apostolic teaching claims. Otherwise, our queries become twisted into deception and we become no better than a corrupt executive seeking to illegally take control of assets.

Michael White has illustrated a dominant trend in religious thinking. He suggests that the Gospels were not written by Matthew, Mark, Luke, and John; he believes all four documents flow from a time after the apostles.[8] Further, he believes that not all of the letters attributed to Paul were indeed Paul's. Regarding Ephesians, he has written,

> Ephesians is not typical of Paul's letters in form, style, or theological language. Stylistically, it is characterized by lengthy sentences that pile numerous synonyms together for ornamental effect and abstract tone in a way uncharacteristic of Paul.[9]

48

He also believes the Acts of the Apostles as history is misleading at the very least.[10] But White is not alone in his conclusion; his suggestion is far from being late-breaking news. Almost fifty years ago another student of Scripture arrived at a like conclusion. He suggested that Ephesians 3:4-5, for example, was composed of language that better fit the decades after the apostles.[11]

In contrast the assessment of the authorship of Ephesians and 1 and 2 Timothy by numerous other students of the New Testament has led to a different conclusion. Donald Guthrie suggests that Ephesians and 1 and 2 Timothy carry "connecting points" to other letters whose authorship by Paul is undisputed. As such, he suggests there is good reason to conclude that Paul indeed penned the letters.[12] Further, Guthrie, Neil Lightfoot, and John A. T. Robinson have described how the letters were included in multiple ancient lists as having been written by Paul.[13] Additionally, Thorsten Moritz has asked why folks believe that Paul wrote Galatians – based on the volume of Old Testament use – but not Ephesians. As he has shown, the Ephesian letter includes more use of the Old Testament than does Galatians.[14]

The second century Christian writers Clement of Alexandria and Polycarp provide us with further evidence. Clement's *Exhortation to the Greeks* contains numerous references to the Ephesian letter, which he calls an "apostolic precept."[15] Polycarp refers to 1 and 2 Timothy, indicating the letters to be from Paul.[16]

In addition to raising valid authorship questions, Michael White's *From Jesus to Christianity* also provides a surprising example of a crucial spiritual issue. White expresses little confidence in the New Testament's historical accuracy. However, he also announces with certainty that "the earliest followers of Jesus were all Jewish...."[17] He speaks confidently that Jesus employed ancient curse formulas in his words.[18] But how does he know? Indeed, how can he announce that Jesus was raised from the dead?[19] If mere human storytelling, then perhaps the resurrection of Jesus is but the myth of another ancient cult. White's study raises important spiritual questions. Can our investigation become spiritually corrupt? Do we ever "use" the New Testament only where it suits us? Do we have license to assess apostolic teaching without taking into account what it claims about itself? As one telling measurement, the Spirit of God is mentioned one time only in Michael White's 508-page book – a quote of Acts 1:8 (page 251).

The feminist Elisabeth Schüssler Fiorenza's *Bread Not Stone* has expressed a similar perspective – and desire to control Scripture. She has revised the meaning of "inspiration," describing it as the general action of God's people in every age. Ironically, however, she has also excluded the original actions of the apostles from her definition. As she writes, "Inspiration cannot be located in texts or books, but its process is found in the believing community and in its history as the people of God."[20] Similar to Michael White's book, *Bread Not Stone* includes little reference to or discussion about the Spirit of God.

The approach makes for an easy path to justifying religious diversity in our day.[21] However, the lack of discussion regarding the supernatural work of God should alert us that something is amiss. Even if we approach the New Testament as literature alone for a time, ultimately, we come face-to-face with the supernatural claims (e.g. 1 Cor. 14:36-38). The language of the New Testament forces a decision. Either apostolic teaching is from God or it is a corrupt fabrication. Either we have examples of the risen Lord's actions or apostolic writings are no more than diverse human reflection – resulting in nothing but darkened, hopeless fiction.

Efforts to "control" inspiration and Scripture eventually begin to look as self-serving as the actions of Gunther Bornkamm and other German theologians under Nazi rule. They announced that Jesus was Aryan, not Jewish. Similarly, the 1996 book *The Hiram Key* proposed that Jesus was a Mason. Holger Kersten suggested in *Jesus Lived in India* that Jesus of Nazareth studied and embraced ancient Hindu and Buddhist teaching. Isabel Brogan's novel *The Novice of Qumran* portrays Jesus as a young Essene, on trial at age thirteen for his radical beliefs. James Tabor's *The Jesus Dynasty* depicts Jesus as Jewish royalty, of natural parents – one being a father who was likely a Roman soldier. Carl McColman's *Embracing Jesus and the Goddess* weaves together the story of Jesus and neopaganism; the author suggests that were Jesus alive today he would be Wiccan. The play *Corpus Christi* depicts Jesus and the apostles as homosexual. All of the various images represent attempts to seize control of and manipulate the Gospel of Christ. When the goal is to control inspiration and Scripture, perilous crosswinds replace a benevolent wind from the risen Lord.

Apostolic Deposit and Gender-Neutral Translation

Related to the issue of inspiration and religious diversity, the question of Bible gender translation has also surfaced of late. Numerous voices have urged that references to God as "Father" be replaced with "parent" or even "mother" within the Bible. The goal has been to use language that is supposedly more understandable or acceptable to more people.

Perhaps one of the clearest assessments of the gender-neutral Bible issue has come from the (now deceased) Bible translator and archaeologist, Lucetta Mowry. As she writes in a 1982 article,

> A development which primarily pursues the feminists' desire for the elimination of "sexism" and other related issues would result not in a translation for the entire Church but in a "Targum," a term which refers to the synagogal practice during Jesus's day of rendering Hebrew texts into Aramaic with the freedom of adapting those texts to satisfy the wishes of a congregation.[22]

Lucetta Mowry summarizes her critique of gender-neutral translations by pointedly suggesting that "the procedure of eliminating all that is offensive to the modern mind and mores is too violent a reaction. To speak of God as Parent rather than Father diminishes the power and effectiveness of the biblical metaphor and would be an unnecessary loss."[23]

Gender-neutral translation efforts also have overlooked a key aspect of the Ephesian letter. Paul announced God as Father to a society familiar with strong messages about the "divine mother." God revealed himself as Father to a society with many similarities to our own. The use of "Father" in reference to the Creator in the Ephesian letter (Eph. 1:2, 3, 17; 2:18; 3:14; 4:6; 5:20; 6:23) provides a powerful, apostolic critique of gender-neutral interpretation in our day.

The Deposit, Our Religious Beliefs, and Christian Life and Teaching

Taking care of the apostolic deposit in our day has presented many with a culture clash. Frequently, people have created a religious melting pot that includes thoughts added by numerous others. When mingled together it becomes something that "feels" right (called "postmodernism" by some). After years of simmering, the concoction seems to work and it seems to keep the melting pot from melting down. However, as Ephesus discovered, not every religious belief or expression has represented truth; some have been saturated with spiritual deception and darkness.

Looking through a pair of economics glasses may help clarify the deception. Consider how quickly all of us become less accepting of someone else's point-of-view when that view includes the theft of our online banking account ID. Similarly, imagine making a deposit at a bank only to return a year later and be told, "Our opinion is that you did not make a deposit. We feel that you only think you did." Would any of us be content with the ethical and financial charade? Not likely. We would look for the documentation that showed the truth of our deposit. Thereafter, we would politely turn the bank officers red-faced with embarrassment and retrieve our money from the bank *post haste.*

Our need, as much as any other, is to approach Paul's Spirit-guided "deposit" just as we approach our financial deposits. But often we do not. Why? The snare we face is to think that in a pinch we can get by without religious views, or we draw a distinction between Paul's teaching and our feelings. We do not see the religious threat that mirrors the thief who hacks into and clears our online bank account. We do not think a thief can "hack into" our religious beliefs and thoughts.

They are, after all, ours; our religious treasure is safe. Not according to the Spirit of the Lord.

A dark lord threatens all of us. One of the gravest threats is to embrace a view of Scripture that allows it to be the changing thoughts of people "about God" versus being revelation "from God." Scripture, however, is no mystical writing, supposedly requiring special knowledge or experience to understand it.[24] Nor was it intended for a chosen few. Instead, it was God-breathed for all of humanity to hear and read.

Another threat has surfaced in the "emerging church" movement. What makes the threat especially acute is that it is woven together with kind biblical teaching at points. The movement has been correct to talk about the importance of relationships as we follow Christ. Justice; one-another living; kindness; reaching out to others. Much of the emphasis in "emerging church" thought echoes Christ's teaching and that of his chosen apostles.[25]

However, at least one of the movement's leaders has drawn a contra-apostolic conclusion regarding Scripture. In his *A Generous Orthodoxy* essay "Why I Am Biblical," Brian McLaren takes a look at Paul's counsel in 2 Timothy 3:16-17. As he writes,

> The Bible, he [Paul] says, is good for equipping people to do good works. It does so specifically through teaching (telling you what is true and right), rebuking (helping you see where you've gone wrong), correction (guiding you on how to get on the right track again), and training in justice (educating you in the skills of staying on the right path).[26]

While he gets at much of what Paul has written, his essay reveals that the "you" he speaks of is completely self-focused. In his understanding God did not breathe Scripture for the purpose of our using it to correct, even challenge, the religious beliefs of others. He pointedly suggests that Paul did not want Timothy to make such use of Scripture. He seems convinced that those who have opened the Scriptures to correct the beliefs of others have acted wrongly – even unkindly.[27] *A Generous Orthodoxy* as a whole maps out his conclusion. So, is he being unkind to challenge unkindness? No, he is justified; some (perhaps many) "Scripture debates" have indeed been unkind.

However, he has also misread Paul's letter. Paul is counseling Timothy to lean on Scripture as he teaches – even corrects and rebukes – others (2 Ti. 3:16-4:5). He also tells Timothy, "Preach the Word; be prepared in season and out of season; correct, rebuke and encourage – with great patience and careful instruction." (2 Ti. 4:2, NIV). *A Generous Orthodoxy* proposes an unlikely portrait of the first century. Were the earliest churches doing no more than copying Gospels and apostolic letters and passing them out to individuals for personal reflection alone? No public teaching? Given that most folks in our day have developed some sort of view of Jesus, taking the path Brian McLaren has suggested presents a remarkable question: why preach? The answer we need to firmly grasp flows through the New Testament. One of our tasks as Christians is to extend the love of Christ through kind teaching – which in some instances challenges and corrects beliefs that folks have embraced.

As an example of teaching closely related to the "emerging church" movement, Mark Love, Douglas Foster, and Randall Harris give a kind and passionate appeal that following Christ be more than book learning. In *Seeking a Lasting City* they urge that people see and participate in the story of God and his creative work and recreative work through his Son.[28] They also urge that churches read the Word and work to reverse the trend toward biblical illiteracy.[29] Indeed, following Christ is more than reading a book, at the same time as we need to hear the Word. Paul describes the importance of Christian life and example and also apostolic teaching and the Scriptures as he urges Timothy to remember both (2 Ti. 3:10-17).

Mark Love, Douglas Foster, and Randall Harris helpfully focus on the "story" aspect of the church, but also deemphasize teaching that includes propositions/beliefs.[30] However, "guarding the deposit" is also part of the church's "story." The Creator and Father wants the church to hear and tell the story of Jesus. He also wants the church to hear and tell the story of the risen Christ as he guides his apostles to teach and to discipline spiritual distortion and rebellion. Limiting the "deposit" to the words and story of Jesus of Nazareth misses the New Testament's message about the supernatural work of the risen Son. The Lord wants his church to hear apostolic teaching that includes belief/doctrine and then tell it to others. An apostolic "deposit" is made up of all of the above. Commanding Christians to cease teaching false doctrines (1 Ti. 1:3) is part of the story as well.

The story of the Christians in Ephesus reminds us of a challenge God's people face. Sometimes our efforts to be gentle or understanding of the people around us can result in our saying little (or nothing) that challenges.[31] Spiritual correction can become some of the deepest pain each of us experience; most of us prefer to not hurt someone else by challenging their religious beliefs. It is likely that Paul was helping a Christian missionary in Ephesus with exactly that challenge as he faced the Asian religions and also Jew-Gentile issues. The apostle counsels Timothy to speak with gentleness (2 Ti. 2:25), but also to speak (2 Ti. 4:2). Speaking the truth in love (Eph. 4:15) requires nothing less, and as well prayer for wisdom.

Finally, we can be tempted to resort to the phrase that seems to resolve issues when all else fails: "that is your interpretation." It has been a comfortable phrase in Western religion, a mainstay when disagreements blow in. But the phrase also represents a deception. It suggests that we cannot collectively understand the words "one dollar" on our currency. Applying an individualist view to the marketplace does not make sense; a "my interpretation" approach to currency and commerce does not long survive. All of us make the effort to achieve common ground for buying and selling. Otherwise, commerce ceases, the grocery basket becomes empty, and our stomachs begin to growl in protest. Similarly, while an apostolic deposit is certainly more than the two words "one dollar," the risen Lord describes his Word in terms of what can be mutually understood (2 Ti. 2:2).

Conclusion

Postmodernism does not "work" at the checkout counter of the superstore – and none of us practice it there. Similarly, it does not "work" in our spiritual search. It represents a dark storm hindering our spiritual voyage. A common basis for commerce has illustrated how people can think and work in unison when all must operate from the same standard. So, why do we think differently in our approach to Scripture? The answer is that we are being spiritually deceived. The experience versus understanding clash that brews in some churches illustrates the deception. Are we to live as Jesus lived? Certainly. Are we also to seek understanding? Certainly, just as did Jesus of Nazareth as he read the Scriptures and acted on what he read.

Paul reveals the value of apostolic teaching when he uses the word "deposit." He writes "To the saints in Ephesus" (Eph. 1:1, NIV) and he uses language that can be understood. We are free to examine the letters. If we decide that they are indeed supernaturally guided, we need to hear them as the counsel of the risen Christ and then teach others.

Chapter Four

Who Are We?
(Ephesians 2-4; 6:10-18; I Peter 2:9)

The large volume of spiritual ideas, movements and groups in twenty-first century America poses a challenge to understanding and embracing Christian faith. Government leaders propose a broad definition of religious truth. Powerful religious fiction such as *The Shack*, *The Secret Life of Bees*, and *The Mists of Avalon* penetrates millions of minds. A nation weary from war just wants peace – including spiritual peace. Religion saturated with phrases such as "inner spark," "divine awakening," or "inner goddess" is becoming commonplace. Christian faith mingled with Eastern religion flows from people proclaiming both Jesus Christ and the discipline of Yoga (a Hindu term for "spiritual union"). Much American and Western religion would find itself right at home in first century Ephesus.

So, how do we get a firm grasp on Christian identity and spiritual truth? Surrounded by a strong current of civil religion seeking peace, dare we suggest that not every spiritual expression is true? Equally important, in seeking some sense of progress and success, how do we run and finish a spiritual race and keep the faith (1 Ti. 4:7)? Paul's letters to the ancient capital city of Asia provide us with powerful counsel. They also let us step out of our society and then compare apostolic teaching and an ancient city to our day and our place. How are Christians distinguished from initiates in other religions? Faced with the constant threat of religious blending (syncretism), how do people keep true to the Lord?

A People in the Heavenly Realms

The apostle to the Gentiles announced that Christians have been made alive with Christ (Eph. 2:5), raised with Christ, and seated with him in the heavenly realms (Eph. 2:6).[1] The Ephesian Christians no longer required an earthly priest or priestess to mediate between them and the supernatural realm. Now they experience the blessing of one mediator, Jesus Christ (Eph. 2:6, 1 Ti. 2:5).

Gone were any other special mediators of divine blessing. Paul announced that Christians have already taken up residency in heaven. They are priests before God. They are themselves a temple of God (Eph. 2:21). Similarly, Peter wrote to the Christians in Ephesus, Asia, and beyond that they were "a chosen people, a royal priesthood, a holy nation, a people belonging to God." (1 Pet. 2:9a, NIV). They are a people who belong to a righteous deity – the Creator of all.

The apostolic teachings of both Paul and Peter have helped Christians weather the powerful religious storms of both the first century and also our day. The apostles announced that the priesthood was not limited to either male or female. Further, their letters carry no hint of the universal priesthood versus "ministry priesthood" tradition of Catholicism.[2] Nor is there any priest/high priest hierarchy among Christians such as Mormonism has constructed.[3] Instead, apostolic teaching was showing the Christians in Ephesus and beyond that all Christians had equal access to the supernatural realm through Christ. The teaching stilled the storm of spiritual deception from the Asian cults and brought a fresh wind for Jews and Gentiles alike.

Fast-forwarding to our day, perhaps no time has more needed to soak up Paul's teaching in Ephesians 2:4-10. The apostle's words speak in-depth about relationship with God and a powerful image, without allowing for a personally defined salvation. Being seated in heaven as priests represents the glorious culmination of God's grace in taking away our sins. Christians' identity as a people "made alive with Christ" (Eph. 2:5, NIV) in baptism stands at the heart of Paul's message for people then and now. Baptism into Christ is more than just symbol. As a supernatural event, it remains a message and experience needing emphasis in a postmodern world.[4] It provides an anchor for people. In the waters of baptism, we are immersed and raised up; God is sealing us by his Spirit (Eph. 1:13), washing us spiritually clean (Eph. 5:26). He is making us priests and priestesses and seating us in heaven! We are participating in the death and resurrection of Christ! (Ro. 6:1-7)

The idea of a glorious people in the heavenly realms seems to also be related to another image Paul uses. He announces that "the manifold wisdom of God" (Eph. 3:10, ESV, KJV, NASB, NIV) is revealed in the church. It is seen in the binding together of Jews and Gentiles as the people of God.

The phrase "manifold wisdom" may not initially strike the same chord in our day that it did in the first century. The word translated "manifold" (Gk. *polupoikilos*) represented the strengthened form of a Greek word that carried the meaning of "many-coloured" as well as "diverse, manifold;" the verb form also included the meaning "of the stars in heaven."[5] The strengthened word was used in hymns composed as part of cult worship, including that to the supposed goddess Isis.[6] So, was Christ's ambassador using the language of the Asian cults to describe truth? Yes, it appears he was – as he used a powerful word to describe the Father's wisdom.

"Manifold wisdom" certainly represents an accurate translation, but it also excludes part of the imagery of the Greek phrase. The phrase carries the idea of both wisdom with countless expressions and wisdom that dazzles. Similar to the radiance of a beautiful diamond, God's wisdom permeates this world with dazzling brilliance. That brilliance is seen in the church. God intends for his people to be the subject of awe and wonder – the image of wisdom that dances with light.

He intends for his people to captivate the eyes and hearts of people drowning in darkness.

A "One Another" People

Paul frequently uses "one another" or "each other" in his letter to the Ephesian church. The concept is a simple one: that of the crew of a ship. Christians are encouraged to think of others and act on their behalf. Further, the apostle's message highlights the importance of depending on others when the ocean swells get large. When the link with the civic, economic and religious security of the province – the Asian cults – gets severed, Paul encourages Christians to see the importance of facing the storms together. Clearly, some who had come to believe in Christ ultimately decided to move back in with the folks they had left – too much abrasion with the 200,000+ other people in the city (1 Ti. 5:15). Undoubtedly, some segment of the Ephesian congregation was struggling with their new faith.

So, what does Paul say to help them weather raging winds (Eph. 4:14)? The list below describes briefly his one another/each other teachings in the letter to the church at Ephesus:

Eph. 4:2   "Be patient, bearing with one another in love." (NIV)

Eph. 4:25   "let each one of you speak the truth with his neighbor, for we are members one of another." (ESV)

Eph. 4:32   "be kind and compassionate to one another" (NIV)

Eph. 4:32   "forgiving each other" (NIV)

Eph. 5:19   "speaking to one another in psalms and hymns and spiritual songs, singing and making melody with your heart to the Lord;" (NASB)

Eph. 5:21   "Submit to one another out of reverence for Christ." (NIV)

The teachings are easy to soak up, but may be more difficult to act on. We live in a society accented by competition and the encouragement to "step out" and get noticed. Competition does not necessarily head us away from "one another," but in a time that couples competition with a focus on "me" and on quick results, it happens too often.

Consider the difference between people who grow into graceful athleticism versus those who take the shortcut of bulk-building steroids. Growth into true athleticism requires hard work, patience, and typically camaraderie – to encourage on a journey that takes time. Athletes who take that path recognize the importance of "one another" far more clearly than those attempting to fast-path their way to strength and success.

A related example comes from Norman, Oklahoma. Sherri Coale, the Head Coach of the Oklahoma Sooners Women's Basketball Team, shares an image of selflessness that is filled with light (partly because she herself is a daughter of light). In her January 14, 2007 Internet weblog, she describes the contribution of Jesse Greadington, an OU student who has freely helped the Sooner women get better on the hardwood. At the same time as the team members have received the accolades, Mr. Greadington's name has not been publicly mentioned – and Sherri Coale wants others to see his role and his example. Yes, he will stand in the background, but with the knowledge that he has contributed to the team's success. And he is OK with that – and keeps coming out to practice and to help.[7]

Jesse's example (along with similar ones by many of the Sooner women) serves as a reminder of the power of "one another" in shaping who we are and what we do – from basketball to teaching Bible classes. A "one another" commitment influences friendships, marriage, parenting, mentoring, spreading the Gospel, jobs, and even highway driving. Paul's "one another" teaching does not rob us of our uniqueness. Instead, it accents our individuality as it counsels that each of us is important because of our ability to help others uniquely. Paul's letter to the Ephesians wondrously holds together the individual and the community aspects of our humanity. The apostle emphasizes what we have been recreated to do in Christ: "From him the whole body, joined and held together by every supporting ligament, grows and builds itself up in love, as each part does its work." (Eph. 4:16, NIV)

Nothing destroys faith in action faster than attempting to follow Christ in isolation from others. Long commutes and work weeks; the growing trend of less intent listening; a darkened world that builds distance between affluence and need. All serve to urge people apart. Even Christians who desire to help can find themselves growing used to brief conversations or impaired vision to those with desperate needs.

The recent writings of select feminists have illustrated the spiritual danger as well. Consider the importance of the narrative of the wife of Zebedee and her two sons James and John (Mt. 20:20-28) – and how little it has been discussed. Two landmark studies of women in early Christianity, *Her Share of the Blessings* and *Women and Christian Origins,* make no mention of the narrative and Zebedee's wife (save in one brief footnote). Why? The narrative is far from flattering. It is the record of a self-centered quest for position and Jesus' kind, patient rebuff of the woman's request and that of her sons.

When one feminist, Elisabeth Schüssler Fiorenza, faces Jesus' teaching regarding selflessness and submission, she suggests that Jesus is speaking to a specific group of people: the people in power, those in charge.[8] In trying to make her case for a feminist dismissal of submission, she overlooks the obvious. Were Zebedee's wife and sons part of the Jewish aristocracy? Is there any indication that the family of fishermen was part of Galilee's wealthy? It is at the heart of Jesus' teaching about denying self that radical feminism shows one of its vulnerabilities. Its agenda, which includes the shifting of power and position, achieves no lighthouse status. Elisabeth Schüssler Fiorenza's study fails the test of "one another" life by its focus on achieving prominence and position.

But to be clear, Jesus' critique was not just of what has shown up in feminism; he was also critiquing selfishness by men as well. The Lord revealed that the entire world was being destroyed by the self-serving desire for position (at times in the guise of service). The watershed decision of submission or position penetrated acquaintances, friendships, marriages and families in Galilee, Judea, Ephesus and beyond.

It also penetrated pocketbooks. The portrait of a game of chance on an Ephesian coin has announced that games of fortune-telling tied to ancient cults probably looked much like our modern games of chance (see Illustration 3).[9] And they probably operated with the same offer of adventure. Lotteries; betting pools; Penny Poker. Each has playfully lured and betrayed the selflessness of Christ's example and apostolic teaching about one-another. The Son of God revealed one of the greatest human adventures: learning about ourselves as we help others. In contrast gambling has illustrated people (sometimes playfully) hoping to receive more than they have put into play; it has revealed human vision pointed in the wrong direction – toward self versus others.[10]

Paul was calling people to actions that would put lives, marriages, families, and finances back on course. Such actions would reveal the best in all, the uniqueness in each. Embedded deeply in African culture is a powerful word that expresses the idea of one-another living: *ubuntu*. The idea is that of a life lived with others and that encourages. It means that we tell people we are glad they joined our worship assembly. We avoid the temptation to let their hair style and choice of clothes, their jewelry and tattoos, their crying child, or their unfamiliar Bible version act as a spiritual distraction or hindrance. Paul was showing people how to weather the rough seas of a deceptive, corrupt, and even lonely world – by all hands being on deck and working and living together (Eph. 4:15-16).

A Unified People

When compared with the American religious idea of "go to the church of your choice," Paul's message in Ephesians 4:1-16 seems strange and out of touch. It probably seemed just as strange and even exclusive to many Ephesians and Asians. Why is he writing to Christians and urging them to be unified? They believe in Christ. Right?

So, are they not then unified over what matters? The apostle's focus on unity reveals an unsettling reality. People could gather in the name of Jesus and yet not be following Christ. Even gathering in the same place did not ensure unity in the presence of the risen Lord.

The apostle writes, "Make every effort to keep the unity of the Spirit through the bond of peace. There is one body and one Spirit – just as you were called to one hope when you were called – one Lord, one faith, one baptism, one God and Father of all, who is over all and through all and in all." (Eph. 4:3-6, NIV). While we do not know all that was keeping the Ephesians from unity and peace, the letter suggests that Jews were challenging Greek/Asians' Christian status. Therefore, Paul emphasized that Jew and Greek were no longer separated in Christ, but instead were one body. The message of one hope echoed his earlier words in Ephesians 1:18.

Additionally, Paul's mention of "myths" in his letters to Timothy (1 Ti. 4:7; 2 Ti. 4:4), together with other clues, points to native Asian religions causing problems as well. It was not enough to say, "I believe in Jesus (and other deities)." Instead, belief in Jesus challenged the Asian cults. Why? The cults were the tools of a dark lord. Paul's words likely unsettled many who were used to the religious melting pot that was Ephesus. The supposed goddess Artemis alone was considered the result of much religious thought melted together. After all, the city was an urban crossroad; 200,000 people had to get along religiously. So, how could Paul expect folks to embrace the idea of one God – when the message showed a lack of acceptance of other deities and the feelings and faith of other people?

The words have challenged American religious thought in our day as well. In addition to worshiping Mary, many have suggested that Shiva, Wakan-Tanka, and Yahweh (Jehovah) are no more than different expressions of the same spiritual being/power. The idea is that Hindus, Native American spiritualists, and Christians believe much the same thing; all are in possession of spiritual illumination.[11] Not according to Paul. The apostle has announced that the Creator and Father has revealed himself through his Son; Jesus Christ is the one mediator between God and humanity (Jn. 8:58; 14:5-21; Acts 4:10-12).

Paul's reference to baptism in his list of "ones" may seem less obvious. Two baptisms? More? It is possible that in addition to Christian water baptism (Christ's versus John the Baptist's, Acts 19:1-5) the question of cult baptism was in view. Little is known of the cult baptisms, but we do know that the event was broadly understood as a purification/renewal ritual (either physical or spiritual).[12] Regardless of which baptisms were in view, Paul was calling the Christians in the province to only one.

Apostolic teaching about baptism couples a washing of rebirth with a spiritual renewal.[13] People who come to believe in Christ and submit to him are passive in the event. Baptism into Christ is an act of God, an expression of his grace (Titus 3:4-7) – without being a sacrament. It is the event where the risen Christ makes his people holy "by the washing with water through the Word." (Eph. 5:26, NIV)[14]

Paul's seven "ones" represent a religious focus that also includes powerful imagery from Ephesian city life. He notes the importance of a bond of peace (Eph. 4:3) to spiritual unity – similar to the bond of love in Colossians 3:14. When he talks about the peace bond, he is using a word that describes something as tangible as a rope securing cargo, a ligament securing muscle, or a coin binding a business transaction.[15]

As much as any city in the Mediterranean world, the city of Ephesus had a need for a token or commercial "rope" that would tie society together. As a hub of commerce and trade, the metropolis faced the constant challenge of keeping economic peace. Perhaps because of its location, the area of Ephesus (ancient Lydia) had developed what appears to have been the earliest use of coinage in history (see Illustration 2).[16] Dating back more than 500 years before Paul's visit, the coinage of Ephesus had become famous. Its fame has reached even to our day where coins from the ancient city typically command both interest and value.

A spiritual peace bond carries far more value than economic oneness. The apostle's teaching announces common belief with peace to be more than wishful thinking; by the power of God it can and does happen. Our time has seen "fundamentalists" being accused of seeking truth without regard for the feelings of folks. "Postmoderns" have been accused of building the world on feelings and relationships alone. Neither action, when true, binds with more than worn, rotted ropes. In contrast Paul reveals what withstands a dark storm: knowledge woven together with faith (Eph. 4:13) and truth braided with love (Eph. 4:15). Such a peace bond challenges a deceived tolerance. Charles Brown's popular song *A Common Love* reminds us of our goal and can lift our hearts. Singing it together better equips us to strive for oneness in Christ that is based on Jesus' teaching and that of his apostles.

A People Under Siege

At times Christians can find themselves surrounded by an illusion of spiritual peace and civility. Paul uses the imagery of a siege (Ephesians 6:10-18) to tear away the deception. He reminds us that God's people stand in the middle of conflict. In using the imagery of a siege, the apostle depicts the unyielding character of Ephesus' enemy and ours. He also announces the emotional threat that comes with a lengthy war. Under siege by a dark lord with an iron will, the apostle urges us to resist, to stand firm – counsel he emphasizes four times in Ephesians 6:11-14. As Clinton Arnold has highlighted in *Powers of Darkness*, spiritual warfare "is a defensive posture. It involves recognizing the supernatural nature of temptation and being prepared to face it."[17] Our situation is desperate at any given moment. Only by the Lord's strength does desperation change to a deep breath, calmed nerves, and renewal.

The idea of a dark siege raises a question unique to our day. What is evil? We know it when we see it in the actions of terrorists and of those who abuse and molest the powerless and the young. We can describe the selfishness of executives who illegally revise company books to siphon off profits. We feel it financially when someone lies to us as part of a purchase or breaks into our house. We hear it in the persuasion of predator lenders. Movie thrillers often depict it as an ancient, imprisoned other-worldly creature that has been freed by some unsuspecting victim. But does evil have more than an ethical, financial, or entertainment character? Can religion or spiritual expressions be evil?

Scripture announces that terrorism, cruelty, selfishness, and theft have a root spiritual issue. Evil represents our ceasing to listen to and obey the Lord. It is what shows up when we pull away from our heavenly Father and cease to hear his counsel, his Word. When we decide to let a Bible collect dust, then we are left with more than merely a literary vacuum; we sow the seeds of what will become evil. Evil has more than a social and civil definition; it is spiritual. And the siege is more than ethical. It is doctrinal as well. The truth for a Western religious melting pot is that evil teaching exists as well (cf. 1 Ti. 1:3).

We may see peace in the diversity and tolerance of a U. S. religious melting pot; the peace is an illusion. Paul's response to Ephesian religion reminds us that not every religious expression represents good. Some are evil, including some expressions in the name of Christ. The Ephesian and Asian Christians were being shown that unsettling reality. After hundreds of years of religious tradition, it was probably difficult for the Ephesians to see a religious threat for what it was – the consequence of human invention influenced by a dark spirit and ruler. Seeing the threat has been no less difficult 2000 years later.

The Lord's "armor" (Is. 59:16-17) to defend against "the devil's schemes" (Eph. 6:11, NIV) reveals what many people cannot fathom; our emotions and thought can be twisted! Just as the Ephesians had been lured into inventing goddesses and gods, so also our view of God and/or religious truth can become an invention, a feat of imagination. But what the apostle announces is that the "God and Father of our Lord Jesus Christ" (Eph. 1:3, NIV) is not a human invention. He is not a system of philosophy or sociology. We do not "get to him" by cleverly invented group rituals, mind-altering drugs, prevailing social custom, university degree paths, or UNIX® terminals and computer commands. Nor do we know him by merely feeling like we do. That was the trap of the Artemis and Dionysus cults (among others); the trap has not gone away. Instead, God calls us to embrace and speak his truth in love (Eph. 4:15).

The Lord urges us to persevere similar to soldiers, athletes, and farmers when they face suffering and hardship (2 Ti. 2:1-6). Our spiritual decision to resist and challenge the efforts of a dark lord will meet a grueling test, much like a runner's in preparing for the ancient *Ephesea* contest.[18] Efforts to prepare for a marathon will pale in comparison. This race is for spiritual life; it is run against a bitter wind from dark lords bent on our destruction. It can pressure us with a spiritual weight similar to the race by a black Olympian in the 1936 Olympics. Are we spiritually blind, mirroring an angry German Chancellor who storms out of a stadium, or do we see with the clarity of selfless love – the response of the German athlete Lutz Long, who embraces Jesse Owens and congratulates him?

In the face of spiritual struggle, the words of Jamie Owens-Collins's song *The Battle Belongs to the Lord* provide a powerful call to seeing reality and hope. We can become deceived by marketing efforts that condense Paul's teaching down to a cell phone ring tone or a method to overcome drug addiction.[19] The song reminds us of the broader character of the siege. The Persian army at Thermopylae boasted that their rain of arrows would blot out the sun.[20] Our spiritual enemy is far more dangerous than the one faced by 300 Spartans. However, this spiritual siege is one the Lord can and does win; we are part of the victory as we obey him and depend on him.

Conclusion

The metropolis of Asia and Paul's letters to the city provide us with a unique window into the ancient world – and our world. We are shown a portrait of God's people living and worshiping in a dangerous setting. The people of Ephesus had developed a strong civil practice of building devotion by way of mingled faiths. Artemis Ephesia, for example, was a "composite image." Her statue captured in crafted stone many generations of Ephesian magic lore, stories, and belief in other deities (such as Cybele).[21] The layers of stories represented self-fulfilling human actions. They allowed Artemis to get folded together with common feelings and thoughts so that the supposed goddess would become familiar to more people.[22]

The apostle's letters suggest that some (or many) of the Christians in Ephesus and Asia are acting similarly. A dark lord is urging them to knead together various beliefs and practices, all the while thinking the results will be legitimately Christian. Let belief in Jesus grow... as it blends together with other religious expressions. Think of "Christian" as comfortable, familiar. Knead red clay with black and eventually the two are inseparable.

Paul's teaching challenges the practice – and allows it no room to "familiarize" Christian faith. He describes a unity (Eph. 4:1-16) distanced from the instruments of a dark lord. Unity is not red and black clay mixed. Nor should the word "Christian" be defined by a dark lord. We can almost hear echoes of the Ephesians' amazement: "Becoming part of the new religion is different from the civil religions of the city?! Our worship cannot be similar to what we have left? What we are used to?"

A similar desire – and deception – ripples through our time. Easy-access information has influenced us. Often we desire that religion be briefly stated, easy to practice, and something that fits well with our present view of things. In the middle of longing for spiritual comfort and rest, we face a difficult challenge. Are we willing to sift through the religious thought and practices around us? Are we willing to follow Jesus even if it brings spiritual shock? What if it means a departure from the beliefs and practices of family or friends?

Paul's letters to Ephesus and Asia help clear our vision about so many different religions and churches. A spiritual siege can blind us regarding our use of language. Certainly, the Lord has a clear view of his people. But what about our view? Many groups wearing the name "church" dot the landscape of our cities and countryside. We are deceived if we believe language frees us from a spiritual siege. A people gathered in the name of Christ can die spiritually. Some of the first-century churches in Asia Minor were facing that very threat (Rev. 2-3).

Just as the word "church" does not protect us from deception, neither does the word "institution" necessarily hinder. Every religious group has a boundary; it is established both by the geography of people gathered and as well by beliefs and practices. Frequently, our struggle about churches as "institutions" represents the wrong focus of our attention, teaching, and prayer. We need to focus on a spiritual siege. Paul reminded church elders that some people would choose darkness (Acts 20:29-30).

Paul's Ephesian letter breathes strong messages about identity even as it alerts us to the spiritual struggles in every place and age. God's Word reveals that the Creator is renewing the world through his Son. He has made his people a holy priesthood by sealing them with the Spirit (Eph. 1:13). He desires for them to be a one-another people, a unified people. But they are also a people caught in a threatening siege. In a world with temptation just moments away, Christians are encouraged to live as children of light.

Chapter Five

Living as Children of Light

(*Ephesians* 4:17—6:9)

No teaching in Paul's letters to Ephesus carries more practical application to building relationships with others than the apostle's words in Ephesians 4:17-6:9. The apostle's teaching speaks volumes about the choices that make or break a friendship, family, city, or nation: truth versus lies; kindness and compassion versus emotions out of control; moral purity versus corruption; sensitivity versus full-tilt sensuality; self-sacrifice versus selfishness. The either-or alternatives people face illustrate the stark difference between living as children of light (Eph. 5:8) or living in darkness (Eph. 4:18). Paul's use of dramatic contrasts allows no negotiating room regarding Christian conduct; he is not talking in shades of gray. So, what was pressuring Christians in Ephesus? What is the importance in our day? What applications should we make from Paul's teaching?

The Dangers of a Darkened City

Paul's words in Ephesians 4:17-6:9 reveal a unity to them that suggests his various teachings are in some way connected. The apostle's uses of "therefore" or "on account of this" in Ephesians 4:25 and 5:1,

7, and 17 link his teachings. Further, Carroll Osburn has provided an important observation regarding the structure of Paul's letter:

> Actually 5:21 governs the entire context of 5:22-6:9, which is related to 5:15-21. Paul restates (see 4:1, 17-24) his appeal for Christian ethic in vv. 15-17 with a call to "take care how you walk." By way of example, he says in v. 18, "*do not be drunk with wine*," but "*be filled with the spirit.*" Five Greek participles follow, each specifying how Christian readers can avoid irresponsible living and be "spirit-filled" people. Three participles occur in v. 19: "*speaking to one another in psalms, hymns, and spiritual songs*," "*singing*," and "*making melody [in] your hearts to the Lord.*" The fourth occurs in v. 20, "*giving thanks always.*" And the fifth is "*being subject to (submissive to / deferential to) one another*" (v. 21).[1]

He has carefully summarized how Paul has sewn together his writing in Ephesians 5:15-6:9. Additionally, Paul provides other messages that tie together Ephesians 4:17-5:21 and suggest a common issue. The apostle's uses of "impure" or "impurity" in Ephesians 4:19 and 5:3, 5 capture the image of a common moral and spiritual storm.

Finally, Paul describes the alternatives of evil conduct and speech or thanksgiving to God in both Ephesians 5:4 and 5:18-20. In Ephesians 5:4 he urges Christians to give thanks as opposed to allowing themselves to be caught in the web of "obscenity, foolish talk, and coarse joking." (NIV) In 5:18-20 he counsels them to always give thanks (and sing) as opposed to getting drunk on wine, "which leads to debauchery." (Eph. 5:18, NIV) The parallel between the two statements suggests a common issue that the Christians in Asia are facing – different waves breaking over the bow, but the same dark storm.

The apostle never names the source of the influence corrupting the Ephesian Christians. He says only that the Ephesians should "no longer live as the Gentiles do, in the futility of their thinking" (Eph. 4:18, NIV). He describes the conduct with general statements/words such as "impurity" (Eph. 4:19, 5:3, NIV) or "debauchery" (Eph. 5:18, NIV), and indicates that the Gentiles have lost all sensitivity and given themselves over to sensuality (Eph. 4:19). He does not identify pressure from one (or more) of the Asian cults on churches in the city and/or province. Instead, he mentions only the general issue of the Christians' former way of life (Eph. 4:22).

The text does, however, provide some clues as to what may have been taking place. For example, 186 years ago James MacKnight suggested that Paul wrote Ephesians 5:18-20 in response to Dionysus cult-like practices among the city's Christians.[2] His conclusion has been echoed by numerous other students of the apostolic letter.[3] The conclusion is based on the alternatives Paul mentions in connection with worship and music. Indeed, the context of the apostle's words in 5:19-20 has carried a strong message even among those not convinced of cult influence in the Ephesian church.[4] Given the prominent place of religion in Ephesus, influence from the Asian cults in the congregation of new Christians would have been no surprise.

Additionally, Cleon Rogers has observed, "It seems significant that the things Paul wrote about in Ephesians 5:19-33 have to do with some matters which played a vital part in Dionysiac worship."[5] Women's studies of late have described how the Dionysus faith shaped both ancient religion and also, to some degree, ancient marriages. Asian society's respect for the powerful cult allowed women to meet and seclude themselves for wine and music-filled gatherings as they wished. Further, it appears the cult served as an influential social club for women; women and girls made up a majority of the cult.[6] So, while some English translations include a break in subject matter between Ephesians 5:18-21 and 5:22, we should recognize no such break in what Paul is writing. It is likely he is addressing selfishness influenced by Asian religion.

Another statement by Paul may reference the Dionysus religion's influence. Paul's "obscenity, foolish talk, or coarse joking" (Eph. 5:4, NIV) and his use of "shameful" in Ephesians 5:12 closely parallel an ancient comment about Dionysus worship. During the popular *Thesmophoria* and *Haloa* festivals to Dionysus (and Cybele, or Kybele), women shouted rude and shameful things to each other.[7] Further, excesses of wine during the festivals were well known in the ancient world.[8]

As additional evidence, history records that initiates in the Dionysus cult were "marked" – "as if stamped for life with a divine seal."[9] Michael Weed has observed that sealing was "familiar to Paul's Gentile hearers who had participated in pagan religious rites in which emblems and tattoos were cut on the body as a "seal" of a divinity's ownership."[10] Indeed, the word Paul used for "sealed" in Ephesians 1:13 and 4:30 (Gk. *sphragizein*) was prominently associated with the Dionysus cult.[11] So, was the apostle being guided by the Spirit to use the familiar cult concept of being "sealed" to help people understand the true God's action on their behalf? Yes, it appears that is exactly what is taking place.

Further, the second century Christian writer Clement of Alexandria reveals that Dionysus worship is associated with the very sensuality Paul mentions in Ephesians 4:19. Clement even uses the same Greek word to describe cult conduct.[12] The spiritual darkness Paul mentions may also represent a subtle reference to the nighttime activities of the cult.[13]

Recent archaeological finds have helped confirm that the worship of the god of wine was prominent in the ancient city (see Appendix C).[14] Evidence indicates that the Dionysus cult exerted a strong influence in Ephesus and throughout the province of Asia. Indeed, religion played a major role in ancient society. So while we cannot know 2000 years later which Asian cults were influencing the early Christians in the region (and beyond), multiple apostolic statements tell us enough (e.g. 1 Pt. 4:1-11). Dark ancient religion indeed brought pressure on early Christianity. Given the issue of drunkenness and the remedy of being filled with the Spirit (instead of with the god of wine?), the matter of shameful speech, and the "sealing" Paul describes, it seems likely that the apostle is addressing deceptive crosswinds from the native Asian religions in his letter to Ephesus.

If this is correct, then we should see Ephesians 4:17-6:9 as having a common theme of the Gospel versus Asian cult belief, thought, and ritual (e.g. 1 Ti. 4:7; 2 Ti. 4:4-5).[15] The apostle's counsel in response to immorality, obscenity, shameful activities, and issues with Christian worship and Christian family life then represent a common response – layer upon layer. Paul is helping early Christians navigate out of a dark storm at sea to discover a bright morning and fair winds. Given the power of the Asian cults, it would have been little surprise to discover that some (or many) of the Christians in Ephesus and Asia were shaping their worship assemblies and feasts and their households into Dionysus-Christ, Artemis-Christ, or other blended religions. But does the apostle's response to a first century issue speak to our day?

The Storm of a Darkened City Blows into Our Day

Looking back 2000 years and earlier to the practices of the Dionysus religion reveals unsettling similarities with our day. For example, our time has been drenched with the same symbolism, the same "obscenity, foolish talk or coarse joking" (Eph. 5:4, NIV) that permeated ancient religion and society. Perhaps surprisingly a specific sexual curse found in our public schools, sporting events, and on our urban highways was also part of a dark storm in the Mediterranean world. Indeed, the sexual symbolism appears to have been closely associated with the Dionysus cult.[16]

From a worldwide perspective, Dionysiac thought continues to show up in numerous places. For example, rock music concerts have used some of the symbolism associated specifically with the Dionysus cult.[17] The growing phenomenon of pole dancing represents a close relative. Similar symbolism has even featured prominently in a 2007 New York City art exhibit – and received a title associating the artwork with the ancient religion.[18] The British Isles remain littered with images associated with the cult.[19] Present-day Indian religious festivals mimic Dionysus religion.[20] Further, ecology's current interest in the mystical

Green Man of Celtic myth hearkens back to imagery in the ancient religion,[21] as does a recent best-selling novel.[22]

In addition to cult symbolism, the sound of music that historically has been associated with Dionysus religion has also found its way into our day. The southern version of hip-hop, called "krunk" (or crunk), is closely linked with the sound of Dionysiac music and ritual – even using a common ancient cult term to describe the music. "Krunk" itself represents a word invented from a combination of "crazy" and "drunk." Krunk is made with high-pitched sounds and deep bass rhythms, similar to the music of Dionysiac ritual. The film *ATL* included what *The Tufts Daily* called "woofer-shattering crunk bass, the bacchanalian, the party-all-the-time mentality and the sharp-tongued shout-outs...."[23] It should come as little surprise that music fans have used the term "bacchanalian" to refer to the crazy-and-drunk character of crunk music. "Bacchus" was the Roman name of Dionysus.

The spirit of Dionysiac music is not, however, limited to Krunk. Rock music promoters Lee and Aime Joseph steer people in the same direction with their *Dionysus* and *Bacchus* music labels. Their *Dionysus Records* website proclaims Dionysus as the god of "Wine, Women, & Wild Behavior" as it announces that the company has been offering "an orgy for your ears for over twenty years!"[24] Similarly, the vocal group *ABBA's* famous song *Dancing Queen* carries images often associated with sensual eastern dance – the offspring of Dionysiac ritual. While seemingly an instance of seeking poetic lyrics, the song's references to tambourines and leaving men "burning" have nudged it close to a powerful ancestor.

January 2008 Internet searches on "cult of Dionysus" and "modern Bacchanalia" found over 800,000 sites/references. The subset of websites represents a diverse collection: Internet forums/groups; an article in *Americana* magazine about the infamous Daytona Beach Bike Week; erotic art collections; studies of Hinduism's Shiva-Dionysus connection; a *Modern Drunkard* magazine editorial about present-day Dionysus cults; information about a gothic band called "Cult of Dionysus."

Additionally, the website collection contains numerous references to the pandemic of intoxication and dishonorable sexual thought and speech on college and university campuses. Linked with "bacchanalian" drinking activity is a promenade of sexual innuendoes – similar to the connections made in the ancient world during worship to the "party god."[25] Coded phrases such as "sausage parties" fill high schools and university and college campuses, as well as websites proclaiming dark campus humor.[26]

The language and symbolism walks too close to ancient Dionysiac religion; it is no coincidence. Satan has had a hand in both. The language gives no honor to man or woman as the Lord's creation – a physical, social, sexual, moral, and spiritual being. It distances itself from the Lord's counsel that people use careful, respectful language to talk about human privacy and intimacy. In short, any notion that our time is far removed from Dionysus religion, thought, and sound needs revision. Few would announce that the god of wine is real. However, much of the mindset, music, speech, and sexual symbolism of the ancient religion whirl through our day with the power it also carried in the first century.

Light in the Lord

In counseling Christians, the Spirit through Paul urges the Lord's people then and now to replace futility and loss of sensitivity with truthful speech (Eph. 4:25) and diligent work (4:28). Their speech needs to be encouraging (4:29), not filled with anger and rage (4:31). They must leave behind even the hint of sexual immorality, greed (5:3), and obscenity (5:4). Instead, they are to become children of light (5:8). Their worship is to carry the sound of spiritual sensitivity and a focus on others (5:18-21).

Paul's encouragement to avoid obscenity and even the hint of sexual immorality is the morning sun burning away a fog that hinders hearts and minds. The Spirit through Paul urges a sensitivity that gives back to human intimacy a sense of mystery. Our lives need mystery untouched by romance novels, pornography and fantasy. Where obscenity, pornography and coarse humor commonize, the Lord guides his creation to guard sexuality. He wants it to be a cool, reviving wind versus stifling equatorial air that gives little relief. Christians are called to light in the matter of our most powerful sensations and drives. The apostle urges us toward honor, selflessness, and obedience to the Lord in the most intimate moments.

Some religious leaders have suggested that part of Paul's teaching in Ephesians 4:17-6:9 has no relevance today (specifically 5:22-33). They have argued that the apostle was speaking to a different society.[27] Others suggest that Paul's words in Ephesians 5:22-6:9 represent nothing more than an effort to pattern the Ephesian relationships after an ancient "household code."[28] A further line of reasoning has proposed that God's ambassador to the Gentiles was applying the only thing he knew – patriarchy – to Christian marriage. The idea is that Paul was limited by what he had grown up with, what he had learned.[29] The suggestions are spiritually nearsighted.

The proposal of irrelevance does not fit the evidence regarding Ephesus and its cults – and the shadows in our day. The worship of the god of wine (and also the Artemis and Cybele cults) emphasized deep emotions, religious experience and eroticism – the very marks of much modern thinking. Most importantly Paul reveals that the ancient cults have the same source as the religious and social deceptions common in our day: "the ruler of the kingdom of the air" (Eph. 2:2, NIV).

Further, the proposal that Paul is "caught" in his time and culture does not fit Ephesians 5:21. Numerous inscriptions in the ancient city have described the frequent efforts of Ephesians to achieve prominence; they sought such even at the expense of the position of others – similar to efforts in our day.[30] The apostle's teaching runs counter to much of Ephesian society. Attempting to confine Paul's teaching regarding male-female relations or other family relations to the society of the day makes no sense of Ephesians 5:21-33; it sidesteps the issue of the spiritual battle going on in Ephesus and Asia. It also avoids the question of the Spirit's power in the heat of the battle – to guide Paul beyond his own religious, philosophical, and emotional limitations.

Feminist scholars have demonstrated with clarity that the ancient Dionysus religion represented a powerful expression of women's religious freedom and influence in the ancient world. The cult had even urged marriages in the direction of an equal rights society. Husbands may have welcomed such, seeing as they expected to get back a more exciting partner after a wives' night out. We should not underestimate the degree to which the cult had influenced marriage in the first century. It challenged Christlike submission. Both men and women probably had been lured to see in the Dionysus cult something of a win-win situation. However, the religion was not building selfless love in marriage. It was destroying such even as it embraced and fed on deceptive short-term bursts of sensuality and sensational ritual.

In response, the apostle to the Gentiles saw clearly the evil in the city and challenged the influence of a dark lord. He was not attempting to mold Christian faith to Ephesian culture, Roman culture, Jewish culture, or any other culture – even an equal rights culture. Ephesians 5:21 turned much of ancient culture on its head. It has had the same message for a present day equal rights America; it has urged Christians to give up their "rights" and live as light in the Lord.

Conclusion

Ephesians 4:17-6:9 announces that the apostle sees evil and darkness in the practices of Gentile living and worship; he is urging God's people then and now to navigate out of dangerous winds. Ray Bradbury attempts to illustrate a similar situation as *Cooger and Dark's Pandemonium Shadow Show* slips into Green Town in *Something Wicked This Way Comes*. The carnival comes at night, lures, and invites. Cooger and Mr. Dark carefully separate out individuals, urge people to brood on their desires, and deceive. The dark duo offer fantasies realized, but give only loneliness, fear and destruction. They provide nothing that builds lasting encouragement, wonder, oneness, and peace.

By contrast, in the Ephesian letter the Spirit works through Paul to guide Christians out of Satan's storm – both then and now. It is likely that the father of lies was presenting enticing alternatives to faith in and worship of the Lord. Christians today have been drenched by the same breaking waves, the same spiritual struggles. The issue of evil has left no academic, religious tradition, or social wiggle room as people have searched the Scriptures in our time. Either Paul was being supernaturally guided in a spiritual war or he was no more than another deceived peddler of religion (2 Cor. 2:17). No more than another cult priest.

For the apostle Christian ethics, worship, marriage, family, and labor relations are under spiritual siege. We live and move in a spiritual reality that is far from peaceful. David Kinnaman and Gabe Lyons's book *UnChristian* shouts that the nation is caught in a spiritual siege.[31] Some desire spiritual darkness. Others are filled with a deep fear and even a sense of hopelessness. It is the irony of darkness that Christians are judged to be judgmental. Equally damaging, some claiming to follow Jesus have decided (perhaps secretly) to give up light – and have done harm to the word "Christian." Followers of Jesus picketing with the word "hate" does not help; ironically, some political activism has given substance to the word "unchristian." While the grace of God stands close to all of us, so also does a dark lord. To this end the apostle to the Gentiles urges Christians to live as "children of light" (Eph. 5:8, NIV).

Chapter Six

Speaking in Song to One Another and to the Lord - Part 1

(Ephesians 5:18-21)

Reading Ephesians 5:18-21 in our day typically has carried with it challenges. First, the teaching seems brief. Second, it sounds like no more than an *ad hoc* teaching, even a cryptic one to some people. It seems thoroughly different from the previous verses. Perhaps for that reason some have looked at Ephesians 5:18-21 by itself, separate from the text around it. Further, drenched as our age and society is with instrumental and digital music, a question about appropriate Christian music may seem absurd to some (or many). What is Paul saying about music and worship? Is the apostle talking about instrumental versus vocal music? Is instrumentation an issue? Did the question even surface in the ancient world? What application, if any, does the teaching have to our day?

What was Prompting Paul to Write Ephesians 5:18-21?

As the previous chapter describes, Paul's teaching in Ephesians 5:18-21 stands at the climax of a longer teaching that ranges from ethics to worship (Eph. 4:17-5:21). It appears that the Ephesian church is stepping into the jaws of powerful, seductive religious blending within their moral conduct, relations with each other, and in their musical worship to Christ. We risk drawing the wrong conclusion if we measure Paul's teaching in Ephesians 5:18-21 by the fact that it is composed of a mere forty-four words (in the Greek text). The apostle's teaching needs to be measured by the threat it surfaces, by the spiritual goal that is at stake, and by the pointed call to submission that follows (Eph. 5:21).

Surrounded by a religious culture rich with music from flutes, tambourines, and kettledrums, it is likely that the Ephesian Christians were bringing Dionysus (and/or Cybele) cult-like practices into their assembly. Some of the Christians may have longed for rituals they had previously practiced. Perhaps eating and drinking the Lord's Supper had seemed the ideal setting for blending Asian cult practices into worship of Jesus. Some of the Christians may even have concluded that cult-like music could help draw in unbelievers who were used to the sounds of the Asian religions. Similar to the conclusions of Dionysus cult members, some may even have urged that the supernatural was guiding them (making little distinction between Dionysus and Jesus). Whatever the motivations for their actions, Paul was sounding an alert by the word "debauchery" (Eph. 5:18, NIV). Christians were allowing themselves to be blown toward spiritual disaster on a rocky coast.

Exposing Spiritual Darkness by Living as Children of Light

As we approach Ephesians 5:18-21, one of the most important views to better understanding the teaching has to do with the parallels Paul uses (All quotes are from the NIV, save verse 19, where the NIV does not catch the message of the Greek participle "speaking," and starts a new sentence; verse 19 represents the author's translation, which compares closely to the ESV and NASB):

Eph. 5:7   "Therefore, do not be partners with them. ("For you were once darkness," Eph. 5:8a)

Eph. 5:17a	"Therefore, do not be foolish,"
Eph. 5:8b-10	"but now you are light in the Lord. Live as children of light, for the fruit of the light consists in all goodness, righteousness, and truth, and find out that pleases the Lord."
Eph. 5:17b	"but understand what the Lord's will is."
Eph. 5:11a	"Have nothing to do with the fruitless deeds of darkness,"
Eph. 5:18a	"Do not get drunk on wine, which leads to debauchery."
Eph. 5:11b	"but rather expose them."
Eph. 5:18b-21	"Instead, be filled with the Spirit, speaking to one another with psalms, hymns, and spiritual songs, singing and making music with your heart to the Lord, always giving thanks to God the Father for everything, in the name of our Lord Jesus Christ."

Additionally, Paul's appeal for Christian thanksgiving in place of evil conduct in Ephesians 5:4 and in 5:18-20 serves as another important parallel in his teaching.

Paul is reiterating the danger and as well the spiritual goal that the Ephesian Christians should share. They need to stop partnering with darkness and foolishness, getting involved with worthless actions, and getting drunk with wine – that leads to debauchery. In place of these they need to seek what pleases the Lord, understand his will, expose the darkness (as children of light, Eph. 5:8), and be filled with God's Spirit, speaking to one another and to the Lord in song. The latter two phrases have raised a cause-effect question. However, the most we should say is that being filled with the Spirit and Christian song are closely associated in the teaching. They are powerful, benevolent wind and willing sails, working together to drive the message of God's love and reclaiming power.

The word "debauchery" that is found in many of our English translations of Ephesians 5:18 (e.g. ESV, NIV) accurately conveys the meaning of the Greek word (*asotia*). However, it is not a word people frequently use. So, typically folks seek out their dictionary or they end up concluding that "debauchery" means "bad stuff" and move on. The simple sense of the Old French word is "orgy," a term that usually catches people's attention. However, "orgy," as we have commonly used the word, also includes sexual activity – which is not in view here. While the Dionysiac mystery rites did include the idea of sexual renewal (for women), the rites were not sexual free-for-all parties.

In Ephesians 5:18 "debauchery" (Gk. *asotia*) points to an event filled with self-centered sensuality and emotion.[1] The Greek word *asotia* is found only three times in the New Testament (Eph. 5:18, Titus 1:6; 1 Pet. 4:4). 1 Peter 4:4, also written to inhabitants of Roman Asia (among other areas), helps us get closer to understanding the word: "They think it strange that you do not plunge with them into the same flood of dissipation, and they heap abuse on you." (1 Pet. 4:4, NIV). In this text the word is translated "dissipation," the idea being that of self-destruction. It mirrors a drunken crew, oblivious to danger, sailing toward crashing breakers and loss of life.

As further help in navigating Paul's teaching, we also have a record of the remarkable assessment made by the Greek playwright Aristophanes. In his play *The Clouds*, Aristophanes used a unique word to describe the composers of "New Music" Dionysiac choruses. He called them "twisters of song."[2] The playwright's description was not intended as a compliment, but as a stinging critique of music to the god of wine. One ancient comment showed that the (so called) New Music to Dionysus was considered to be without virtue; it was shameful.[3] The judgment of some of the Greeks was that it was morally self-destructive.[4]

Aristophanes' critique was intended to show that the chaotic character of the music, written to emphasize the lyrics, together were destroying respect for others and urging decadent behavior.[5] The "New Music" playwrights were attempting to use bold new sounds and words to build a wild, throbbing excitement; they were attempting to satisfy crowds of worshipers gathered on behalf of the party god of the ancient world.[6] Much like the production of numerous present-day music videos, new choruses to Dionysus likely had the goal of being more sensational, more sensually inviting than previous choruses.

Centuries later Paul's teaching announces a similar issue – perhaps the result of similar cult worship. He is counseling the Ephesians to leave behind worship practices urged by a bursting, destructive sensuality. Perhaps surprisingly, the Lord's ambassador contrasts "debauchery" with song that speaks to others and to God in thanksgiving. Instead of being a bright sky and a fair wind, Christian worship in Ephesus (and perhaps all of Asia) is becoming a dark storm. Paul is revealing how worship in music is one way a group of people reveal their spiritual (and moral) character: either light and thanksgiving or darkness. In Ephesians 5:18-21 he is declaring the ethics of music.

Good Music, Good Song

For Western society all of this may not initially ring familiar to our ears. On a day-to-day basis, we may feel somewhat removed from ancient cult worship and the setting of Paul's contrast of debauchery versus good song. We may not initially grasp music and song as good or evil. For example type "ethics of music" into an Internet search engine and the results focus on music sharing and copyright law. In contrast Ephesians 5:18-21 announces a spiritual war that involves music.

C S. Lewis provides some help in *The Magician's Nephew*. The English storyteller paints a powerful image regarding the moral and spiritual elements of music and Genesis chapter one. In the story Lewis illustrates the event of creation by the great lion Aslan singing Narnia into existence. The song of Aslan is far more than merely pleasing sound or "just music." It carries a majestic and powerful goodness as the expression of Aslan's moral and spiritual character. Aslan's song that speaks Narnia into being is good music, good song.

Similarly, Genesis one declares that creation, as the work of a good Creator, is itself good (Gen. 1:4, 10, 12, 18, 21, 25, 31) – and therefore its music is good. The speech of songbirds is good, not just in terms of the quality of sound, but in a moral and spiritual sense. Why? Their speech is the result of a good action by a good Creator. A whale singing; a chorus of frogs at a pond's edge; the song of morning stars (Job 38:7); the sound of little children singing to the Lord. Each illustrates the music of a good creation – the good sounds of the Lord's creative work. The last stanza of Henry van Dyke's poem *Joyful, Joyful, We Adore Thee* illustrates well Job 38:7 and creation's song:

> Mortals join the mighty chorus, which the morning stars began.
> Father love is reigning 'ore us; brother love binds man to man.
> Ever singing, march we onward, victors in the midst of strife.
> Joyful music leads us sunward in the triumph song of life.[7]

Mr. van Dyke is not describing creation's song, accompanied by instrumental sounds. Instead, he is announcing creation's song as song that all of humanity should join, in praise to the Creator.

In the same way, our congregational worship in song to the Lord possesses a moral and spiritual character as well. Its moral and spiritual quality is wrapped up, not only in obeying Paul's Spirit-guided teaching, but also in the fact that it is the music, the song, of God's creation. Our sounds as male and female; made in his image. God intended for human song to him and to one another to be good. The song of his creatures in praise to a good Creator was intended to be good music – not in an aesthetic sense alone, but more importantly, in a moral and spiritual sense.

Human song, however, faces a real spiritual threat. The threat has nothing to do with missing a note. Instead, it surfaces as God's creatures lose sight of the moral and spiritual character of their song. We face the spiritual danger of allowing good human song to degenerate into little more than sensual and sensational music – and perhaps no song. Why? We live in a world under spiritual siege; the siege can have a devastating effect on us and on our worship to God.

In contrast to good song, consider how Dionysus cult-like practice seems to have been leading some (or many) in the Ephesian church into self-centered worship. Far from being good music, individualism and sensational worship were tearing apart their religious community. But they were blind to the spiritual danger, just as cult worship had been for centuries. Dionysus worshipers had believed, in the strongest emotional terms, that the god of wine was guiding them. In actuality the thought had served as an example of spiritual deception – which has happened in our day as well as theirs.

Stephen Guthrie has asked important questions regarding why Paul places speaking in song in opposition to spiritual darkness, debauchery, and getting drunk with wine. Why the association between song and light? "Why *music* in particular? Why is song an apt response to sensuality? Why should darkened hearts be met by tuneful voices?"[8] His answer to the questions directs us to the force of Paul's teaching: "the children of light are singing people, not *despite*, but *because* music engages body and sense."[9] He suggests that body and senses, as well as mind, need to be reoriented toward God, which happens as we sing.[10] As he further suggests from Paul's light versus darkness teaching in Ephesians 4:17-5:21,

> The sensual have, both literally and metaphorically, lost their senses. It is the alcoholic who is least able to appreciate the wine he drinks. It is the lecher, the playboy, who is least able to perceive and respond to the beauty of his lovers. The work of the Spirit, then, is to remake us from sensual people into sensible people.[11]

Song Then and Now

Further, the context of Paul's teaching regarding music, specifically Christian song, provides more than a look at ethics and spiritual growth. It also reveals an ancient struggle not so different from our own. Some may be inclined to ask if an issue with instrumental music even surfaced in the ancient world. Everett Ferguson's important survey of the writings of Philo and Philodemus reveals that it did. An interest in song/vocal music extended beyond Christian worship in Paul's day. For example, the church historian notes that, "Philo's preference for vocal music and his description of the musical practices of the Therapeutae [ascetic philosophers] provide close parallels to early Christian practice."[12] Additionally, he writes, "It appears that there was a common cultural assumption, at least among the educated, on the priority of words and so a special regard for vocal music."[13] A commitment to learning or to a simpler lifestyle appears to have prompted some in the ancient world to think more deeply about the importance of human song.

Similarly, in our day numerous sociologists, music teachers, and psychologists are urging that we give a renewed focus to vocal music. For example, Joan Russell has assigned herself the task of researching vocal music, believing that song provides a unique means of building cultures.[14] Her research has echoed the familiar comment by the seventeenth century Scottish statesman Andrew Fletcher: "Let me write the songs of a nation – I don't care who writes its laws." As a further look at song's importance, Wendy Moore has documented the use of song for relaxation, overcoming depression and anxiety, and even treating clinically serious mental-health problems.[15] Maria Sandgren's recent research into the health of vocalists has announced a similar message. She suggests that vocal music has a profound and positive effect on emotional wellbeing.[16]

Moore's and Sandgren's studies talk not only about the importance of song in our day, they also echo a crucial time in American history. The nineteenth century American statesman Frederick Douglass observed that the songs of an enslaved people were not always songs of joy. More often they were songs that expressed hearts in pain and with deep longing for a better future. Powerful hymns such as *There is a Balm in Gilead* announced the hopes of thousands of American families powerless to change their earthly situation. Similarly, John Steinbeck reminded a nation of the importance of song with these words:

"The songs of the working people have always been their sharpest statement and the one statement which cannot be destroyed."

We also hear the message in a simple story from ancient Macedonia. A Christian writer tells of two men singing in prison. A nighttime earthquake erupts under the area of the prison, causing significant structural disruption. Cell doors break open and even chains come loose. Inmates can storm the guards and break free. Remarkably, they do not. Luke records Paul's emphatic words to a jailer who is responding to the threat: "Don't harm yourself! We are all here!" (Acts 16:28, NIV) The narrative is filled with revealing messages. None is more revealing than that of prisoners listening to the spiritual songs of Paul and Silas.

The impact of songs on first-century inmates; slave families singing to God; the relationship between song and wellbeing; song as a builder of culture. Each reveals the power and importance of song. Gladly, in our day the thought of leaving the "real singing" to the trained vocalists is beginning to elicit warnings of danger. Reaction is growing against a vast technology and/or roaring sensuality that threatens to drown out our voices. Those who believe we can have sensibility together with sensual freedom are missing a crucial message from others who see and hear efforts to unmake or diminish us.

Conclusion

Writing a century and a half after Paul, Clement of Alexandria described the power and lure of sensual music in the ancient religions of his day: "Under cover of music they have outraged human life, being influenced by daemons, through some artful sorcery, to compass man's ruin."[17] Just as music commanded a powerful role in the ancient Asian cults, so Paul has announced the importance of song in the Lord's renewing darkened people.[18] In Ephesians 5:18-21 we have nothing less than an echo of Ephesians 4:17-24 and 5:4. Paul is helping the Ephesians understand one way that God rescues them from insensitivity. He is describing in Ephesians 5:19-21 one of the ways that

Christians are made new in the attitude of their minds. He is revealing Ephesians 4:23-24 applied to Christian worship.

Dan Burr's song, *Make Me New,* echoes the apostle's message
even as it captures something of the spiritual thirst of our day. The
spiritual song serves as a powerful reminder of one of the means God
uses to mold and shape his people to be children of light. Therefore,
we should expect Satan to exert an iron will in order to try to stop or
to corrupt such a powerful means of renewal. The corruption of
human song is exactly what was happening in Ephesus and what has
also happened in subsequent centuries.

Chapter Seven

Speaking in Song to One Another and to the Lord - Part 2

(Ephesians 5:18-21)

When Paul tells the Ephesian church to expose "the fruitless deeds of darkness" (Eph. 5:11, NIV), he does not leave them with an abstract idea, but makes it something they can visualize. Just as he tells them to be careful how they live (Eph. 5:15), he also tells them to be filled with the Spirit, speaking to one another and to the Lord in song. He is calling them away from music and conduct that is dishonoring God and fragmenting them. Their character as children of light will be seen in their goodness, righteousness, and truth. (Eph. 5:9) It will also be seen in their worship together.

Psallein, Generality, and Cult-Like Worship

What should we make of Paul's phrase "singing and making melody in your heart to the Lord" (Eph. 5:19b, KJV)? A great deal of attention has focused on whether or not Paul is talking about instrumental music in his teaching. The question has also prompted discussion about New Testament authority and the question of doing or not doing something where the New Testament is silent. Marcus Barth has been representative of those who have concluded that Paul was urging instrumental music's use.[1] Everett Ferguson,[2] Jack Lewis,[3] and William Woodson[4] have been representative of those who have concluded that Paul was teaching that Christian assemblies should include vocal music only. The conclusion represents a commitment to the divine character and authority of apostolic teaching and the New Testament as a whole.[5]

Students of the Ephesian letter have looked closely at Paul's use of the Greek word *psallein* in the phrase "making music in your hearts" (Eph. 5:19b, KJV). In early Greek culture, the word was associated with making music on a stringed instrument.[6] It was often used with this sense in the Greek translation of the Old Testament (the Septuagint). However, the apostle's use of *psallein* has diverged from this meaning in Ephesians 5:19. Indeed, the apostle to the Gentiles has made use of the common phrase "sing and make music" found in the Septuagint, but with a revision which points to vocal music only.[7] Paul has modified *psallein* by "with your heart to the Lord" (Eph. 5:19b, NASB) and then added the phrase about thanksgiving to God the Father and submission to one another (Eph. 5:20-21, NIV).

What was once worship "on an instrument" (e.g. Psalm 27:6; 57:7; 2 Chronicles 29:25) is now "with the heart." The Spirit is guiding Paul to counsel Christians away from Asian cult practice. Given apostolic use of Psalms, it appears the Lord is also calling Christians to a reshaping of Israel's temple worship. As LaGard Smith has observed, "Carefully examine the context of the passages which deal with singing as an expression of Christian worship and you quickly discover how closely singing is linked with the "internal."[8] The apostle announces that now the temple of the Lord is not wood and stone but the Lord's people (Eph. 2:19-22). God's people are the temple in which he lives by his Spirit. Equally important the sound resonating from the temple of the Lord, Christ's Church, is to be the sound of voices.

Paul does not encourage the instrumentation that is common in the city's Asian religions. Instead, Ephesians 5:4 and 5:18-20 announce that the church in Ephesus should distance itself from dark conduct and replace it with thanksgiving. In response likely to pressure from deeply rooted religious practices, Paul was issuing clear guidance for Christian ethics, lifestyle, and worship. He was urging the Christians in Ephesus and Asia to worship the Lord, not in sensually corrupting worship, but in song that would teach and encourage others and honor God. As Herbert Presker has written concerning the alternatives,

> The fundamental difference between early Christian fullness of the Spirit and the orgiastic enthusiasm of Hellenism is indicated in Eph. 5:18. The life and liturgy of Christians are not marked by sensual ecstasy or Bacchantic [Dionysiac] frenzy (μεθυσκεσθαι οινω) but by infilling with the Spirit (πληρουσθε εν πνευματι). The distinction could hardly be more succinctly expressed: orgiastic enthusiasm on the one side, and on the other the fullness of the Spirit that finds liturgical expression in praise and thanksgiving (5:18-20) and practical expression in αγαπη [love] (5:21-6:9).[9]

Presker has summarized well why Ephesians 5:18-21 represents a teaching whose importance far outweighs its brevity. Paul appears to be contrasting sensual Dionysus cult-like activity with song through which the Spirit works. In doing so he is providing powerful counsel regarding one way that Christians are renewed by God to be children of light.

Was Christ's ambassador critiquing instrumental music, moving the Ephesians away from it or no? While much has been made of the fact that Paul does not specifically mention instrumental music, what Paul does say and why he says it provides the answer. Yes, it appears he was counseling them away from their instrumental music – and showing them the spiritual danger of what they were doing. Dionysus (and Cybele) worship was filled with the sound of flutes, tambourines, cymbals, and drums. In contrast to "debauchery," the apostle to the Gentiles emphasized speech and song by all. With the ancient cults fill-ing the background of the scene, the contrast paints a powerful foreground image.

Indeed, our day may have underestimated just how much the Ephesian church's assembly had degenerated into a pool of sensational worship. Dionysiac worship used vocal tones mimicked by instruments to announce various aspects of cult ritual. Low tones, such as those from drums, announced possession by a supposed deity.[10] However, we should also take note that Paul is addressing more than the instrumentation in and sound of cult-like worship. The root problem that he writes about in Ephesians 4:17-5:21 is a thirst for the sensual. The use and sound of instruments in Dionysus worship represented an accomplice to the issue of sensational religion. The same was likely true for the Ephesian assembly.

Additionally, it is important to realize that what Paul writes in Ephesians 5:18 represents a generality, similar to Ephesians 4:19 and 5:3-5, 11. The apostle's use of generalities and euphemisms in the letter represents at least one way we should understand some of the "silences" of the New Testament. The apostle uses generalities in Ephesians when addressing Asian cult practices, such as Dionysiac religion. Indeed, the New Testament contains none of the ancient Greek words prominently used to describe Dionysus cult symbolism and ritual.[11] Indecent behavior, foolish talk, coarse joking, "impurity,"[12] (Eph. 4:19; 5:3, 5), getting drunk on wine and "debauchery" (Eph. 5:18) are how Paul describes the traps facing the Ephesians. The ambassador of the Lord generalizes the specifics, saying enough to call the Ephesian congregation away from the spiritual danger. In contrast to how they have been living and worshiping, he urges them to live as children of light and sing to one another and to the Lord. His emphasis is on what they should be doing as opposed to all that they have been doing.

Paul, however, was not unique at this point. The second century church teacher Clement of Alexandria provides a similar example. While urging people away from "drunkenness" to "sober salvation" in *Exhortation to the Greeks*, he generally describes conduct and attire, but leaves the religion unspoken initially.[13] He talks only about the "frenzy-stricken one," wands, ivy wreaths, and fawnskins.[14] However, no question existed as to the religious danger he was describing; the Greeks and Asians knew exactly what was on his mind. He was urging people away from the pervasive and powerful Dionysus cult; he names it later in Chapter Twelve of his essay. Both Paul in the first century and Clement in the second century were helping people navigate out of the powerful storms of the Asian cults.

Singing to the Lord as a Unifying Action

The months prior to World War II provide one of the most powerful examples of the importance of song. In October 1940, American educators saw a nation of young people in desperate need of encouragement. They also realized that a new generation needed to better grasp their roots. So, they urged a national movement of folk song as a means to offset propaganda attacks from select foreign presses. They counseled the nation's schools to use upbeat, joyous song to replace discouragement and fear in the hearts of young people. They urged students to sing together![15]

The clash in American race relations has witnessed a similar lesson. While the struggles of skin colors and dialects have sapped a nation's strength for generations, song has helped wounds to heal. For more than half a century, Muscle Shoals, Alabama has reverberated with the sound of harmony by musicians determined to overcome division and express unity. Races blending their voices. Blacks and whites combining their creativity. Millions of people have been the welcome recipients of lyrics by Aretha Franklin, Eric Clapton, Carrie Underwood, and numerous others. Song by people under siege has revealed something crucial about our humanity.

Joan Russell has announced a similar message from a religious setting. She traveled to Fiji in order to hear vocal music in a Fiji worship assembly. What she witnessed was the powerful unifying force of Fiji society – song that pulled together children and parents, young and older, male and female. She observed that upon entering a worship assembly in Fiji, she was handed a songbook by a member – an invitation to join in. No one left out or left behind; people drawn together. As she recorded from her experience, part-singing invited full participation by all members of the community because all vocal types found a place in ensemble singing.[16] She highlights the importance of the cultural goals for the people of Fiji and how those goals translate into their worship. As she writes, "For the survival and well-being of the community, the common good is valued over the individual good...."[17] A first century B.C. Greek papyrus preserves a like message: "Music has power to check faction and disturbance... and whoso liveth is soothed by song."[18]

Stephen Guthrie concludes his study by observing the close relation not only between light and song but also between singing and unity.[19] Unity in song represents one of the ways a congregation of people reveal they are children of light. God desires that we, by our song, would join the rest of his creation as the good sound of his good work (including those of us who cannot carry a tune!). It is only a good sound, however, when it is also the sound of a people acting with solidarity. No organ/band/orchestra. Even the song leader deemphasizing the role.

The many religious assemblies in our country that include special vocal groups and/or bands/orchestras announce that much of the nation remains insensitive to a group perspective. People assembled to worship can fall prey to an entertainment mentality. As the *Goshen College Bulletin* has well suggested regarding congregational worship versus Handel's *Messiah*,

> Music for worship has different goals than religious art music. Worship music can, and hopefully does, have artistic merit. But artistic merit is not its only goal; its ability to serve the function of worship is the primary goal – worthy music that becomes part of worthy worship.[20]

Our day knows the same spiritual threats as previous periods; people begin to believe that the praise team or the folks next to them who are singing meet the need of the 1000 (or the 100) gathered to worship. Some cannot imagine that a spiritual threat exists to the group (and to themselves) should they decide to just listen or mumble through a song.

As one sign of increased sensitivity to unity in worship, the "emerging church" movement has observed the danger and begun to react to it. Dan Kimball, for one, highlights the action of moving a band/orchestra to the back of a building, out of sight. As he writes, "Not only does this keep the band from being the focus of attention, it also adds to the sense that we are all worshiping together as a community without any of us being more significant than the others."[21] "Emerging church" thought at this point is headed in the right direction. Taking the crucial step of no instruments, all singing, probably seems incomprehensible to many. It probably seemed such in Ephesus as well. Paul's words in Ephesians 5 should keep us alert to one of the most powerful spiritual expressions in the world today: a church singing together.

Given the unifying power of song together, we should not be surprised by Satan's efforts to hinder such expressions. For example, recently, I tuned in to watch the telecast of a large Houston religious assembly, which included an orchestra and choir. As I watched and listened to the music and noticed how the assembly was listening and enjoying, what also caught my attention was who was missing from the assembly. As the cameras panned across the thousands of people gathered, I saw many adults, but no children. The worship assembly had the complexion of thousands of couples on a date, listening to a concert. The action of bands/orchestras and choirs – and often listening by everyone else – fits our time. It also hollows out our spiritual growth. The irony is that our day searches for deep spiritual experiences, but often ignores one of the most powerful.

Children's presence and their singing in a church assembly represent a telling measurement of a church's oneness and light. Churches that are sensitive to the spiritual needs of all include in a worship time songs that are familiar to children and teens. We allow spiritual danger when we think and act otherwise. Perhaps imperceptibly, it tears at the fabric of a church's unity when our children desire to sing and try to sing, but stumble. Equally serious, we can believe that their spiritual needs are met by separating them out of all (or many) of the assemblies.

The Lord intends for a church's times of song to urge unity between children, teens. and adults. He wants our gatherings in song to be times when all take part – when we know oneness as a family (cf. Eph. 3:14, 4:15-16). Our assemblies need to know the Lord's blessing from singing simple songs that our children know well, songs young people know well, and songs that adults know well. Our gatherings need to allow all to speak and encourage one another. In addition to singing simple children's songs in the assembly, if we are not already doing so, perhaps we can also allocate time in Bible classes to teach our children verses of songs familiar to adults.

We face a spiritual threat older than ancient Asian religion when our children or teens feel left out or assemblies divide into music players versus singers. Guided by the Spirit, Paul saw the spiritual danger the Ephesian church was facing. The Spirit saw just as well the same danger we have faced 2000 years later. Every age has had a great need to see clearly the importance of unity.

Paul's teaching may not be an easy thought to accept or act out in a nation that typically values diversity, "stepping out," and freedom above community. Nor does it necessarily meet the expectation of our emotions, which can serve as our ultimate measuring rod of spirituality. However, even if we do not "feel" the difference and have to walk by faith, what the apostle writes is filled with light.

Conclusion: Singing as Children of Light

Ephesians 5:7-21 announces one of the most powerful teachings in Scripture about the Spirit's work in every age. However, it has often been ignored or read over quickly, save for a discussion of instruments or vocal music only. Why? It forces people to walk by faith, similar to trusting that prayer is more than speaking into the air. We are being pushed to depend on faith in the unseen as opposed to what may captivate our senses. We may talk about walking by faith; our thirst for the sensual and the sensational brings us face-to-face with one of our most challenging tests.

Concert halls on wheels; great-sounding digital music players; home theaters. Easy-access sensuality drenches our society. Our senses are part of our humanity and not necessarily a hindrance to our spiritual growth. But selfish desires can also represent the medium of temptation. As Paul writes, "You were taught, with regard to your former way of life, to put off your old self, which is being corrupted by its deceitful desires...." (Eph. 4:22, NIV) The demise of ancient Asian religions should not suggest that we discard Paul's words in Ephesians 4:17-5:21. Instead, the apostle's teaching represents important counsel even now. "In a speech-debased world, the language of worship creates a distinctive people living for the sake of others."[22] Singing to others and to the Lord as part of his good creation represents a powerful expression of good humanity – one that a dark lord seeks to silence.

Singing in the twenty-first century remains crucial to renewing our senses, unity, and declaring the Word. In a time when many are less familiar with the Bible, a church singing Scripture provides a powerful means of teaching and encouraging. One self-professed religious dropout and mystic spiritualist, Joan Borysenko, emphasizes that very point. She comments that people singing Scripture together – no instruments, band, or chorus – represent one of the few powerful, encouraging memories for her from the Jewish synagogue of her youth.[23] Similarly, consider what a visitor to a church sees and hears as they are handed a songbook or are pointed to a projection screen. The entire congregation singing together; no instruments. If a special singing group exists in the church, during the worship assembly it is embedded in the church as a whole. The oneness presents a warm invitation to visitors to join the singing as the church sings to them.

The apostle emphasizes to the church in Ephesus that the sound of the Lord's temple is to be the sound of voices. The popular song, *Come Let Us All Unite to Sing*, captures well Paul's message at the same time as it urges us to lift our voices together:

Come let us all unite to sing, God is love;
Let heav'n and earth their praises bring, God is love;
Let every soul from sin awake,
Each in his heart sweet music make,
And sing with us for Jesus' sake, For God is love.

Oh, tell to earth's remotest bound, God is love;
In Christ we have redemption found, God is love;
His blood has washed our sins away,
His Spirit turned our night to day,
And now we can rejoice to say, That God is love.[24]

In his letter to the church in Colossae, Paul writes that the church's singing serves as a form of preaching (Col. 1:28; 3:16). Singing carries that same purpose when the singing is by a Praise Team that is leading an assembly; the team is preaching. Preaching the Word was to be more than the work of an apostle, prophet, or evangelist; it was also to be the work of an entire church singing together. We need to see ourselves as an assembly of people each with a responsibility to sing to others and to the Lord in thanksgiving. Ephesians 5:19-21 announces wondrous counsel that guides us to being children of light, declaring God's Word as a unified people, and praising the Lord.

Chapter Eight

Marriages and the Clash of Faiths and Rights

(Ephesians 5:21-33)

Ephesians 5:21 and the example of Christ's love for the church lay the foundation for Paul's remarkable teaching about Christian marriage. In our day people have questioned the meaning of "head" applied to the role of husbands (Eph. 5:23) as well as submission by wives (Eph. 5:24). What does Paul say about husband-wife relations in marriage and what applications should we make for our day?

Eden or Ephesus?

Paul writes Ephesians 5:21-33 for a city facing spiritual and social destruction. Similar to our day, Ephesus likely was a city filled with people hoping for a break – a pleasurable diversion from work or a financial lift. Many were chained to the massive estate complexes of the Artemis cult, the city's public works or medical facilities, or its various shops. Most people probably ended up working long hours and just getting by. Their marriages were managed with efficiency, just like their jobs. Minimal talk; just enough to get someone's attention or give directions. Not much energy left to really get to know her; not even interested in her thoughts. With time marriage tasted like the same lunch day after day.

Little guesswork is required to see Ephesus under the shadow of a dark lord. Marriages darkened by the Asian religions had left people conditioned to brief bursts of pleasure. Similar to our day of reality TV, movie thrillers, or sports spectacles, the religious cults had brought thrills and festivities, but they did not satisfy long-term. People hoped their relationships would, but probably found them stagnant or decaying as well after a few years.

In contrast Paul's teaching about Christ's love and care for his bride, his people, his church pushed people back to Genesis 1-2 and the beginning of humanity.[1] The opening chapters of Genesis and the portrait of creation was intended to scatter darkness from Israel and from the ancient world. In a world saturated with sin, the Lord began his Word to his people by revealing the almost untouchable, unimaginable. Man and woman; male and female; without sin. Those first minutes, hours (days, weeks, months, years?), what were they like? "This is now bone of my bones and flesh of my flesh; she shall be called woman for she was taken out of man." (Gen. 2:23, NIV) The words announce a mind filled with joy and wonder at seeing one who is like him.

When I think of those first moments and what man and woman must have experienced, on occasion I think of words from the vocalists Brooks & Dunn's *My Maria* about woman as a miracle work.[2] The words do not get close to Genesis 2:21-23, but they head us in the right direction. The astonishing potential and intellects of man and woman blending; their interest in each other; their wonder at the animals around them; soaking up the sights and sounds of a new world. Reading Ephesians 5:21-33 should help us soar once again. However, the words also carry risk. We are being called upon to give up something for someone else. In a world used to functioning by "rights," control, and competition, we are urged to focus on another's best interest.

Marriage Shaped With Towels

With the powerful Asian cults near-at-hand, the Lord's ambassador to the Gentiles urges Christians to do the almost unthinkable. He applies "submission" in his teaching to both husbands and wives. Those who have attempted to separate Ephesians 5:21 from 5:22-33 (and 6:1-9) have done a disservice to Paul's teaching. The verses are intimately entwined; Ephesians 5:21 serves as the guiding rudder for the ship of husband-wife, parent-child and master-slave relations.

Beyond the relationship of 5:21 to what follows, a good bit of discussion has focused on Paul's teaching about the roles of husbands and wives in marriage. Related to the question of submission, some have suggested that "head" (Gk. *kephale*) in Paul's teaching is referring to the husband as the "life-source" for his wife.[3] The idea is based on the fact that "head" in ancient Greek literature often referred to the source of a river; typically it did not mean "leader."[4]

The word meaning from ancient Greek literature has been suggested as the basis for an equal rights view of marriage in Scripture. As the thought goes, either a husband or a wife can lead the family since Paul is not talking about leadership. The idea that either can lead and that hierarchy is a consequence of sin has deeply penetrated religious teaching in our time. As one example the religious novel *The Shack* announces the conclusion – even putting the idea into the mouth of God.[5]

Thinking of language alone, a translation of "life-source" or "source" could be correct. However, it does not fit what the apostle is writing in Ephesians 1:10 and 1:22. In his first two uses of "head," he is describing a position of authority – Christ's authority. As one proposal, Gordon Fee has suggested that Paul "switched gears" between Ephesians chapters one, four, and five. In Ephesians chapter one he clearly had "authority" in view. In chapters four and five he did not.[6] But would the Ephesian Christians have understood the transition? The straightforward meaning makes the most sense of the letter; Paul uses "head" with the same meaning throughout the letter.

The apostle is using "head" in Ephesians 5:22-25 as a metaphor for leadership or authority – similar to the use of the word in the

Greek translation of the Old Testament.[7] As James Thompson forcibly writes, the use of "head" in Ephesians expresses "a hierarchy of being that is a development of, but not a radical departure from, the earlier instructions [in 1 Cor. 11:2-16]. This hierarchy is the basis for social relations within the church and family."[8]

It is a hierarchy shaped with love. That is the difference between social structure shaped by Christ and the twisted fashions of a dark lord. The leadership Paul describes in marriage gives up life for another; it expresses a love that sacrifices – even to death. I. Howard Marshall has summarized Ephesians 5:21-33 carefully:

> Like Colossians 3, this passage teaches a requirement for a husband to love and care for a wife, which was certainly compatible in the first-century context with a position of authority over her (just as parents love their children). What we have here, then is another example of "love-patriarchalism," in which the traditional elements of submission by the wife to her husband is required, but with a remarkable development of the motif of self-giving love as the dominant characteristic of the Christian husband.[9]

I. Howard Marshall and Carroll Osburn, as two voices, have also suggested that while Ephesians 5:21 has continued relevance, Ephesians 5:22-33 has been surpassed by our equal rights culture.[10] As I. Howard Marshall writes,

> From patriarchalism we have moved to love-patriarchalism, and the road is open to mutual love between brothers and sisters in Christ. This final step was not taken by Paul, any more that he took the step from accepting slavery to recognizing that his own teaching contained the seeds of its inevitable abolition, but this is the direction in which the evidence clearly points. Mutual love transcends submission.[11]

The argument is careful and it sounds good to a people who are part of an equal rights society. Indeed it may represent the dominant conclusion in the early twenty-first century. However, that does not make it true to Christ. Jesus gave up "rights." He submitted himself even to death on a cross. He gave himself up for his bride.

Paul probably sounded as astonishing to the Ephesians as he has sounded to many people in the twenty-first century. In actuality, Ephesians 5:21-33 probably represents a bold response to first-century domestic freedom nestled in the Dionysus cult, similar to the view found in an equal rights America. Mutual submission has challenged both times and places. Paul is challenging a wife to yield freedom she thought was hers. He is also challenging a husband to submit his leadership to his wife's best interests.[12] As LaGard Smith has emphasized, "the husband is not the head of his wife as an *autocrat* but as a servant...."[13]

Ephesians 5:21 breathes cool air into a sweltering society. It displaces every social expression. Patriarchy (as it has frequently been expressed); equal rights; feminism. All disappear. Paul's words echo the example of Jesus who used a towel to craft his kingship (Jn. 13:1-17). The apostle of Christ emphasizes that it is by "washing feet," not claiming water rights, that marriages and families follow Jesus. The risen Christ reveals through Paul that both men and women are to see that following him dictates a way of thinking and acting that breaks the spiritual and social deception of a world drenched in darkness.[14]

One of the challenges is that we live in a world where headship often translates into loveless domination. So what about that? What should a Christian woman do in a house of abuse and/or infidelity? Cynthia Dianne Guy provides careful counsel to women as she points to the example of Abigail (1 Sam. 25:2-42). She urges courage in the face of harsh, bitter circumstances: "If a husband does not fulfill his responsibilities, his wife must – whether it is working to pay the rent, training the children, or (like Abigail) protecting her family from harm. As she strives to submit herself to her own husband as unto the Lord, God is her help."[15]

Many of us – men and women alike – can find plenty of justification for clinching our fists or burying our heads in seen or unseen pain when we think of Paul's teaching in Ephesians 5. Do husbands give up the sports telecast to listen to their wives, especially when the subject their wife is sharing seems distant to their sphere of interest at the moment? Do wives recognize that when he is up to his elbows in grease either under the hood or under the sink, that moment may not necessarily be the best time to talk about an issue or a hurt? He is trying to fix her kitchen or her car – because he loves her (but maybe he needs to just take a break, stay filthy for twenty minutes longer, and listen when the subject comes to her mind).

Typically, we are a time-pressed people and the time pressure can serve as the setting for temptation. "Husbands, love your wives" does not mean "love her after the game is over" or "love her after the job is done." Instead it translates to "love her as her need surfaces." In fact she may be raising an issue or hurt during the game telecast or during a task as an unconscious test of care and love.

What Ephesians 5:21-33 reveals is that both husbands and wives have a challenging road in following God's counsel regarding marriage. Both will know the temptation to seek their own way, carve out independence – the very things the Dionysus cult promoted among women. Both first-century men and women had prayer and work ahead of them. The situation has not changed 2000 years later.

Perhaps one portrait of what many Americans have allowed to happen and what needs to be has erupted from the pen of the fantasy novelist Robert Jordan. In his bestseller *The Eye of the World*, he writes about a long distant, almost forgotten time. He describes a struggling village that has forgotten courage and self-sacrifice. A storyteller comes and reminds the village of who they used to be and who they need to become again. They need to follow the example of an ancient king and his queen. The two rulers are described with the words, "Bravery and beauty and wisdom and a love that death could not sunder."[16] While fantasy, the story speaks volumes to our society from a heart that loves his wife (see the dedication) and longs for paradise. Jordan has attempted to show a weary, unraveling Western culture a glimpse of how things should be. Paul's writing in Ephesians 5:21-33 is no different, save that it is composed of far more than fantasy.

How Can This Be Happening?

My vantage point for the last two decades has allowed me to see a unique slice of how marriages go. While far from being a marriage and family counselor, I have had the opportunity to work with numerous new employees of a Fortune 100 company – each of them easily characterized as among the brightest and best. No small number of young women have been single when starting their first job. I have noticed that many have gotten married no more than three years into the job – to a coworker they have met or as a result of a relationship started in college, or earlier. Many of the marriages have endured and even prospered (about 50% – matching the national average). However, what has surprised me is how many marriages to kind, intelligent, pretty, and athletic (and frequently deeply religious) young women have crumbled within less than two years – in every case the result of a husband's infidelity. It has felt like I was seeing an epidemic unfold. Almost without exception, women have shown deep religious moorings and ethics, only to be stunned by a husband's lack of self-control and resulting infidelity.

Recently, a shocking scenario unfolded too close to home – in a small Texas town. A man was recorded as he issued instructions and paid a hit man (undercover policeman) to kill his wife – a lovely, spiritually- minded woman and physician. She was stricken with grief and stunned by the lies and hidden life of the man she thought loved and protected her.[17] Unfortunately, while the event represents an extreme scenario, the root spiritual disease and the resulting secret life probably characterizes many men and women in our time.

I feel like I am looking into a pit of darkness when I think about the majority of a generation of young men and women. I have seen in my own daughter and sons the frequent frustration, even anger, at the high school sex talk. Some of it boastful lies; some of it true to every detail; all of it corrupting minds. The situation may not be new, but the past ten years may have carried the nation along to moral bankruptcy much faster than we had previously been getting there. It is likely that Internet-based pornography and newsstand eroticism have pulled on a large percentage of the nation's boys and men. If parents and other adults have been tempted to minimize all of this, they should work through those feelings – and promptly shred them.

We are in the middle of a pandemic as a nation and the threat is far greater than flesh-and-blood terrorists or a viral outbreak. The terrorist leader in this case is Satan and his weapons are visible on many magazine covers and Internet advertisements. Pop music vocalists; international supermodels; actresses; elite, sensual athletes. Our society is drenched with the images. Toned and ripped advertising is eroding self-images and hope.

Equally dangerous, the lie of sanitized pornography meets young men and women in sensual music videos, movies, the clash of modernized "gladiatorial" games, and a tsunami of "hard-body" imagery. It captivates in the name of "sports." And since sports are often beneficial, it represents one of the nation's most dangerous siren-songs. The images weave themselves into the minds of teens and adults, endangering the ability to build selfless, healthy, Christ-centered relationships. At the same time the mental self-control in many men (and women) is being stripped away at mach speed. Marriage becomes one of the victims.

Marriages That Prosper

At the same time as I have seen the "How can this be happening?" situations, I have also received the pleasure of seeing marriages that have prospered – and a bit of why. The "why" has represented no secret: men and women who know and give selfless love and who act with spiritual and moral constancy. I have heard numerous young women speak about their husbands with both love and admiration. It has not been just a case of "saying the right thing." Instead, what has shown up in their faces is genuine love for the young man they have married. They have talked about his quick mind, humor, playfulness, and/or athleticism – and in every case his religious and moral constancy. As the actress Courteney Cox has quipped, "Honesty is the key to a relationship. If you can fake that, you're in."

Typically, these women have also served well as kind supervisors, team leaders, managers, or coworkers. Far from seeming degraded, they have appeared happy and it has transferred to her work. In one case, I am aware of a woman who managed a manufacturing facility and who gladly submitted to her husband. Why? She loved and trusted him. Having watched them interact with each other, what has been clear is that they have given themselves to each other – because they first gave themselves to the Lord. Marriage contains a hierarchy, but it is hierarchy shaped by Jesus Christ – fashioned in love, not hammered out by force.

Conclusion

The risen Christ announces that marriages, families, and as well his church are shaped with towels (Jn. 13:1-17). What has become clearer with each passing year is that mutual submission is far from the "society breaker" that feminism and equal rights have suggested. Instead, it represents a remarkable foundation that allows both men and women to soar in their jobs and their marriages. Men who have consistently spoken of their wives with eyes that light up – who compliment her in the presence of coworkers – in every case have been men respected among their coworkers. Even if the respect has remained unannounced, it has shown up on the faces of people as a man walks by or as he chats with others. Walking as Christ walked brings a light unmatched by the festivities of a holiday party.

Nothing in Scripture suggests that women should be limited to their homes as their sphere of work. The Word emphasizes that their homes represent their most important sphere of work (1 Pet. 3:1-6; 1

Ti. 5:14); it also announces the positive examples of women working and serving beyond their family role as well (Lk. 8:2-3; Acts 16:14).

Additionally, Scripture has said that women should submit to their husbands, and husbands to their wives by leading with love – just as Christ loved the church. Perhaps the great irony the nation has struggled with is that the more marriages are built on-the-fly and shaped by power struggles, the less secure is our society in general. Conversely, where marriages are framed by serving love, the more towns, cities, and nations prosper. Secured and strengthened by each other, both men and women bring their unique talents, intellect, and perspectives to their workplace. Whether managing children and families or working beyond their homes, both prosper.

When men invest themselves in keeping their eyes and hearts focused on the woman who has given herself to them, the Lord will use that selflessness and self-control. He will lift a marriage above the economic strains, time pressures, health challenges, and personality differences that test every relationship. Praying to the Lord and reading Scripture together as husband and wife builds a bridge between two lives that can handle great pressure.

Thinking of her and treating her like a miracle work will bring blessings to both wives and husbands. Listening; loving; acting with moral courage and an unyielding commitment to marriage vows; fixing her kitchen sink or her car. All demonstrate a leadership that will bring marriage closer to Eden – by the power of the Lord.

Chapter Nine

Parents, Children, and the Spiritual Storm

(Ephesians 6:1-4; 2 Timothy 3:14-17)

Thunderstorms can become one of the most frightening events for children. A flash of lightning and a thunderous boom can break sleep and send little ones to parents' bed – for good reason. The sights and sounds express power far beyond their control. In such moments a parent's presence surfaces as a place of security unmatched in this world.

Parents can face the challenge of recognizing that at times children see spiritual storms more clearly than do they. Fathers and mothers may become numb to a fallen world, lacking alertness to what unsettles children – and what should unsettle adults as well. As a result, often children will seek safety from a spiritual storm, but parents are deaf to the howling winds their children hear. Perhaps they have heard a spiritual storm for decades and the winds have become part of the common noise in their lives. So, instead of responding to their children's fear, parents brush off the threat and watch the dark movie, etc. Children learn to do the same.

Additionally, twenty-first century popular religion in the U.S., similar to ancient Ephesus, has not always represented a healthy environment for our children. The religious expressions intended to capture their hearts have ranged widely from good witches to MTV-mimicking musical productions proposed as worship to God. Some have gulped down factually corrupt Bible stories told by animated vegetables. They may even have picked up books such as *The Secret Life of Bees* or the *ABC Book of Shadows* without knowing the dangers carefully woven into what they read. Adding to the situation, much of the Bible teaching they hear remains confined to a Sunday Bible class. All this can happen in a day when they want and need more time to talk with their parents and others about the Word of God and about the creation around them.

Further, much of middle school and high school meets many of our children as a seven-year party of sensuality and perhaps even sexuality. During the party many of them sense deeply that they need to grow religiously and morally, but they can also feel a lack of confidence and self-control to get there. With the national virginity-at-marriage statistic hovering at the ten percent mark, parents have good reason to be alert. Add to this the persistent drinking on college campuses and we have an age that knows the same spirit that was part of ancient festivals to the supposed god of wine. Indeed, in our day "Bacchus" (Dionysus) is used as an acronym and perhaps some subtle humor by one college campus organization attempting to deter alcohol consumption by young adults.[1]

So, what steps can and should parents and church leaders be taking to help children grow spiritually healthy? How can we help them discern evil? How do we counsel them without frustrating them (Eph. 6:4)?

Ephesians 6:1-4 and Spiritual Nurture

Paul uses a mere fifty-one words when addressing the subject of parents and offspring, but his words tell a great deal. Fathers are singled out, with the command that they avoid exasperating, or angering, their children – but instead nurture them in Christ. The word "exasperate" (Eph. 6:4, NIV) is used only two times in the NT (Ro. 10:19,

Eph. 6:4).[2] "Training" (Eph. 6:4, NIV) is found six times (Eph. 6:4, 2 Ti. 3:16, Heb. 12:5, 7, 8. 11).[3] The balancing act is no easy one or Paul would not have needed to provide apostolic counsel. As one student of the text has written, "Parental love which coddles, spoils a child; barbaric discipline crushes."[4]

We know little about ancient education, but do have glimpses. Everett Ferguson has provided one informed look. He writes that most schools "were small and private, the work of a single teacher who received a fee from his pupils, except in some of the cities where rulers or wealthy citizens endowed educational institutions."[5] Additionally, the Gospels reveal the importance of Scripture in the education provided by God-fearing parents and other teachers (Lk. 2:41-52).

The apostle never indicates that he is focusing on headship in the role of "father." Given this father's experiences, it is more likely that Paul focuses on fathers because here the greatest need exists for his teaching. If the greatest need focuses on fathers, then in our day much is also tied to the pace of the families they lead.

In the last thirty years our children have learned well from their parents and their society. Waiting for someone to finish a thought can be something they and we barely tolerate. Our society appears to be growing fond of the idea of investing as little time as possible in someone else – be it a waiter, coach, or coworker (or even our children). We will still wait in line for a hot dog at a high school football game and rarely raise a complaint. However, the idea of relationships patiently built or Scripture slowly read is fast becoming foreign. The phenomenon of the declining literacy rate in America may represent an important parallel.[6] We may be close to correct to blame much of it on the cell phone and text messaging. Whatever the reason we are reaping the whirlwind of impatient conversations and teaching. Fast ethical decisions, impatient dating, even fast marriages, and fast failures have often followed.

Doing What is Right

Beyond the responsibility laid on parents, Paul also gives responsibility to children. He tells them to obey their parents and honor them (Eph. 6:1-2). Paul's letters give no indication that the apostle is responding to an issue of parent-child relationships in the city/region. However, given Satan's work in every age, it would be no surprise to find that Ephesus and ancient Asia had faced issues with children and teens seeking to free themselves from restraints. Indeed, one ancient source recorded that the Dionysus cult, with its emphasis on freedom and sensuality, was especially popular among the young.[7]

The apostle's words carry an important message for our day as well. Paul emphasizes what is "right" (Eph. 6:1) and therefore what is wrong. The teaching represents a clear ethics decision, but one that may be lost on many teens and young adults in the early twenty-first century. The areas of challenging ethical decisions fill our land. Casual lies between friends; cheating in classes; stealing copyright-protected music; sensuality out of control. "Right" is difficult to identify when "wrong" is in question.

Our day has become intimately associated with the absence of thought about ethics.[8] The issue is not a matter of "situation ethics." Instead, ethics is becoming a concept that is genuinely foreign to many teens and young adults. Why? One sociologist has suggested that a decline in dialog between adults and youth has contributed. Further, an increasingly dominant focus on technology and computing skills is replacing time to wrestle with ethics decisions, urged by literary readings.[9] Discussing religion and spiritual ideas in place of reading the Bible has a hand as well. Paul highlights the importance of the Scriptures in shaping Timothy (2 Ti. 3:14-17); they are no less important 2000 years later. The developing vacuum in ethics education is leaving numerous young adults bailing water and having limited ability for finding and repairing holes in the hull.

Beauty and the Most Dangerous Beast

We do not know the degree to which ancient Ephesus struggled to distinguish right from wrong, but we do know that Artemis worship held its own moral pressures. For example, some (or many) of the girls of ancient Ephesus got lured into the beauty culture associated with the patron goddess of the city.

History tells us that the attendants at the Temple of Artemis were attractive virgins – projecting a kind of at-a-distance sensuality. Similarly, given the sensual, sexual emphasis of the spring festival to Artemis, it is likely that recipes for ancient aphrodisiacs were discussed even between mothers and daughters. While Ephesus may not have been characterized by pornography on every street corner, it was probably a city bathed in sensuality. Many of the magazine covers in our time probably echo the sensuality of the ancient city. Satan, described as a beast on the prowl (1 Pet. 5:8), has been at work for millennia.

Some years ago as I was talking with my oldest son about dating in high school, one of his conclusions rang loudly. I was doing some casual probing during his Junior year and he said, "Dad, there are not many girls at school that I am interested in dating." I asked a question related to Katy High School being a large Texas 5A school and his response put an exclamation point in my mind. He talked about how he thought many of the girls at school had been cute when they and he were in eighth grade. Then he shared words I will not forget: "Dad, a lot of them have changed. Their eyes don't sparkle anymore." We talked a good bit more about the hurt he felt at hearing the high school sex talk. He talked about how it made him sick, how it caused his stomach to knot up.

Three years later my youngest son shared the same thing with me and often exhibited the same symptoms. He talked about the sickness and anger he felt when someone would talk disrespectfully about one of his friends – a pretty, happy girl who was keeping her high morals. Corruption of what the Lord made good brings pain that should stay with us – whether it is a young man or woman who compromises their heart or a cool, clear stream turned foul. And why does it happen?

The campus organization BACCHUS helps reveal part of the dark answer. At least one prominent source of moral pollution is parties where alcohol and sensuality flow freely; they invite a lapse of judgment and resulting ethical corruption.

The belief that sex before marriage is healthy or that intense high school and college female and male sensuality is not even noticed these days is a lie that is older than ancient Ephesus. As the Song of Songs expresses, "do not awaken nor stir up love until love itself shall please" (2:7, *The New Berkeley Version*; see also 3:5 and 8:4). G. Lloyd Carr has suggested that the sentence carries the meaning "don't start the process of loving exchange until the opportunity and appropriate occasion is present."[10] That appropriate occasion in the Song of Songs and in the presence of the Lord is called marriage.

C. S. Lewis captured well just how spiritually important was the matter of human affection and attraction – and as well how great the potential for godly joy and hope. In his book *The Screwtape Letters*, one of Satan's servants, Wormwood, is having some trouble with the human subject assigned to its "care," and Screwtape (another demon) is providing counsel. It seems that the human subject – a Christian man – has found himself captivated by a young woman and in the worst kind of a relationship possible (according to Screwtape). She does not even appear in Wormwood's report (because the demon is hiding the situation...)! So, Screwtape does some research of its own, only to find the following information about the young woman. The information sends it spiraling out of control with rage at how things are taking shape:

> Not only a Christian but such a Christian – a vile, sneaking, simpering, demure, monosyllabic, mouse-like, watery, insignificant, virginal, bread-and-butter miss. The little brute. She makes me vomit. She stinks and scalds through the very pages of the dossier. It drives me mad, the way the world has worsened.[11]

So, what is the translation of Screwtape's dossier from "demonese" to English with a Christian perspective? She is a Christian beauty! A virgin. She loves the God of heaven and earth, cares about others, and quietly helps. Her smile, her eyes, her truthfulness, her modesty and uncompromising moral values, and her kindness have sent dark forces scurrying for a cover story for their failure. She has lit up the world around her and captivated a young man's eyes and heart.

C. S. Lewis saw how crucial to faith and spiritual growth were moments of affection and male-female relationships under construction. By the sheer power of our senses and our humanity, those moments could cause people's hopes, and even spirituality, to hang in the balance. As Lewis well pictured, they represented moments and relationships that dark forces remained highly interested in subverting, distorting and destroying. At the same time, affection and godly relationships built represented one of the greatest joys in the world. Consider the power of two people with common spiritual hope and with a common goal with which to fill all of life. Together, they would light up the world even more! The goal should spur parents to spend time with their children. They need to listen carefully to what sensuality their children are seeing and how they compare the surrounding world with the counsel the Lord has provided.

Fun, Games, and Superheroes

In addition to formal education and cult beauty contests, Ephesus knew fun and games as well. The discovery of coins from the ancient city has provided its own glimpse into Ephesian entertainment as well as its mingling of commerce and religion. Well-preserved examples of a coin minted in the city depict two boys playing the ancient game of *Astragali* (Knucklebones) at the foundation of the *Artemisium* (the Temple of Artemis). Coins from as early as the fifth century B.C. include imagery of knucklebones being associated with the Artemis religion. If we look at our practice of engraving coins with the images of important individuals or events in our history, then the presence of a children's game pictured on an ancient coin should grab our attention. The game must have been a prominent, frequent, well-known part of Ephesian religion and society.

Knucklebones represented a form of fortune-telling and probably as well entertainment. The game was played with four elbow bones from a goat, with meanings attached to how the bones landed when tossed.[12] Similar to our game of dice and the roll of "snake eyes," Knucklebones tosses could take on meanings varying from good fortune to calamity. Some of the bones even had the names of supposed deities carved into them.[13] We do not know whether children and teens took the tosses seriously or rather saw them as actions where they would laugh and tease each other about a given roll. It would be no surprise to learn that both elements came into play. It may be that the older they got, the more they made emotional (and perhaps economic) investments and developed some form of faith in associated cults.

Boys in our day carry the same interests in games – be they board games, those of the video variety, or the type that requires a field or court. We are reminded of one of the ways boys learn as we watch their amazing split-second decisions in a sports event. Boys' feet and minds are directly connected; typically, they are thinking and learning when their feet are moving! Indeed, the recent trend in some parts of the nation away from public school recess typically has placed boys at a learning disadvantage.[14] They need "run time." As Derek Kidner quipped regarding Psalm 127:3-4, "The greater their promise, the more likely that these sons will be a handful before they are a quiverful."[15]

Perhaps for that reason a superhero cape can often be found among a given boy's dirty clothes. Leaping from a tree branch or swinging on a rope are some of the ways boys learn – and even calculate as they develop basic engineering skills. But they can learn more than distance and time calculations as they grow. Sometimes they learn New Age religion – without knowing it. For example, the cartoon adventures of *Captain Planet* feature nothing less than Gaia concepts – a form of Earth Spiritualism – dressed up in superhero costumes. Equally as dangerous, music videos and video games at times feed them messages that mimic those of decadent ancient religions – such as the Dionysus cult. Keeping them (and their parents) from a dark, spiritual "sucker punch" remains crucial to spiritual development.

All of this reinforces what most parents sense. Children need to grow spiritually in order to filter through what they see and hear. They need to hear the Word in ways that allow their bodies and minds to digest the message well. Reading the Word in a Bible class is important; so also are opportunities for them to learn by activity. Consider, for example, the place of the Feast of Tabernacles (Lev. 23:33-44) or Passover in Jewish learning. Constructing a house out of sticks or eating a meal quickly while recalling the Exodus provided an enduring memory for children as they were growing up. Our children benefit from illustrations of the interaction between God and humanity; often, they need imagery to help them grow spiritually. It helps them as they mature – like the change from a delicate ball of gray fluff to the regal red or orange plumage of a cardinal sailing on the wind.

Training and Instruction in the Lord – in Song

Similarly, singing carries significant power in teaching children. Public school teachers and Bible class teachers alike have learned to couch some of their most penetrating teaching in the rhyme and melody of songs. Letting children or teens sing together provides them with a way to learn as they express their emotions and their energy. It unites them and allows them to contribute versus listening only. Perhaps for that reason numerous public school teachers have returned to an emphasis on vocal music as a means to teach.

One skilled, nurturing preschool Bible class teacher, Lora Laycook, left an enduring legacy of teaching-by-song. Her teaching and her song digest *A Treasure Chest for Bible Teachers* have influenced at least two generations of children and teachers. Countless children have grown up rolling through their minds the songs she taught them. Jesus' frequent reference to the Psalms in his teaching suggests similar childhood experiences of singing to God by the Son of man.

Extending Bible teaching in song and praise into our worship assemblies remains equally important for our children and teens. Bringing into our assemblies the opportunity for all to sing – young children included – represents one of the most powerful, unifying experiences for a church, a family of God worshiping together. To add a simple children's song or a song especially enjoyed by teens to the list of songs for a Sunday assembly represents a simple action with long-term memories for our children.

Conclusion

Teaching our children patiently, counseling them when the spiritual storms come, and teaching with sensitivity as to how they best learn represent three key characteristics of spiritual instruction. Typically, mothers are well aware of the needs; fathers may be challenged more to keep the needs in mind. Perhaps for that reason Paul directed his instruction to fathers (Eph. 6:4).

Further, our children will remember the times parents sang with them in a Sunday assembly, especially when they were feeling hurt. They will remember attention to moments when they were spiritually unsettled by what they saw and/or heard in the world around them.

Perhaps at the top of the list, they will remember times of spiritual comfort when someone close to them dies. It is likely they will come to a time in their life when they feel the death of Jesus acutely. It is then that they will need a parent, guardian, or friend most. They will need help to work through the pain and guilt of what they have done that is wrong and the fact that someone had to die for them. The words of the song *Jesus Loves Me* may ring in their mind. Parents will have reason to rejoice when they see young hearts singing *I Stand in Awe of You* as they mentally visit Gethsemene, Golgotha, and an empty tomb.

Chapter Ten

Men, Women, and the Church's Worship and Work - Part 1

(Luke 10:38-42; Ephesians 2:6; 1 Corinthians 11, 14)

Few religious topics have urged greater discussion in the early twenty-first century than women religious leaders. The reason? Religious thought and action among many groups continues to take a path that is counter to American equal rights thinking. Many women have expressed hurt and anger at the notion that women do not have the same right to speak as men in the religious assemblies of some churches.

Equal rights advocates have suggested that the barriers previously raised in our nation hindered the Gospel of Christ from being properly heard. In their judgment to teach that Paul's messages in Ephesians 5:22-24 and 1 Timothy 2:11-12 have relevance in our equal rights society represents nothing less than evil. They believe such teaching is wrong.[1] They strongly suggest that Paul's teaching was intended only to guide until we reached a free and matured society – with freedom of speech and equal opportunities for all.

In the balance, those who challenge an equal rights view of Paul's teachings react with similar zeal. They have suggested that equal rights advocates are yielding to the surrounding culture. As Carroll Osburn has well observed, the discussion surrounding Ephesians 5:22-24 and 1 Timothy 2:11-12 actually represents part of the broader discussion of equal rights and the Bible.[2] So, what does the New Testament announce regarding the spiritual status of women? What was the Ephesian church experiencing and what is the meaning of Paul's response? What relationship does the teaching have with Paul's teachings in 1 Corinthians 11:2-16 and 14:33b-36? Finally, what, if any, application of 1 Timothy 2:9-15 should we be making in our day?

Challenging a Corrupt View of Women

Listening to the answer to the first question often represents a rough road for women. Part of the challenge of reading the New Testament has come in the form of distractions as dangerous as the deceiving winds of the Ephesian cults. As one example Tertullian, an early third century religious leader, called women "the gateway of the Devil."[3] He was not limiting his comment to immoral cult members. His shrill language included even Christian women. Ironically, in making his general assessment he himself had fallen into a dark trap. His writing revealed that he was as much a gateway of the Devil as were women he had met who had influenced his view.

Further waves of insult and harm have washed into our day from Augustine and from medieval Dominican thought. The fourth century religious leader proposed that women were only in the image of God when they were married; if single they were not![4] The fifteenth century Catholic document *Malleus Maleficarum* suggested that women's sensuality inclined them toward evil. Both Tertullian and Augustine, as well as some Catholic teaching, have been the focus of feminist attacks – for good reason. The teachings have corrupted the Word of a good Creator.

The birth of Jesus announces the beauty and purity of Mary in the sight of the Lord. The teaching that Mary remained a virgin – untouched by the supposed taint of sexuality – clashes with Mark 3:20-32. The Gospel of Mark makes clear that Jesus' mother and brothers came to see him during the early days of his public ministry. At least initially, they judged that Jesus' actions were inappropriate and had come to take charge of him. Given the Gospel narrative, no reason exists to suggest that Mary and Joseph experienced no sexual relations. Similarly, does the Gospel of Luke announce that Elizabeth was 'tainted' by the birth of John? Does Jesus ever hint at such a corruption of sexuality in women (or men)?

What the Scriptures announce is that woman was created good and beautiful. Sensuality and sexuality were created good by a good Creator. The Gospels clash with the belief that something in women is amiss. It challenges religious teaching that casts a shadow on the sensuality and sexuality of women. The powerful image of the glorious bride of Christ dispels such shadows (Eph. 5:25-27 and Rev. 21:2). Certainly, temptation that preys on our emotions can contribute to the decision to sin. However, human sensuality – both male and female – represents no natural evil.

A similar corrupt view of womanhood is illustrated by the (apocryphal) *Gospel of Thomas* (not written by Thomas). The supposed Gospel includes the following supposed dialogue between Jesus and Peter:

> Simon Peter said to them "Let Mary go out from among us, because women are not worthy of the Life." Jesus said: "See, I shall lead her, so that I will make her male, that she too may become a living spirit (πνευμα), resembling you males. For every woman who makes herself male will enter the Kingdom of Heaven.[5]

Nothing in the New Testament matches the above words. It is possible that the author of the apocryphal gospel is echoing Galatians 3:26 and the idea of sonship. However, the author has missed Paul's message as much as have equal rights advocates in our day. While the *Gospel of Thomas* suggests that women must "make themselves male," that is exactly the opposite of what Paul is writing in Galatians 3:26-28. The apostle is announcing that no gender, race, or social barrier limits God's work. All who have been baptized into Christ are God's people. Women do not need to "make themselves" anyone! Jesus Christ gives them wondrous status as members of his household. The writer of the *Gospel of Thomas* was guilty of nothing less than harmful, even cruel, corruption of Jesus' glorious work and apostolic teaching.

Satan has twisted a good creation and distorted Scripture in every age. The painful, historical fact is that many kind, spiritually minded women have had to put up with post-apostolic evil for 1900 years or more. So, it is little wonder that female followers of Christ and unbelievers who are interested can, at times, feel bone-weary from looking for calm off a stormy sea of spiritual deception.

Galatians 3:28, Ephesians 2:6, and a Royal Priesthood

When people think of New Testament teaching about the status of men and women, frequently Galatians 3:28 has come to mind. The text indeed announces wondrous blessing – and spiritual status in Christ. It is, however, no announcement of civil and legal rights. Instead, the apostle's teaching has everything to do with being freed from sin and given the status of heirs in God's household. For all of her bombastic assessments of Christianity, the feminist Mary Daly's critique of much religious thought about Galatians 3:28 is correct. She has argued that the teaching is no more an equal rights slogan than is 1 Timothy 2:11-15.

As a result of being made righteous by Christ, both male and female are priests before God. Apostolic teaching announces no ministerial priests, such as were common in the ancient world. Indeed, that is part of the purpose of Galatians 3:26-4:7 – to dispel such concepts. It announces that Christians are heirs; they are spiritual offspring with the highest of status. No longer does gender or race define God's household; tattered clothing and empty pockets present no barrier to his love. All are priests. In Christ all may come before the throne of God (Eph. 2:6, 1 Ti. 2:5, Heb. 8:1-10:17, 1 Pet. 2:9). Indeed, the idea of a ministerial priest separate from a church "laity" corrupts Galatians 3:28 and Ephesians 2:6. Apostolic teaching knows no mediator save Jesus Christ (Acts 4:10-12).

Consider the implications for our day. When a Christian woman goes before the throne of God in the quietness of her household or her seat in a worship assembly, she is acting from a royal position that knows no higher. She comes as a result of her status as a priestess at the right hand of the Creator of the universe. Taking up the spiritual reality Paul announces in Ephesians 2:6, suddenly eyes of faith can see a house or church building filled with light that dazzles – as the glory of heaven explodes into this world. The reality is that she is seated in heaven and speaks from a position unequaled by earthly roles. Allowing our spiritual understanding to be shaped only by who visibly leads a worship assembly misses what the Lord sees. No action by a president, judge, health care professional, athlete, Congresswoman, professor, news anchor, or actress has had (or will have) equal or greater significance. "Brotherhood," while certainly no derogatory word, carries no greater importance than "sisterhood" in Christ.

The ancient world balanced to a great degree on the life and work of its priestesses and priests. It held them in high esteem as mediators between earth and the supernatural realm. If our day often has replaced the role of a priest with a banking, judicial, or medical role,[6] it has also failed to see the status and responsibility given to both priests and priestesses of Christ. We need to keep close in heart the words "royal priesthood" (1 Pet. 2:9) and Paul's teaching in Ephesians 2:6. Christians – both men and women – have the gift from the Lord of an astonishing spiritual status and responsibility in this world.

The Portrait of Women in Luke and Acts

The Acts of the Apostles provides a view of the early church that parallels apostolic teaching about the priestly status of men and women in Christ. Luke, the traveling companion of Paul, charts the spread of the Gospel and the work of the Apostles (and many others). He shows the promise fulfilled of a spiritual blessing to the entire world (Acts 1:8; 10:47-48; 11:20-21; 13:46-47; 15:12-18; 28:25-28). As part of the portrait, Luke also reveals that Christ captured the attention and hearts of many first century women. He makes clear that a significant number of prominent women in both Thessalonica (Acts 17:4) and Berea (Acts 17:12) became believers. In addition, he records Lydia's conversion in the Macedonian city of Philippi and also her persuasiveness and hospitality (Acts 16:11-15).

During the past thirty years, numerous religious feminists have given considerable attention to Luke's Gospel and the Acts of the Apostles. They have anticipated that the large number of references to women in the writings would carry important messages about women in earliest Christianity.[7] In short, while some have overstated Luke's purpose,[8] perhaps ironically their studies have helped shed light on the writings.

Luke's Gospel uniquely records Jesus' culture-shaking response to the actions and words of two women of Bethany, Mary and Martha (Lk. 10:38-42). Mary's actions as a student at Jesus' feet are commended. Feminists have been correct that the narrative represented no small message. It provided a new view of women as legitimate students of a rabbi; gone was the deep-rooted image of only boys and men being students of the Scriptures.[9] Both men and women were to be involved in searching the Scriptures and listening to the Lord's teachings.

Similarly, Luke also communicates the role of women in the early church. Mary Rose D'Angelo has suggested that the Acts of the Apostles was written both to edify and encourage women and also to educate them regarding the boundaries of discreet behavior.[10] She has suggested that Luke's narratives of the actions and contributions of women are accompanied by a description of the limitation of their roles.[11] While she is not enamored with the message, she believes that Christian women "in large part accepted the propriety of limitations that gender placed upon them – and taught it to their daughters."[12]

Turid Seim has also contributed an important study of Luke's purposes in the Acts of the Apostles. Her survey has suggested that the

Gospel of Luke and Acts clearly highlighted and promoted the learning, contributions and faith of women. Prophetesses (Acts 21:9); Dorcas (Acts 9:36-42); Damaris, an Athenian with some relationship to the Areopagus (Acts 17:28); Priscilla (Acts 18:26); women who were devoted to listening to the Lord's teaching and searching the Scriptures (Acts 17:11-12). All are part of the message of the Word spreading. Women are to be involved in the activity; they too are missionaries.

Seim has suggested that Luke was providing a double message. He was portraying men and women as having equal status within the body of Christ; both were priests before the Lord. However, he was also describing strict boundaries for women's activity in the Jewish and Mediterranean worlds.[13] The feminist surveys have highlighted carefully how the Acts of the Apostles carried two clear messages. Women were to be involved in learning and spreading the Word. However, limitations also existed regarding their teaching role in some public spheres. So, what should we make of Paul's teachings in light of the history that Luke writes?

Corinth and Ephesus: The Story of Two Cities

Many students of the New Testament have suggested 1 Corinthians 11:2-16 to be the key to understanding all of Paul's teachings regarding women and teaching the Word. Most have concluded that Paul was permitting prophetesses to speak in the worship assembly in Corinth.[14] They have proposed that the text guides us to see 1 Timothy 2:9-15 (and 1 Corinthians 14:33b-36) as addressing unique situations. The idea is that Paul was not limiting women teaching men in the assembly *per se*. After all, he is endorsing their doing so in Corinth. Paul is not telling them to stop in 1 Corinthians 11:2-16. Instead, he is only telling them how to dress. Correct? So, he must have been addressing an attitude issue among some (or all) of the women in worship assemblies in Corinth (and Ephesus).[15]

In an effort to eliminate apparent conflict, some have also suggested that 14:33b-36 was not part of Paul's original letter.[16] However, the various manuscripts of the letter show that the question is where 14:33b-36 fits in chapter 14, not whether Paul wrote the teaching.[17] 1 Corinthians 14 has to do with supernatural speech and we should recognize that Paul continues to talk about such in 14:33b-36.[18] So, how do we reconcile 1 Corinthians 11:2-16 with 14:33b-36? Is there a unique situation in the Corinthian assembly?

The questions hinge on whether prophecy and prayer are always associated with Christian worship assemblies. An alternative does exist. 1 Corinthians 11:17 guides us to better understand 11:2-16. Verse seventeen urges us to rethink the scope of Paul's teaching in 11:2-16. As Everett Ferguson, for one, has suggested, we should recognize an important contrast between 1 Corinthians 11:17 and 1 Corinthians 11:2-16. He proposes that 11:2-16 has to do with public settings in the city of Corinth – not the setting of a Christian worship assembly.[19] The apostle's focus in 11:2-16 is on propriety in public; verse seventeen signals a change to a focus on the Corinthian worship assemblies.

So, if 11:2-16 has to do with public settings in the city, what was prompting the apostle's counsel? It may be that ancient cults were putting pressure on propriety. For example, women's hair often figured prominently in ancient cult worship. The second century A.D. traveler Pausanias tells us that one Corinthian cult statue was covered with offerings of women's hair.[20] Further, historical evidence suggests that, similar to Ephesus, the Dionysus cult thrived in Corinth prior to Paul's time and probably in the first century as well.[21] Intoxication, long, waving hair, and frenzied speech characterized the worship.[22] It is likely that the city's streets were very familiar with high-octane Dionysiac religion. Its cult members were known for their public religious displays, often unattached to a temple.

Given the message of Acts, we should see Christian prophetesses as involved in teaching about Christ in public settings within the city – similar to Dionysus priestesses. Perhaps they were even teaching where cult leaders were seen and heard. Paul's reference to uncovered heads suggests that he is contrasting the Christian prophetesses with commonly seen female cult leaders. It appears Paul is praising the Christian prophetesses of Corinth for their "street" evangelism, but counseling them regarding their attire. Further, 1 Corinthians 14:33b-36 may have been written to address the influence of Dionysiac religion in the Corinth church. The Dionysus cult played a prominent role in the city life of Corinth as well as Ephesus. So also did the sensual activities of the priest-esses of Aphrodite.[23] Given the religious winds blowing in the city, the apostle's guidance regarding propriety by women spreading the Word publicly in the city would have been no surprise.

Further, Paul is not talking about private, family worship settings – where the question of veils would not have arisen.[24] Instead, the Christian prophetesses of Corinth are being urged to conduct their public teaching (including teaching among groups of women) with propriety. The apostle is also instructing women to show propriety as well wherever they pray in public. Our equal rights mindset has impressed onto the text messages about women's leadership in Christian assemblies that Paul was not giving. It is only at 1 Corinthians 11:17 that the apostle turns his attention specifically to worship assemblies. He confirms in 14:33b-36 that Christian prophetesses should remain quiet within the assembly; they should not be teaching/preaching in mixed groups of adults.

1 Corinthians 11:2-16 and 14:33b-36 paint an important portrait of the Spirit of God at work, guiding when difficult questions surface. First, the apostle guides Christians to understand the general matter of headship and Christian propriety in public settings within the city. Then, he confirms the role of prophetesses in Christian assemblies. If anyone wants to draw a different conclusion, Paul reminds his readers that what he writes is the Lord's command.

Conclusion

Remarkably, among Luke's many portraits of the conversions of women, he provides no portrait of women in the capital city of Asia. Luke's lengthy narrative (Acts 19) about Paul's work and the many converts in Ephesus includes no mention of women. He mentions twelve men who spoke in tongues and prophesied (Acts 19:6-7), but no women. It is certainly possible that Ephesus and Asia did not have Christian prophetesses. However, in the very place where it is likely that he could have described public religious leadership by Christian women, Luke provides no record of the work of women. Luke's record of Paul's stay in Corinth reads the same way.

Similarly, Paul's letters to Ephesus and Colossae include little mention of individual women converts in the capital city and province; Nympha may be the only example (Col. 4:15). Further, it is in focusing on Ephesus that Luke provides a record of Paul's interaction with elders (Acts 20:13-38).

In comparison with the warm, positive descriptions of the Christian women of Macedonia (Acts 16:13-15; 17:4, 10-12), Luke's almost complete silence about the Christian women of Ephesus, Asia, and Corinth is remarkable.[25] The women of Macedonia, especially Lydia, provide a portrait as important as that of Mary (Lk. 10:39, 42). In describing Lydia's persuasiveness, Luke uses a word found only one other time in the New Testament; it is used to describe the disciples' response to Jesus and his teaching (Lk. 24:29).[26] Mary; Mary Magdalene; Joanna; Susanna (Lk. 8:2-3); Tabitha (Acts 9:36); Lydia; Priscilla (Acts 18:26); Mary, Jesus' mother (Acts 1:14); Philip's four daughters who prophesied (Acts 21:9). The portraits and examples are intended to both encourage and teach Christian women.

More than merely recording history, Luke was emphasizing both the new role of women in learning and in spreading the Word in private settings and some public settings. He was also describing the limitations to the role of women in congregational worship settings. Luke's Gospel and Acts present women with the goals of searching the Scriptures and teaching others. However, they are to avoid taking a leadership role in a church and prophesying in the church's worship assemblies.

The message in Acts represents one that some may dismiss as patriarchal and provincial. Does it matter what the Acts of the Apostles says about the male leadership of the churches in the first century? The question illustrates a powerful challenge to Christianity in our time. As we have seen, part of the answer has nothing to do with a specific point in time and everything to do with how we see God. How do we view the Creator's wisdom? Does the God who made us love both male and female perfectly? Does he treat male and female equally?

The questions that equal rights advocates press also ignores what we now know about the ancient world. First century religious culture was not as thoroughly patriarchal and supposedly dissimilar to our time as some have suggested. Ephesian and Corinthian religion included significant expressions of female authority and leadership, similar to much popular religion in our day. The Dionysus and Isis cults, in particular, fashioned such roles for women (see Appendix C).[27] The Artemis cult may have as well. As such the messages of Acts and of Paul's letters to cities familiar with religious leadership by women should catch our attention. The apostle was speaking to a religious culture in some ways like our own.

On the same canvas as Luke's dual portraits in Acts, Paul paints an important portrait of female coworkers (e.g. Ro. 16). However, the apostle's words have also prompted feminists to suggest that Phoebe and others like her led churches.[28] Given what we see in Luke's portrait of women's roles in the early church, this conclusion misrepresents Paul's purpose. The apostle gives no indication that his female coworkers led churches, but he does want congregations to be aware of the contributions of women in spreading the Word. However, the conclusions of feminists at this point do introduce us to the intense discussion that has focused on Paul's letters and especially his teaching in 1 Timothy 2:11-15.

Chapter Eleven

Men, Women, and the Church's Worship and Work - Part 2

(1 Timothy 2:8-15; 2 Timothy 3:15)

Was Paul providing a broad teaching in 1 Timothy 2:11-15 or was he instead addressing a specific, local problem only? Was his teaching intended for Ephesus (and perhaps Asia) alone? What is the application, if any, of 1 Timothy 2:9-15 for Christians in the twenty-first century? Evidence from the second century illustrates that the work of women preachers (e.g. prophetesses among the Montanists) remained a live question just a short seventy-five years or less after Paul's death. Fast-forwarding to American religious culture, some have argued that limiting the role of women has distorted the Gospel. So, what was Paul saying in his first letter to Timothy?

1 Timothy 2:11-12: Learning About the Lord

Students of 1 Timothy 2:11-15 have drawn varying conclusions regarding what was happening in the Ephesian church that prompted Paul's teaching. Some have proposed that Paul was addressing the influence of wealthy women who were exercising too much authority.[1]

Another writer has suggested that Paul was teaching the Christians in Ephesus to avoid self-indulgence.[2] Carroll Osburn has proposed that the general issues of false teaching (1 Ti. 1:3, 4:1-3) and domineering women were disturbing the Ephesian church.[3] Similarly, another historian has suggested that dominant women, perhaps influenced by the Artemis religion, were ruling over men in the congregation and Paul saw a need to halt the behavior.[4]

Those who have emphasized an issue of dominant women have pointed to the rare Greek word *authentein* that Paul used in 1 Timothy 2:12. The uncommon word has acquired as much attention as an unsecured sail in a storm. The Greek word typically has been translated as "usurp authority" (KJV) or "have authority" (NIV). Carroll Osburn has suggested that it carries the stronger meaning of "domineer" (*New English Bible*).[5] Given what we now know about the word, he and others are likely correct that it has a meaning stronger than "have authority." Paul could have used a more common word with the meaning of "have authority," but he uses a rare word that describes someone who chooses to "exercise authority" (NASB).

Carroll Osburn suggests that it should carry the sense of dominance in the text and that we should see it as modifying "teach." His proposal leads to a translation of "teaching domineeringly."[6] The idea is that Paul is guiding toward an attitude of "peaceableness/quietness" instead of one that is domineering.[7] However, this would have left the Ephesian congregation with an interesting question. When was a woman teaching men with an attitude of peaceableness and quietness and when was she not? Also, it leaves an awkward relationship between verses eleven and twelve.

What we make of women not being permitted to "exercise authority" parallels "must be silent" (1 Ti. 2:12b, NIV). Further, 1 Timothy 2:12 elaborates on what Paul is directing in 1 Timothy 2:11. As Neil Lightfoot has observed, the latter command reiterates "learn in quietness" (1 Ti. 2:11, NIV); the relationship of the verses "makes it clear that her submissiveness consists of her not being permitted to teach or have authority over men."[8] 1 Timothy 2:11, not 2:12, represents the important beginning of the instruction. "Learn in quietness" (1 Ti. 2:11, NIV) does not mean "teach in/with quietness."[9]

While it is possible that some of the women were disagreeing with some of the men, we do not need to know the specifics. It is enough to understand something of the religious culture of Ephesus and Asia. It is likely that some of the Christian women of Ephesus (and Asia) were acting with a strength of will developed from years of cult leadership. 1 Timothy 2:11 makes clear that Paul is directing the Ephesian women toward learning and submission in the assembly, not a peaceable leadership role. Women who previously had led worship devoted to Dionysus, Isis, or Artemis would have understood the apostle – even if surprised by the teaching.

The teaching probably surprises no less in our day. Learn only? Submission? In a time filled with male and female ability and confidence, the teaching swims against a strong current. But the apostle is not saying that women should avoid teaching the Word. Instead, he is announcing the purposes and roles within church assemblies. Cynthia Diane Guy has highlighted well that a woman "is not violating Scripture by teaching or having authority over men outside the spiritual realms of church and home."[10] Dorothy Patterson offers that the apostolic boundaries of 1 Timothy 2:11-12 "will make a woman's learning, and the outworking of that learning, most meaningful to her, most edifying to the kingdom, and above all most God-glorifying in the overall schema of the Father's plan."[11] One of the challenges – for both men and women – is to look beyond deeply-embedded deception to see how the Word can and will best spread. We can expect to be hindered and deceived in that task, just as was the Ephesian church.

Finally, the KJV translation of "usurp authority" (Eph. 2:12) is possible, but only if we recognize what the translators likely were hoping to achieve. They were attempting to render the unique word close to the meaning of "domineer." However, some have missed the message and suggested that if a man gives authority in an assembly to a woman, she is not usurping authority.[12] This also misses Paul's corresponding message for women to learn. According to what Paul writes, men do not have purview to give authority; that is not the meaning of the apostle's teaching.

1 Timothy 2:13-15: The Basis for Paul's Teaching

Beyond the specifics of 1 Timothy 2:11-12, what Paul makes clear is that female submission in the assembly is based on Adam being formed first, then Eve, and Eve being deceived. 1 Timothy 2:13-15 serves as the mast and rigging for the mainsail of Paul's teaching in 1 Timothy 2:11-12.

Carroll Osburn suggests that 1 Timothy 2:13-14 represents no more than a use of Jewish rabbinic tradition to emphasize that women should not be leading men astray. As he writes, "Paul does not draw from Gen. 1-3 a universal principle from the historical Eve, but an ad hoc analogy from the later caricature of Eve in Jewish tradition."[13] But is the analogy true? No, it is a rabbinic caricature without historical foundation in Scripture. So if Paul is using it, why would he do so? Is it because of his rabbinic training?

Ultimately, Carroll Osburn's suggestion raises an enormous question. Did the Spirit of God guide Paul to use Jewish opinion about Genesis 1-4 as opposed to the truth of Genesis 1-3? Or equally devastating, was Paul hindering the Spirit's guidance in the teaching? No matter what conclusion we draw regarding Paul's sources (I believe he is using Genesis 1-3, not rabbinic tradition about Genesis 1-4), the point is inescapable. Paul is basing his teaching on Adam being formed first, then Eve. He believes it is truth from God. It is the foundation of what the apostle teaches and no discussion of rationale, method, or source changes the teaching. Either he is an apostle speaking for the Lord and by God's power or he is no more than another Jewish teacher struggling for answers in a Gentile world.

Other equal rights advocates have argued as well against Paul's use of Genesis 1-3 and a creation order in 1 Timothy 2:13. However, their arguments have left them with nothing but mud for footing – because Paul could not have been clearer. It is here that equal rights advocates have faced one of their greatest challenges – and temptations. Roger Nicole, for one, concludes that by leaning on Jewish tradition Paul stumbles in making his case![14] Ironically, many feminists have been more candid about what 1 Timothy 2:9-15 is teaching than have some Evangelicals and some Restorationists. Why? The feminists have already concluded that 1 Timothy has represented nothing more than human reflection.

1 Timothy 2:13 has become one of the watersheds of Christian understanding in the early twenty-first century (see Appendix B). It has taken shape as a window into how people see the authority and actions of the risen Jesus and apostolic work and self-understanding. Did the risen Christ have the power and wisdom to guide the apostles through the Spirit? And was Jesus successful? While it is but one verse, 1 Timothy 2:13 has affected American religious thought similar to the magnitude of shock waves it likely caused in first century Ephesus and Asia.

Paul is making clear to the Ephesian church that men are to be leading and women are to cease teaching men in the assembly. Instead of teaching, women are to be learning. Further, the apostle gives no indication that he is limiting his teaching to Ephesus (and Asia). Instead, the reference to Adam and Eve announces a teaching with authority that stretches across the earth and across time – to the twenty-first century as well. Our equal rights society is not far removed from the religious culture of ancient Ephesus. Additionally, the New Testament provides no comment that what Paul writes is in conflict with the Lord's wisdom.

In addition to the frenzy of discussion that has surrounded 1 Timothy 2:13-14, Paul's words in 1 Timothy 2:15 have raised their own share of debate.[15] Students of the text have suggested diverse conclusions: 1) women will be saved by having children; 2) women will be kept safe through the childbearing process;[16] 3) woman will be the means by which God's Son enters the world and brings salvation. The teaching may represent Paul's addressing false teaching in the congregation relative to avoiding marriage and having children (1 Ti. 4:1-

7; 5:14). In response to false teachers, the apostle makes clear that childbearing and general domestic responsibility represents the Lord's will for women.[17] He may be using "childbearing" as a general term, looking back to Eve and the Lord's command to replenish the earth.

As to applying 1 Timothy 2:11-15, it makes little sense to suggest that Paul's words were addressing only his day and only God's people in Ephesus and Asia. History announces that the struggle with gender roles and leadership has had more than a first century character. For example, it rippled into the second century and surfaced in the Montanists of Asia Minor and the religious group's prophetesses and leaders.[18] The threat of Montanism became so serious that it spurred the collection of apostolic writings in the second century. Church leaders were attempting to diminish and overcome the movement's false teaching and practices. An equal rights religious culture has had numerous cousins.

Focusing on the Unseen

1 Timothy 2:8-15 is one of those texts where strong cultural currents can close a person to all that is being said. Certainly, Paul's teaching says much about gender roles, propriety, and modesty. However, it also says a great deal about focusing on the unseen. The apostle to the Gentiles is counseling the Ephesian congregation to look up – to the heavenly realm. He is urging the Christians in the region to leave behind the powerful visual trappings of the native Asian religions and look to the true God. And he is counseling his people how to help others look up.

Men are to lift up holy hands in prayer. Women are to dress modestly, with propriety, and with actions of goodness to others. Both are to focus their eyes on the risen Christ. The teachings complement as Paul guides the Christians in the city to displace sensual, selfish religion and turn hearts to the unseen Creator. So, does this mean that men should be lifting up holy hands in prayer in our time? Yes, it does – either that or they should be bowing down (Phil. 2:10). Is Paul telling Christian men that the only form of acceptable prayer is by lifting hands upward? No, but he is emphasizing that men leading the assembly need to lead people to focus their hearts upward. Egyptian wall paintings of religious rituals with hands held high tell us enough to know that the practice was not unique to Jewish worship (cf. Ps. 63:4, 134:2).

Paul's instructions to women to avoid calling attention to their attire – but instead to good works – gives further guidance to the Ephesian church and to Christians today. The Ephesian assemblies needed to represent a clear departure from the frenzied, sensational worship that was characteristic of the Asian religious cults. The Christians were to be a people known for their selflessness, propriety, gentleness, acts of kindness to others, and their focus on the unseen God. The Lord's temple is nothing less than his people (Eph. 2:21-22).

The need has not changed 2000 years later; people still can be deceived by corrupt religious visualization. Even within the most plain of church buildings, our attention can be pulled to the sensational. As an example, recently I listened to a passionate, articulate sermon that urged people to think about God. However, the irony was that while the lesson filled the meeting place with impressive mental images, it represented a bank without assets, a vault without valuables. The thirty minutes of teaching included no statement from Scripture. Similar to the threat Ephesus faced, the lesson lost an apostolic "deposit" to what seemed more influential.

The native Asian religions knew well how to draw people; centuries of practice had crafted captivating, sensual systems of ritual. It is naïve to think that pressure from the Asian cults was not bearing down on believers in Christ, urging them to appear inviting to unbelievers by leaning on familiar expressions of sensational religion. With no intention to court darkness, elders/pastors, preachers, and teachers face exactly the same threat today. Efforts to appeal to unbelievers can begin to lean heavily toward the sensational. For example a place of worship near where I live recently announced itself by a message that probably would have resonated with the ancient Asian cults. The sign in front of the building said simply, "Christians Gone Wild."

To Go Where Only Women Can Go

One thread of evidence from the ancient world sheds considerable light on a role that Paul's female coworkers (e.g. Phoebe) may have played in spreading the Word. Sarah Pomeroy has noted that women-only religious gatherings were common in Rome.[19] The broader Mediterranean world knew a good bit of similarity – especially the province of Asia.

Barbara Goff has added to the portrait by observing that women gathering for Dionysus cult activities functioned as something of a women's city-within-a-city (see Appendix C).[20] Also, from what we know of at least Dionysiac religion, women-only cult gatherings would have been off limits to men, or at least men would have been unwelcome.[21] However, the female coworkers of Paul would have been warmly greeted and been able to do what Paul, Barnabas, Silas, Luke, and Timothy could not – at least initially. It may be that Phoebe, Euodia, and others went where only women could go in the ancient world – into gatherings of women devotees to Dionysus, Isis, Artemis, and Cybele.

In our day, the example of women working as a city-within-a-city remains significant. As an all too common scenario, many women live without a husband and it is unlikely that these women will welcome a team of men into their homes. Instead, the church's greatest opportunity to reach out to help women heal is probably by means of the care and support of other women.

Additionally, sometimes the warmth and nurturing character of many women allows outreach in a place where men likely would be less successful (e.g. in a medical care facility).[22] In a world filled with spiritual breakage, often women (and men) struggle to listen to spiritual teachers and friends – and ultimately to the Lord. Women can uniquely help other women leave what can be deep spiritual darkness. The deeper the dark, the more women initially may need the help of other women. In the middle of frequent time-pressure and other trials, similar to a midwife or nurse's help during childbirth, the nearness of another woman can represent crucial assistance.[23]

None of this represents late-breaking news. However, the growth of Wicca and other forms of mysticism provides an important signal as to the urgency. The church at the beginning of the twenty-first century has faced a culture and a task similar to what Paul faced throughout at least Roman Asia. The presence of women-only Dionysus religious groups as well as goddess worship groups had made it more difficult to reach women, suggesting that women reaching women needed to happen.

Given an equal rights culture and the hurt in many women, teams of women evangelists may represent one of the church's most important mission efforts in the early twenty-first century. Guidebooks such as *Woman to Woman* represent an important resource for churches as women prepare to reach out to other women.[24]

Further, if not already in place, churches need to consider tailoring Bible study environs to provide more women-only classes (including classes for teenage girls). Certainly, for decades many congregations have been providing women's studies during the week, often during the day. Both these kinds of studies, together with evening and Sunday studies, will match teachers to needs as women spread the Word.

Nurturing and Teaching Children and the Work of Women That Some Feminists Have All But Ignored

Our nation has a history filled with the quiet sacrifices of women who have cared for, educated and helped heal both their own children as well as those of many other families. America has witnessed remarkable selflessness by women who have cared for people caught in life-threatening epidemics. They have served as peacemakers on the playground and rescued children from learning disabilities. They have inspired many who themselves became healers, educators, builders, and leaders in subsequent decades.

I continue to recall the examples of many kind women who helped to mold and shape me and who rescued me from infections, broken bones, illiteracy, discouragement, and ignorance. No small tasks. I suspect such tasks have too quickly been overlooked in our day of jockeying for places of prominence and visibility. CEO; judge; university professor; researcher; project manager. All are important, but no more important than the women who have risked their lives for a next generation and kept a nation healing and learning through its history.

It is one of the dark, insidious paradoxes of our time that the very women who have cared for and educated a nation have not even received an endnote in the feminist literature I have read in the preparation of this book. Gladly, in the past decade, the situation seems to have finally shifted some. Our nation appears to better recognize the value of mothers, teachers, and medical professionals, as well as the importance of our children.

Some years ago, as I was teaching an adults Bible class, I made a suggestion regarding children's Bible classes. I offered that if women were to cease spiritual teaching of our children at home and in Bible classes, I believed the church would be no more than a shell of itself within one generation. In response, a former elder spoke up to offer, "Bruce, let me suggest that I think that is too long. It would happen in less than ten years." His comment led to important discussion as the entire class reflected on the crucial work of teaching children. I will gladly defer to a former elder's perspective here. Ten years or less. One decade. The observation is not one I am recommending we test.

For all of the important work of elders/pastors/overseers, evangelists, and deacons, what surfaced in that morning Bible study is the imperative of teaching children (1 Ti. 5:10; 2 Ti. 3:15). However, the work of teaching children can get lost, on occasion, in the middle of a busy world. Why? The children typically cannot articulate how important it is. Further, parents may not see the work accomplished on a given day in their Sunday rush. And finally, the teachers typically do not announce what they have accomplished. However, take the work away and we will see the consequences develop at an unsettling pace.

Probably no work announces a Christ-like selflessness more than a woman who spends many hours preparing to teach children. I suspect no group of people are better equipped to tell the same story of Jesus in ten different ways – all captivating and filled with song. Teachers light up the world of our children. They encourage our children. They may even be the only close-at-hand contact for some children who are in a desperate struggle to understand God's love and his Word. As a result of their work, many children are spiritually rescued by the Lord and in turn become equipped to spread the Word as well.

Conclusion

Joan Borysenko's *A Woman's Journey to God* breathes of kindness, intelligence, a deep understanding of women's medicine, and as well deep spiritual desire. It also seems to reflect the character, thought, and emotions of many women. The book flows out of Dr. Borysenko's *Gathering of Women* retreats, which she designed to help women heal physically, emotionally, and spiritually. The retreats have served as a popular gathering place for women angry at their religious roots, often defecting, and in search of a different answer.[25] It is likely she has sifted out a key learning as she discusses the importance of a place of intimacy, love, and safety where women can pray aloud with one another.[26] She also encourages women to be sensitive to the pace often urged by jobs, cell phones, and text messaging. She comments that equal rights has brought its own new danger; time-pressure coupled with frequent isolation in jobs is threatening one of womens' strengths: building strong relationships with others.[27] As a result she counsels women to take time to speak to God and to one another about the pain and the pressures in their lives.

Out of her personal search and her attention to the hurts in many women, Joan Borysenko has also suggested that, "One of the hallmarks of feminine spirituality is the permission to celebrate God in any form."[28] She has concluded that religion for women must be mystical and it must include the events and cycles that are crucial to women. The search for God/Goddess must be of the heart.[29] And yet in all of her searching and throughout *A Woman's Journey to God*, her heart does not consider the empty tomb of Jesus. She describes travels to meet a Hindu holy man and to practice Native American spiritual rituals. However, she describes no journey through the Gospels. She believes the New Testament narratives about Jesus – and all of the Bible – were written "by men for men."[30] She does not see the importance accorded women in the Gospel of Luke and the Acts of the Apostles. And she misses the power of Paul's words in Ephesians 5:21. She seems to refuse to mentally and emotionally look inside a first-century tomb, see the folded burial cloth, and consider the words of the angel: "He is not here; he has risen!" (Lk. 24:6, NIV) Perhaps her Jewish roots interfere with her search, but for whatever reason, she explores numerous claims to the supernatural touching our world, but not the claim of a risen Jesus.[31]

Joan Borysenko is not alone. The resurrection of Jesus has rarely surfaced throughout the feminist religious literature I have read as part of this study. Jesus' teaching is heartily mentioned by many feminists where he supports women. However, the times when he kindly rebukes a woman are ignored. Feminists typically do not embrace his every word. Why? The pain of any rebuke may seem too great for some. Additionally, I suspect in some cases it is because they have not yet walked to the entrance of the empty tomb and accepted the meaning of the event: his Kingship, his total spiritual authority. Instead, they seem to "grant" him a limited authority as his words fit their beliefs and goals (sometimes by mixing in the question of Scripture's reliability). Feminists, however, are not alone. Men have felt the temptation as well to hear Jesus at points without bowing to him as the risen King.

The rare mention of the resurrection of Jesus should sound an alarm. It gives us an unmistakable glimpse into a dark lord's work. Satan has been using the oppressive actions of self-destructing, loveless men and the hurt in women to bring about spiritual blindness, deception, and eventually a sense of hopelessness. Joan Borysenko's *A Woman's Journey to God* serves as a powerful illustration of one of the great needs early in the twenty-first century. Christian women need to reach out to other women. They need to help hurting women pray and help them consider the empty tomb and grow in faith in the risen Jesus. They need to counsel women wearied by pressure to find healing in the comfort of a Lord and older brother who will stand with them. He came and he rose from the dead as a man – but also as human. He knows and understands the needs, thoughts, and emotions of both men and women. He has the power to heal wounds and renew our minds.

Spiritual renewal helps us see the spiritual reality of all that surrounds us (2 Cor. 10:4-5). It helps us see the truth of a spiritual war that surrounds us, pelts us, and endangers us like the frigid, blowing sleet of a winter storm. It also helps us avoid forcing 1 Timothy 2:9-15 into an equal rights mold. The teaching urges men and women to help others look up to the risen Lord. Paul's purpose is far more encompassing than teaching and leading adults in worship assemblies. He calls attention to how the Lord wants every expression of our humanity – including the clothing we wear and the kindness we express – to help spiritually guide people to the risen Jesus.

Luke provides an important portrait of the faith and life of female disciples in the first century and makes it clear that the work of women was crucial to the spread of the Word. Many who had been deceived by decades of Artemis, Isis, Cybele, and Dionysus worship needed the help of other women to unravel themselves from powerful cults. The church needs to continue to act on a similar situation in the early twenty-first century.

Luke also highlights the contributions and importance of women in helping by serving others (cf. Acts 9:36). Women who followed Jesus did likewise. Whether helping heal sickness, feeding and clothing individuals, nurturing children, translating a Bible lesson for the hearing-impaired, or worshiping the Lord in song and quiet prayer, each action honors the risen Lord.

Early Christianity also knew women who applied their unique skills to "beautiful writing." They practiced the art of making visually inviting manuscripts so that many would have the opportunity to read the Word.[32] Similarly, in our day the number of Christian women who apply their remarkable creativity and language skills to writing and editing gladly grows.

At the center of the worship and work of the church are the wisdom and the will of the risen Lord. The empty tomb stands in the middle of the war of light versus darkness and the purposes of Christ's priests and priestesses. In 1 Timothy 2:8-15 Paul counsels both to act in ways that will nudge peoples' eyes and hearts upward. The roles of each are fashioned, not by the prevailing spirit of the time, but by the King who knows and loves male and female perfectly and who has given to both the mission of spreading his Word.

Chapter Twelve

Church Elders Then and Now

(1 Timothy 2:15; 3:1-7; Acts 20:13-38)

Few events affect the equal rights tenor of the nation like the actions of religious groups excluding women from leadership of churches. In the past three decades our nation has seen a growing number of religious groups revise their practices and appoint female pastors/elders. Paul's teaching in 1 Timothy 3:1-7 stands at the heart of the question of women elders/pastors. It also stands at the center of understanding the role of elders/pastors – both in the earliest churches and also in our time and place.

1 Timothy 3:1-7 may seem to represent an abrupt change of subject in the letter. Paul moves quickly from talking about women bearing children to discussing the role of elders/pastors. However, rather than see an abrupt change, Paul's message should prompt questions regarding the role of elders. What connection did 1 Timothy 2:15 have to congregational leaders? Also, what does the apostle say regarding church elders? Finally, what are the applications of Paul's teaching to church leadership for our day?

Women's Health Care and Ancient Ephesus

Medical issues would have come to mind as Paul urged Christian women to have children (1 Ti. 2:15). Judging from inscriptions that have been discovered to date, the Ephesians placed great weight on such matters – similar to our day.[1] Indeed, Ephesus served as one of the three great medical centers in the ancient world. Its Museum (Gk. *Mouseion*; i.e. college) of doctors and professors was famous.[2] The city's location near a swampy, coastal area – with associated insect-borne disease – may have contributed to the situation.

The first century was stalked by significant dangers associated with the birth and care of the next generation.[3] Women with child; the life-threatening event of labor; the care of infants and children. All had the supposed attention and protection of Artemis.[4] Additionally, the medical cost for a midwife's services reveals that service demand likely exceeded supply.[5] Valerie French has suggested from her study of ancient gynecology that the dangers of childbirth "must have made it an occasion of great anxiety for everyone concerned. The death of a woman or her baby was an all too common occurrence."[6] A recent archaeological find has further illustrated the at-risk situation of a woman bearing a child. A sarcophagus placed near the road between downtown Ephesus and the Temple of Artemis included the remains of a third century A.D. Ephesian woman, estimated to be thirty-five years of age. She died in pregnancy and was buried with a six-month-old child – perhaps the consequence of a common illness that had impacted the family.[7] In light of the challenges, the Ephesian women had a need to see a Christian alternative to the care of a supposed goddess.

The Person and Role of Elders in the Ephesus Church – and in Churches Today

Immediately following his statement about childbearing, Paul moves to talk about overseers (or elders, pastors, or bishops; the titles represent synonyms in the New Testament[8]). His words provide an important message in Ephesus. Surrounded by the power of the *synedrion* – the council and comptrollers of the Artemis cult[9] – Paul uses a word that conveys the idea of a family leader as opposed to a member of a council of priests. Indeed, it should catch our attention that the apostle did not use the term *synedrion* in describing the group of men who were to lead a congregation of Christians. Numerous religious groups in our day have departed from clear apostolic teaching to establish what mimics the ancient council of priests. However, they have done so without God's counsel.

Elders/pastors/overseers were to be men who watched over and cared for a church. They carried something of that role in their homes. However, Paul calls specific attention to their work within a congregation. Unlike the pagan cults, the Lord established his people in churches that were to mimic homes and family units. Churches were to look for men who led their homes in love and appoint them to be elders/pastors.

Paul uses specific language to describe the role of men entrusted with the care of a Christian congregation. He writes, "If they cannot manage their own household, how can they care for the church of God?" (1 Ti. 3:3, NIV) Interestingly, he uses two distinct words to carve out a powerful mental and emotional image of the work of elders/pastors. First, he tells Timothy that elders need to be men who manage their households well; he then translates this role to their work in the Ephesian church by means of a different word from "manage." He uses a word that expresses the idea of "care for." The use of the word (Gk. *epimeleomai*) in the New Testament is rare; we find it used only one other time (Lk. 10:34). So, why did Paul use distinct words in his teaching?

Certainly, he is emphasizing nurture and care versus general management of an estate. He may also have been using language common to Ephesus. The root of "care for" is closely associated in the Greek language with the word for "bee" (Gk. *meli*). The Liddell & Scott Greek-English Lexicon catalogs no less than two pages of words that have *meli* as their root.[10] The prominence of bees and honey in the

Greek language seems no accident. Honey was the source of a sacred liquid[11] and an integral part of ancient facial and medicinal ointments.[12]

Closely associated with the *meli* family was a group of words that had *mele* as their root, The root word *mele* carried the idea of a "good friend" – a relationship described by the pleasant taste of honey.[13] Paul's use of "care for" in 1 Timothy 3:3 is rooted in the word for "good friend" and carries with it the sense of taking care of a close friend.[14] Given the bee's prominence in Ephesian thought, it seems more than coincidence that the apostle uses a word closely associated with honey, medical lore, and the idea of sweet friendship.

For men and women who had leaned on and worshipped their supposed caring, nurturing goddess, they had a need for a powerful substitute: a human being. The apostle was urging them to select men who would actively look to the needs of a congregation of people. He was counseling men to courageously show care when physical and spiritual struggles came and marshal resources to help.[15]

Beyond Paul's focus on care, he also pointedly describes qualities that together may seem like a formidable list:

Above reproach (NIV); blameless (KJV)

the husband of one wife

temperate (NIV); vigilant (KJV)

self-controlled (ESV, NIV)

respectful (NIV); of good behaviour (KJV)

hospitable (ESV, NIV)

able to teach (ESV, NIV)

not a drunkard (ESV); not given to drunkenness (NIV)

not violent, but gentle (ESV, NIV; See also Ephesians 4:31.)

not quarrelsome (ESV; See also "bond of peace" in Ephesians 4:3.)

not a lover of money (ESV; See also Paul's focus in 1 Timothy 6:3-10, 2 Timothy 3:2 and the temptation of money-centered religion.)

He must manage his own family well (NIV; See also Ephesians 5:21-33.).

See that his children obey him with proper respect (NIV; See also Ephesians 6:4.).

He must not be a recent convert (ESV, NIV)

He must be well thought of by outsiders (ESV)

The list highlights a man's relationship with his wife and children, his social conduct, his economic perspective, and finally his religious status as a believer. The attributes describe one who is "an example to be followed; a teacher from whom to learn; a shepherd whose voice one heeds; a protector from wolves; a leader to whom one submits in humility because he is God's steward; and an older man to whom due respect is gladly given."[16]

Paul's final meeting with the Ephesian elders serves as a strong reminder of the rationale for the qualities. The men have a significant responsibility: "Keep watch over yourselves and all the flock of which the Holy Spirit has made you overseers. Be shepherds of the church of God which he bought with his own blood." (Acts 20:28, NIV) The person and work of elders is to reflect the peace that binds and the truth and love of Christ (Eph. 4:3, 15).

Elders/Pastors, a Provincial View, and the "Emerging Church" Movement

The historical evidence about first century Asia Minor reveals that Paul's teaching should not be taken merely as going-with-the-flow counsel. However, both equal rights advocates and feminists have proposed exactly that conclusion. Carroll Osburn, for example, has suggested that women can serve as elders/pastors in an equal rights America – because the New Testament is only reflecting the culture of its day. As he writes,

The NT does not speak regarding women in leadership or preaching capacities. All named evangelists in the NT are male, as are all elders. However, as there is no validity to the

151

"order of creation" argument, this situation should not be viewed as a "pattern" mandatory for all times and places, but merely as reflecting the culture in which the NT events were played out. Scripture does not teach that it is sinful for a woman to preach or serve in a leadership capacity.[17]

The arguments by equal rights advocates can seem valid when people suggest that we are 1900 years removed from the original setting of apostolic teaching. Many have proposed that 1) our day looks very little like first century Ephesus and 2) Paul's patriarchal starting point has limited application to our equal rights culture. However, the research regarding Asian and Ephesian culture by feminist scholars and others presents solid conclusions. First century Asia and twenty-first century Western religious culture bear remarkable similarities.

While imperial society generally was patriarchal, the evidence shows that Ephesus had created a good bit of distance from that culture in some of the Asian cults. It is likely that many Ephesians and Asians would have accepted women religious leaders (with or without male leaders). Centuries of submission to Artemis had prepared the general population for women who possessed special religious status. Building churches around that status would have seemed an easy cultural decision in reaching the Asian population for Christ.

Beyond the power of the Artemis religion, the Dionysus and Isis cults appear to have known even stronger frameworks of feminine leadership. A man leading a Dionysus worship festival probably would have seemed to the gathered women like an apprentice showing expert chefs how to cook. It is likely that the Christian converts from the Dionysus and Isis cults would have accepted female religious leadership of churches as well (see Appendix C for more information about the three Asian cults).

The "emerging church" movement has drawn a conclusion about women elders/pastors similar to Carroll Osburn's, but for a different reason. Ray Anderson has suggested from 1 Corinthians 11:5 and Paul's mention of Phoebe and Junia as co-workers that the apostle must have allowed women to serve as church leaders. He suggests that the New Testament contains two "narratives:" a narrative of restriction, but also a narrative of women as elders/pastors. He sees the restrictions for some reason in Ephesus as limited (see Appendix B for more information); he concludes that the narrative of co-workers should be given priority in guiding "emerging churches" today.[18]

As we have seen from a review of 1 Timothy 2:9-3:7 and 1 Corinthians 11, Paul's guidance to both Ephesus and Corinth reveals a message other than two diverse, conflicting "narratives." The apostle's counsel and command to the two cities/regions carries consistency and mirrors what we read in the Acts of the Apostles. The apostle was teaching that men, not women, should act as elders/pastors.

When we come to Paul's letters to Ephesus, we should see them for the dramatic spiritual challenge they displayed. The Ephesians (and Corinthians) would have felt confronted by an important spiritual decision as they read the letters. Was the apostle speaking for the true God in 1 Timothy 2:9-3:7 or acting as no more than a religious peddler of Jewish patriarchy? Was Paul getting "off-track" and losing his grasp of divine revelation in his teaching to Ephesus? Similar to the early twenty-first century, some (or many) of the women and perhaps men in the Ephesian church – especially the Gentiles – likely felt surprise (or more) at the restriction of church leadership to men. However, Paul does not indicate the teaching to be limited to Ephesus or Asia. Instead he bases 1 Timothy 2:9-15 and 3:1-7 on the same foundation: "Adam was formed first, then Eve." (1 Ti. 2:13, NIV) He lays his instructions on the foundation of God's creative action.

In addition to gender leadership questions, Mark Love, Douglas Foster, and Randall Harris have raised a proposal also closely associated with the "emerging church" movement. They have suggested that apostolic guidance to the earliest churches was diverse; the Spirit's message was varied.[19] Specifically, they have suggested from a look at 1 John 2:27 that John was calling some churches to a model of leadership different from Paul's in his letters to Roman Asia (1 and 2 Timothy). As they write, unlike Paul's letters to Timothy, there is no interest [in John's letters] in identifying office holders to maintain the traditions handed down from previous witnesses. To the contrary, the beloved elder in 1 John reminds these Spirit-directed Christians that they have no need for anyone to be their teacher (1 John 2:27).[20]

They are far from alone in their conclusion. Indeed, their proposal of diversity in apostolic teaching represents a growing conclusion in present-day study of the New Testament. It provides a comfortable foundation from which to view religious "diversity" in the West. For example, Paul Trebilco's recent study of earliest Christianity in Ephesus proposes such diversity,[21] as does that of Helmut Koester.[22]

However, while it may be comfortable, it also raises – but does not answer – crucial questions within the history of earliest Christianity. Does "diversity" extend to the Jew-Gentile tension – and the event of Paul opposing Peter (Gal. 2:11-14)? How does "diversity" in apostolic teaching differ from division? Further, in 1 John 2:27 was the apostle saying that the Christians to whom he was writing did not need to read his letter? Churches did not need to listen to an apostle or church leader, nor seek out reliable people to pass on the Word? The questions illustrate how our missing the specifics of John's message results in a dead-end. John was not telling his readers to cease reading his letter – or listening to elders. But similar conclusions may have helped nurture second century Gnostic belief. Gnostics were convinced that higher knowledge of God came as a result of special enlightenment or illumination.[23] A heightened emphasis on mystical learning and knowledge propels the "emerging church" movement in the same direction in our time (see Appendix D).

So what is the apostle John teaching? The surrounding verses highlight that John is dealing with a specific false teaching. Individuals claiming to be Christians are teaching that Jesus is not the Christ (1 Jn. 2:22). They are announcing that Jesus did not come in the flesh (1 Jn. 4:2-3). The teaching had dramatic impact on Christian doctrine and life. If Jesus did not come in the flesh, then he could not actually have been killed – sacrificed on behalf of humanity. In response John emphasizes that Jesus is the atoning sacrifice (1 Jn. 2:2). Who he is represents the "truth" John writes about in 1 John 2:20 in connection with the anointing Christians have received.

When we get to 1 John 2:27, we should read it differently than Mark Love, Douglas Foster, and Randall Harris suggest in *Seeking a Lasting City*. John writes, "As for you, the anointing you received from him remains in you, and you do not need anyone to teach you." John is saying that they do not need to have a teacher teach them about Jesus coming in the flesh. The apostle is not talking about the whole of apostolic teaching and Christian doctrine. Instead, he is talking about specific Christian doctrine and the false teaching his readers have heard. John is not announcing that human teachers are now unimportant. Instead, he is writing that what his readers have been taught about Jesus in the flesh they do not need to hear again (as a different message) from men. They need no more than what they have already received. They have heard the truth; now they need to look to the Spirit as they think about what they have already heard from God's teachers.

The diversity that Mark Love, Douglas Foster, and Randall Harris have proposed from 1 John 2:27 misses the specific issue John addresses. It also unnecessarily breaks up continuity within the teaching of John and Paul. Nothing in the New Testament gives the signal that the apostles or the earliest churches departed from the practice of appointing elders/pastors to help, teach, and encourage in each church.

The history of the earliest churches reveals that followers of Christ allowed themselves to be blown by deceiving winds (Eph. 4:14) even while Jesus and the apostles taught. The Jew-Gentile tension has revealed the impact when apostles acted differently, and should not have. We are shown a portrait of the impact on the church in Ephesus and the division – not just diversity – that occurred.

The wife of Zebedee and her sons (Mt. 20:20-28); Jewish Christians in Jerusalem (Gal. 2:11-13); some of the Christians in Ephesus and Corinth (as well as other locations). All were spiritually deceived. Further, the second century saw many intelligent, deeply-motivated followers of Christ discard apostolic teaching at points in order to join a supposed new "breaking in" of the Spirit known as Montanism. Mark Love, Douglas Foster, and Randall Harris have provided an accurate and pointed observation that the movement illustrated nothing less than unfaithfulness to God's story.[24] It hindered the work of God in the second century.

The deception has not ceased just because we are far removed from ancient Ephesus, Jerusalem, Zebedee's family, or Montanism. While we typically get more comfortable calling spiritual corruption what it is when it is more distant, it nevertheless exists in our day and our neighborhood. It wears the clothes of people we know – and that makes it uncomfortable. It is more than just the word "Gnosticism" or "antichrist" (1 Jn. 2:18). It walks in the shoes of an acquaintance, friend, or relative. It occurs when people hear the Word of God, but they neglect to let it mold and shape them. They war against it at some point. Whether by powerful cultural, religious, or financial pressures, they allow themselves to be blown off-course. Dismissing apostolic teaching represents nothing less than a course change from inviting seas to howling winds, forty-foot swells and destruction.

Conclusion

In Ephesians 5:21-33 and 1 Timothy 3:1-7 the Lord is guiding his people to loving leadership by men in both marriage and in his church. It would have been easy to follow the cultural practices that prevailed in Ephesus and Asia and allow for female leadership within the earliest churches.

It would have been equally effortless to attach a title such as "*Synedrion*" (council of priests) to a church's leaders. Instead, Paul provides guidance to Timothy that the elders/pastors of a congregation are to be men whose love for their families will provide a powerful foundation for them to care for and guide Christ's church.[25] In the same way as a man is to lead his family in love, he is to help lead a church to follow Christ.

Finally, Paul's teaching highlights that the model of churches having a pastor – one person – misses the point of what the apostle is saying. The Lord's chosen ambassador teaches that a congregation is to have leadership provided by multiple elders/pastors. It is a simple teaching that carries the message of the church's early growth (Acts 14:23; see also Titus 1:5). However, cultural patterns and strong currents of religious thought continue to try to revise the teaching – along lines that are more culturally familiar.

Encouragingly, some who had chosen different models of church leadership are moving back to apostolic teaching. Mark Dever, for one, has written and urged that,

> In order to help Christians in this dark day to turn our soaring sermons and thundering denunciations into more than just a bunch of hot air but into incarnated corporate witnesses to the glory of Christ, we need help. And one crucial means of help God has given His church we continue to ignore to our peril – the provision of multiple elders to give careful, faithful, brave servant leadership to our churches in days filled with danger and opportunity.[26]

Paul's words in 1 Timothy 3:1-7 should echo loudly 1950 years later. Through the writing of an apostle, the Spirit of God is drawing a distinction between spiritual status and congregational leadership. The risen Lord is also guiding his people to a means of spreading the task of teaching, counseling, and helping others among multiple leaders in a church. His words should be heard, honored, and acted on as what they are, the counsel of God.

Chapter Thirteen

Glorious Bride, or Prostitute?

(Ephesians 5:25-27; Revelation 19:7-8; 21:1-14)

In the early twenty-first century, the church finds itself striving to spread the Word within a nation seeking quick answers to serious issues. We are drenched with news of an environment that is breaking and a fractured economy built on restless consumerism. We find ourselves facing broken or fractured relationships and the eroding of religious authority. At the same time, spiritual efforts to reach people caught in the breaks have included dramatic changes. Some groups have revised their worship practices, invested in mysticism, or even aligned themselves with goddess religion or other New Age expressions. What is prompting the changes? Are they healthy or threatening to the church's identity? What is the Spirit's counsel to churches and to people needing help?

Fueling the Spiritual Storm

Certainly, evil remains at the root of national and personal issues (Ro. 3:23). With time and experience people discover that self-help books or a course in psychology does not suffice to fix all of the breaks. The issues are deeper than a matter of attitude. Spiritual and ethical corruption affects us far more deeply than stubbing our toe as we get out of bed.

However, another crisis is also helping fuel the spiritual storm in peoples' lives. People are reading and understanding the Word of God less today than a generation ago. As the *National Endowment for the Arts* has stated in their November 2007 report *To Read or Not to Read*,

> The story the data tell is simple, consistent, and alarming. Although there has been measurable progress in recent years in reading ability at the elementary school level, all progress appears to halt as children enter their teenage years. There is a general decline in reading among teenage and adult Americans. Most alarming, both reading ability and the habit of regular reading have greatly declined among college graduates. These negative trends have more than literary importance. As this report makes clear, the declines have demonstrable social, economic, cultural, and civic implications.[1]

The erosion of literacy; students who are unable to grasp a novel;[2] a growing impatience in the classroom.[3] The symptoms surround us and point to a common national issue in the early twenty-first century. A generation after Neil Postman's accurate critique of television in *Amusing Ourselves to Death*, much of the nation is losing its mental and ethical footing. We are stumbling towards being people who give extended attention to very little. Many dash through hundreds of cell phone text messages in a given day. We read in bits and pieces. A weblog; a newspaper article. We scan read; we skim.

The American literary critic Sven Birkerts has observed from his own college students that many seem to have a fragmented sense of time, a reduced attention span, limited confidence in explanatory narratives, and an absence of any strong vision of the future.[4] He has suggested that the problem is related to our electronic age. He is partially correct. While it is true that CRT computer displays are hard on the eyes, LCD's are more comfortable. Further, paper-like LCD displays are getting close to being affordable. Soon, we will be able to unroll an LCD, adjust the type size, and comfortably read from numerous digital books. But will we?

The issue is related to technology, but it involves more. We get caught expecting/wanting the learning process itself to be easy and efficient – matching the technology. We can "get to" information quickly. So, learning ought to be equally quick, perhaps even effortless. Brief marketing sound bites further add to the expectation that everything is available in small capsules. "Less is more" advertising battles for mindshare and steadily conditions us. And if the subject proves complex? Well, it is obviously not worth our time; we move on to something else.

As a result we fall prey to a dangerous addiction. Too often our learning becomes broad, but superficial – miles wide, but inches deep. As Jerry Seinfeld has suggested, "A bookstore is one of the only pieces of evidence we have that people are still thinking." He may have been exaggerating for humor sake. However, unfortunately, he has snagged some truth. Bookstores' financial bottom lines have declined of late and any notion of replacement by the Internet is fictitious. Further, the addiction of superficial learning carries with it other complications as well; we are more likely to draw incorrect conclusions. We may even end up feeling a sense of inadequacy over time – because we do not allow ourselves time to think and learn.

So, what is the impact on spiritual learning? In a day when the New Testament is readily available, similar to an acquaintance of mine, many have never read a Gospel or listened to one read. Indeed, in a time of text messages and sound bites, reading a Gospel may seem intimidating. We desire spiritual growth that fits our conditioning. For a growing number of people, that translates into listening to brief stories about Jesus. For the same reason, we probably give less time to listening to the counsel of the risen Christ as he speaks through apostolic teaching. However, the choices leave people with little more than a meal of pastry and coffee on the run. After awhile it is not enough.

Not only, however, does reading Scripture and the idea of a Bible study group erode away early in our century, so also does the action of following the risen Christ. Extended listening and attentiveness have declined along with extended reading.[5] In addition to declining literary interests, people are finding that their ability to converse has suffered as well. Large volumes of brief reading have contributed to eroding listening skills. People understand each other less. And mysticism represents no more than a spiritual deception as people think they follow Jesus, but find with time that they really do not know what he taught or who he was.

Finally, we misjudge the storm if we believe it to be generational. It is not. The recent studies by the *National Endowment for the Arts* reveal that the nation as a whole is being affected. We are all – adults, young adults, teens – being influenced by a dangerous addiction to effortless watching, listening, and reading.[6] The practice is helping fuel a raging spiritual storm – that shows no mercy.

Navigating the Storm

In the face of both national issues and an obvious discomfort by some (or many) with extended reading/listening, some churches have sought alternatives. In many cases efforts to "revision" Christian worship with strong imagery, contemporary story telling, and what fills the senses are right-spirited actions. However, they can also represent actions that urge people in the wrong direction. For example, one voice within the "emerging church" movement has gone so far as to suggest Scripture reading to be less relevant in our day.[7]

Churches choosing to minimize extended reading, preaching, and teaching from the Word probably see themselves helping people by doing what will seem comfortable – even captivating. People in a visual age seek images. So, churches can be pulled to focus on the visual and the sensational. However, while images are powerful, in the absence of something more they produce no more than shallow religion. As a result people can end up ill prepared to face a spiritual storm and breaking waves.

Christians need to help others adjust the sail area, secure the hatches, and navigate carefully through the large swells. Churches need to make frequent use of extended public reading of Scripture (1 Ti. 4:13; 2 Ti. 2:7). As John Mark Hicks and Bobby Valentine have highlighted, being the church beyond the apostolic age depends heavily on churches reading the Word – listening to the Lord.[8] Reading the Scriptures provides the means for churches to both tell the story of God's saving actions and also nurture a longing for Christ's return. Extensive use of brief anecdotes and contemporary stories may be more welcomed and more comfortable to many people. However, a comfortable direction leaves hatches open, sails mismanaged, and a spiritual voyage in peril. Efforts to provide religious teaching through media-rich worship experiences devoid of reading from Scripture represents a vault without valuables. What spiritual "deposit" are churches then guarding?

Further, churches need to keep a firm grasp on the character of their music in worship to the Lord. Christian singing may seem foreign to those who have sung little throughout their lives. Many may prefer listening to someone else sing and/or play in a worship assembly. However, taking that path represents the wrong spiritual direction. Churches need to lift their hearts and voices in vocal music to God and to others. And they probably need to talk often about the spiritual importance of song – for all. The very singing that may not seem comfortable is one tool the Lord uses to spiritually revive people (Eph. 5:19-20).

In a time when hearing the Bible read at length is at risk, singing songs composed of Scripture represents one of the most powerful means for individuals and churches to spiritually grow and teach others. Teaching and preaching composed of extended Scripture reading mingled with spiritual songs can help people as they "unlearn" shorter attention spans (that being most of us). As Calvin Stapert, for one, has carefully urged, shallow-rooted American society urgently needs to sing the Psalms more often. Such worship remains one of the ways people engrave on their minds the Word of God.[9] Church leadership needs to guide people to act in ways that are less comfortable in the short-term so that they spiritually benefit more in the long-term.

Sven Birkerts has made the sage observation that the worship assemblies of churches remain some of the last places in the country where the "deep time" of extended public reading takes place. Indeed, for that reason he suggests that churches represent nothing less than oases of depth and wisdom.[10] Extended public reading of the Scriptures continues to represent an action desperately needed early in this century, even if many do not initially see the benefit. Reading the Word at length will also help us navigate out of the squalls of misunderstanding and "that is your interpretation" thinking.

History also provides an important lesson. Early Christian doctrine and mission efforts in Asia Minor appear to have faced some of the same issues as have churches in our day – albeit for different reasons. Deeply rooted goddess religions appear to have challenged apostolic teaching in the late first century and early second century (and beyond). The cults probably represented a comfortable heritage for many people. Montanists, for example, appear to have taken the path of comfort and reacted strongly to "patriarchal Christianity." It is likely that some Gnostics made similar decisions. Seeking divine help through Mary or worshiping Mary represented a further departure from the Spirit's counsel (see Heb. 4:14-16, 10:19-25), but probably touched hearts. Each represented people falling prey to the same spiritual traps as had worshipers of Artemis, Isis, or Cybele. Each walked away from apostolic teaching and embraced the seemingly comfortable lies of a dark lord.

Churches need to accept that they may be judged "out of touch" with the prevailing desires of the day by seeking first the Kingdom of Heaven and by patiently hearing the Word of God read at length. Part of the healing comes as we personally strive for a simplicity fueled by prayer and reading Scripture. As the busy wife of a church elder, Patty Amyx has counseled that prayer and reading the Word provide means the Lord uses to help us through confusion and emotional turmoil.[11] The Spirit's work to remake people as "children of light" (Eph. 5:8) will indeed heal, but it will take time; it will take people committed to listening to Scripture and also lifting their voices in song to the Lord. The Lord's time may not match people's impatient hopes; we need to urge people to wait upon the Lord (Isaiah 40:31). We can follow Christ only if we first listen to his teaching at length over the roar of deceptive crosswinds. So, what does the New Testament say about the identity of the church, surrounded by the storm of Satan's work, the ancient cults? What is its message for our day?

The Bride and Wife of Christ

Ephesians and the book of Revelation (to Roman Asia and beyond) speak with feminine imagery that is unique in the New Testament. The feminine images of the church carry shimmering beauty: glorious bride (Rev. 19:7-8; 21:2, 9) and wife (Eph. 5:25-27; Rev. 21:9). The bride described in Revelation 21 is "beautifully dressed for her husband" (Rev. 21:2, NIV). She is no impoverished bride, trying to find a clean blouse and jeans without holes for her wedding. Instead, she has been given fine linen to wear (Rev. 19:8). Her husband is the King of Kings.

The phrases "a radiant church" (Eph. 5:27) and "beautifully dressed" (Rev. 21:2) represent two powerful expressions in English and just as much in the Greek language. The word "radiant" in Ephesians 5:27 is based on the root of the Greek word for "glory." The word was also used to describe fine clothes in Luke 7:25 and as a description of the wonderful things Jesus was doing during his ministry (Lk. 13:17). Finally, Paul uses the word with the sense of "honor" in 1 Corinthians 4:10. All the meanings reveal various facets of a word that generally describes royal character or glorious splendor.[12] Similarly, the phrase "beautifully dressed" conveys the idea of "adorned." The word serves as the origin for our English word "cosmetics."[13] But a bit of rouge does not begin to get at the meaning.

Beautiful eyes; a warm smile; a dress and countenance that announce purity, dignity, and kindness. Letting the portrait unfold helps us begin to see the bride of the risen Christ. The Lord is revealing with powerful, captivating images the majesty and beauty of God's people as bride and wife[14] – because Christ is groom and husband. She has been made radiant – morally and spiritually – by him. As Paul writes,

> Husbands love your wives just as Christ loved the church and gave himself up for her to make her holy, cleansing her by the washing with water through the word, and to present her to himself as a radiant church, without stain or wrinkle or any other blemish, but holy and blameless. (Eph. 5:25-27, NIV)

The portrait is intended to be personal. The Lord has spoken in an image of feminine glory and dignity, not as a detached, distant image, but as one close at hand. Christians are who they are because they have been raised with Christ (Eph. 2:6). They have collectively participated in the revelation to John of the heavenly city coming "as a bride adorned for her husband" (Rev. 21:2, NIV). They are part of the wedding portrait!

Given the prominence of the feminine images of Ephesians 5 and Revelation 19 and 21, the absence of the word "queen" in reference to the church is striking. Neither Paul's letters nor the Revelation to John include phrases such as "queen of heaven" or "queen of the universe." Indeed, the word "queen" (Gk. *basilissa*) is never used in the New Testament to refer to the Lord or his people. The title "Queen of the Universe" was used to refer to Artemis Ephesia;[15] later "Queen of Heaven" was bestowed on Mary, the mother of Jesus.[16] However, neither the church or Mary is described with that title in apostolic teaching.

The title of "queen" in relation to deity – specifically Artemis – carried familiarity in first century Asia.[17] So why the absence of a term the Ephesian Christians would have embraced easily? In contrast to the Ephesian speech about their patron goddess, the Lord reveals feminine images that carry constant dependence. Unlike a patron goddess who can rule independent of a god, the church's status of bride and wife are related to the risen Christ, to the King. She is who she is because of him, not independent of him. Indeed, the New Testament's message should impress deeply. It is unique, so unique that some could not accept the apostolic teaching and distorted the Word by making Mary "Queen of Heaven" (see Appendix D for more information). In place of such religious distortion, Christians need to focus on Revelation 19 and 21 and the image of Christ's church.

As the wife of Christ, she is no weary, depressed, threadbare woman buried in work and pain, and forgotten by her husband. Instead, as his radiant wife, Christ loves her – even to sacrificing life for her. Now he reigns as her risen husband, crowned with glory and honor, and she with him, at his side. That is the message of Ephesians 5:25-27 and Revelation 19 and 21.

The New Jerusalem is nothing less than God's dwelling place with his people.[18] "John is not describing an eternally secure place. He is describing eternally secure people."[19] The people of God will be at the heart of his new creation.[20] The Lord's letter to the church in Philadelphia identifies the New Jerusalem as personal, not political (Rev. 3:12). Revelation 20:9 adds to the portrait, where beloved city stands in parallel with the camp of the saints. Revelation 19:7-8 shows us that the Lamb's bride is God's people. Revelation 21:9b-10 completes the portrait of the Lord's people, where the New Jerusalem, the bride, and the wife of the Lamb are one and the same. The New Jerusalem is not only a portrait of the future (Rev. 21:4), it is also a portrait of now.

The Bible is not, however, discriminating against men in its description of the church as bride and wife anymore than in the phrase "You are all sons of God" (Gal. 3:26, NIV). Instead, the language announces the relationships God has chosen in describing his relationship with his creatures. In the same way Jesus has completed God's revelation to his creation. In his words, "Anyone who has seen me has seen the Father." (Jn. 14:9, NIV) While God is spirit, he has revealed himself through an act of love – as the heavenly Father who has "given birth" to humanity and to his divine Son.

The Prostitute

In stark contrast to the glorious, majestic imagery of the bride and wife of Christ, Jeremiah announced that Israel had been consumed by spiritual deception:

> The children gather wood, the fathers light the fire, and the women knead the dough and make cakes of bread for the Queen of Heaven. They pour out drink offerings to other gods to provoke me to anger. But am I the one they are provoking? declares the Lord. Are they not rather harming themselves, to their own shame? (Jer. 7:18-19, NIV)

The goddess cult of Ashtoreth (Astarte, Ishtar) had lured Israelite families to their destruction. The phrase "queen of heaven" sounded majestic, beautiful, and powerful; that was part of the seduction.

Similarly, Revelation 17:1-6a describes the prostitute, a woman dressed in purple and scarlet and glittering with jewelry. She held in her hand a golden cup "filled with abominable things and the filth of her adulteries." (Rev. 17:4b, NIV) Subsequently, the Revelation declares that she and a beast she rides will war against the Lamb, "but the lamb will overcome them because he is Lord of lords and King of kings – and with him will be his called, chosen and faithful followers." (Rev. 17:14, NIV) Whether Ishtar, Artemis Ephesia, or the great prostitute, the texts describe a similar seductive trap. They describe, not beauty, truth, and love, but a lie – and destruction.

In the first century the trap was adorned with the opulence of a massive, marble structure – the largest and perhaps richest in the ancient world – and by worship of Caesar.[21] As owner of "the common bank of Asia," the Artemis Ephesia religion held sway over much of the economy of Roman Asia. Its secured vaults, estates, livestock herds, vineyards, and powerful religious system had shaped an intimidating cult.

While we do not know how Ephesian hearts felt about the idea of a goddess, it is likely that the religion was as real to them as the deposits in the temple. They probably associated some form of supernatural power with the Temple of Artemis. Others likely had invested themselves as fully in the Dionysus cult (and other cults). The Ephesian Christians needed to visualize their new royal status as bride and wife of Christ. They no longer needed to appeal to or deposit coins before an imaginary goddess in a stone building northeast of downtown. They sat enthroned in heaven itself, with Christ as their mediator (Eph. 2:6). They needed to see that they were the temple of God (Eph. 2:21). It was God who had given them a deposit (Eph. 1:13-14)!

The Battle For Our Hearts and Minds and the Mystical Work of God

Revelation 21 was written to encourage and to captivate the faith and imagination of churches in Asia Minor. It was intended to boldly stand out in a region filled with the opulence of Ionic temples built as the centerpieces of powerful native religions. It was given by God to fill the church's sails with a cool, fair wind and speed it safely over the highest swells.

In a time drenched with talk about an "inner goddess," Christians face an urgent need to reflect on the images as much now as 1900 years ago. Perhaps congregations should take more time to picture the Revelation to John, allowing the feminine image of the church as bride and wife to increasingly shape faith.

In contrast to the wondrous portrait of the church as the Lord's bride and wife, spiritual prostitution has blown into our society just as it had in the first century. Powerful religious movements and thought that resemble, in ways, the Artemis cult of Ephesus or the Dionysus cult captures peoples' hearts. Wiccan and New Age Spiritualism; prayer to Mary as "Queen of Heaven;" the blended religion often characteristic of the "emerging church" movement. Each seduces.

In our day goddess religion has announced its own form of both nurturing care and corrupting independence from the Creator and Father. In *The Twelve Wild Swans*, Starhawk and Valentine write,

"Once in a month, and better it be when the moon is full, shalt thou gather in some secret place, and celebrate Me, who is queen of the Wise." So begins the Charge of the Goddess."[22] Sue Monk Kidd's 2002 novel *The Secret Life of Bees* has further illustrated how strong, passionate voices have connected motherly nurture and healing with thought about goddess religion in our time. Her bestselling novel has sold over five million copies and been translated into numerous languages. Equally important is who has read it; increasingly, the book has found itself in public school reading lists.

Goddess religion and other expressions of religious mysticism get wrapped in the same desires as those that drenched ancient Ephesus. Our day wants some form of tangible interaction with God. We want to see, hear, or feel deity. In contrast the Lord's Word reveals that we interact and know the supernatural in ways that will lack the tangible character we often crave. It is called faith.

Does the supernatural penetrate our world? Yes, in more ways than we can ever know. Is it "mystical?" Yes, as people often think of the word, God's work is indeed mystical. It defies our senses or stands beyond the stretch of our reasoning – even when it takes the form of "natural." For example, the Lord uses the Hebrew prophet Jeremiah to describe God's moment-by-moment sustaining of Creation – what we call "laws of nature" (Jer. 31:35-36; 33:19-26). Paul describes the work of God in "sealing" Christians when they are baptized (Eph. 1:13; 4:30). By such they become God's possession. He writes that the Spirit of God helps us as we pray (Ro. 8:26-27). He also teaches about the Spirit's work in renewing Christians as they sing hymns to God together (Eph. 5:19-21).

However, knowing that God's work is "mystical" and depending on mysticism to know God are two different things. God counsels us to listen to Scripture, to hear his Word. He tells us to meditate on his work, his creation. He urges us to fix our eyes on his Son. He counsels a path different than the "mysticism" prominent in our day. The irony of what Scripture teaches is that we are to seek the Lord in ways that are not "mysticism" and trust him as he acts in ways that are indeed mystical.

Can we know just what he is doing? Perhaps, with time, similar to Paul's comment about Onesimus coming to Rome. But he wants us to walk by faith. The Spirit through Paul counsels us to see the power and love of God; the Creator has raised us to heaven itself! (Eph. 2:6) While we may not be able to see our status, Paul urges us to trust that the spiritual message is true. When we sing songs such as Stuart Townend and Keith Getty's *In Christ Alone*, we teach others and praise the Lord even as we declare our wondrous status by his power.

Conclusion

In contrast to a security founded on the common bank of Asia or the illusionary experiences of the Dionysus religion, the Lord has guided his people to look to him for spiritual truth. It is his Spirit who can and will guide through raging spiritual storms – that include the dangerous ocean swells of money-centered religion (1 Ti. 6:3-10, 2 Ti. 3:2).[23]

Paul declares that a supernatural being who loves perfectly has adopted Christians. Further, he has given a "deposit" that looks forward to a glorious future that is eternal in the heavenly realms in Christ Jesus. Unlike the religious deception in Ephesus and in our day, the Father has provided true hope, wealth, and power in Christ. He has demonstrated that power by an event like no other: Jesus Christ's resurrection. As we participate in Jesus' resurrection through baptism, the Father reveals that we are raised with his Son and seated with him at his right hand (Eph. 2:6)! By Christ's resurrection, life and immortality are brought to light (2 Ti. 1:10).

The Spirit through Paul has revealed to Christians the goal and means of living and worshiping unified as children of light. God the Father has revealed the unifying teaching of "one Lord, one faith, and one baptism" (Eph. 4:5, NIV). Additionally, his Spirit has announced the importance of community worship where people are renewed through unifying human song, untouched by sensational desires (Eph. 5:19-20). Singing together to one another and to the Lord is one of the ways God spiritually remakes us, recreates us.

171

Further, our heavenly Father has revealed in Jesus a leadership and love that shapes family (Eph. 5:21-6:9) and church with a towel (Jn. 13:1-17). The tension between equal rights and apostolic teaching guided by the risen Christ provides a crucial test in our day. Is the church willing to listen to the Lord in the middle of the howling winds of popular religion and social thought? The word "feminism" is not necessarily evil; it can positively affirm the uniqueness and talents of women and urge that the Lord's gifts to all people of life, freedom, and happiness not be stolen away. However, it can also proclaim "rights" and seek to unravel a biblical message of the Father's model of loving leadership by men in their families and in the church. Early in this century we feel an inviting trap; many of us sense a strong pull to place our feet where a dark lord directs. We are being urged to believe that leadership by men in worship assemblies represents no "mark" of being authentic disciples of Christ.[24] Numerous voices suggest that spiritual authenticity can show itself by women taking leadership roles in worship assemblies and as church elders/pastors as well.

We have faced the same threats as those that were carefully woven into Ephesian and Asian religious culture. The threat urged a deaf ear to some apostolic teaching and some of the message of the Acts of the Apostles. It helped splinter Christianity in Asia Minor in the second century. Some feminists (and others) have suggested the splintering took place because the church lost its way. They have suggested that some apostolic teaching distorted Jesus' teaching. Their judgment misguides.

Both man and woman are made in the Creator's image (Gen. 1:27). He has given dazzling uniqueness and intellect to each. He has brought them together in marriage to complement one another. However, sin has hindered and terrorized both. Only in Christ do both begin to complement and love one another as Christ has loved them (Jn. 13:34-35). At the same time, God the Father has also described different roles and responsibilities for men and women within the family and within his spiritual family.

The Lord's wondrous letters to Ephesus through Paul provide wisdom that announces their inspiration by their unique teaching. They challenge every society and every age by urging people to "submit to one another out of reverence for Christ." (Eph. 5:21, NIV). They lay the foundation for a wondrous society in the actions of the King who washed feet and even gave up his life. They tell us of a spiritual war that surrounds us and endangers us, churning up projectiles like a massive tornado. And they announce God's protection. In the face of such danger, the Lord's people have an urgent need to sing together, pray together, and hear a message of peace and love with faith from the Father and the risen Son (Eph. 6:23). May the Lord bless our growth in Christ and our efforts to spread his Word.

Illustrations and Map

Illustration 1: Coin stamped with an illustration of the Temple of Diana Ephesia (117-38 A.D.)

Illustration 2: Electrum coin stamped with an illustration of the Ephesian city symbol: a bee (5th Century B.C.)

Illustration 3: Coin stamped with an illustration of two boys playing Knucklebones (Gk. *Astragali*) at the foundation of the Temple of Artemis (193-211 A.D.)

Illustration 4: Coin stamped with an Artemis image (48-27 B.C.)

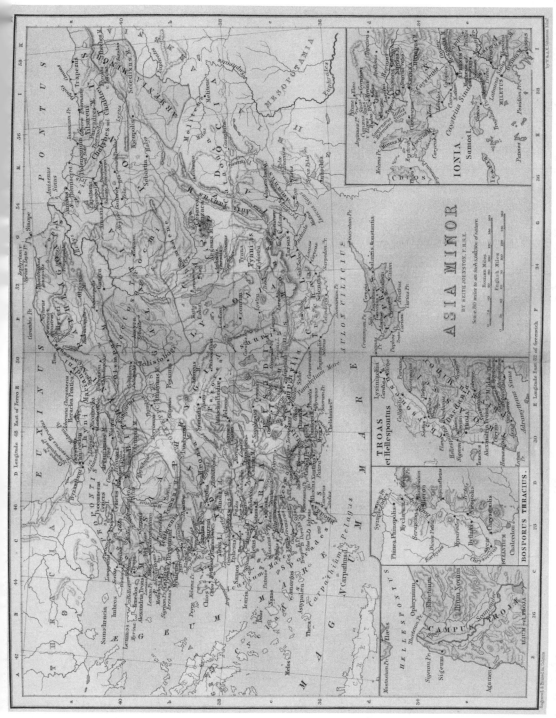

Map of Asia Minor

Appendix A: Discussion Questions

1. **Adopted by God, and the Blessing of Hope, Wealth, and Power.**
   A. When Paul writes his long sentence of Ephesians 1:3-14, what issue is he addressing in Ephesus? How would you describe the economic status of the city in Paul's day?
   B. What was the significance of seals among the ancient cults? When are Christians sealed as the possession of the risen Christ?
   C. What is the deposit guaranteeing our spiritual inheritance?
   D. Why is there so much emphasis by Paul on the idea of spiritual "riches" in the Ephesian letter? What do Christians face today that calls for us to keep that message close at hand?
   E. What caught your attention from the description of power in the Asian cults? Where do people see religious power today?
   F. What is the danger Paul describes of a form of godliness without power (2 Timothy 3)? How does it form?
   G. How would you describe a Christian faith stripped of Christ's resurrection?

2. **Our Glorious Father, the Eternal, Immortal, Invisible King.**
   A. What do you see as the importance of Paul's frequent reference to God as "Father" in the Ephesian letter?
   B. What do you think present-day goddess worshipers mean by the "inner goddess?"
   C. How can we help people who have a painful or poorly-developed image of the word "father" read about their good Creator and Father in Scripture?
   D. How does Jesus reveal that a gender-neutral Bible is no more than a spiritual deception? (Jn. 14:9)

E. What gets in the way of dependence on God? How can we avoid an "on-off" method of listening to the Word – listening to only the parts we are ready to hear?

F. How do children help us see that "feeling" we know God does not necessarily make it so?

G. How do we get beyond depending heavily on our feelings? What role does the Word (and even creation's "voice", e.g. Psalm 19) play in helping us avoid a mystical approach to knowing God?

3. **Guarding the Deposit: Taking Care of the Lord's Teaching.**

A. What does Paul mean by referring to apostolic teaching as a "deposit?" How does Paul tell us that we can lose the deposit?

B. How do people try to gain control of divine revelation? What are some symptoms of such in our world?

C. What are some reasons to have confidence that the New Testament indeed represents God's Word? How can we encourage security as people raise the subject of "lost books?"

D. What happens when we try to grab religious thought in short slices of time? What takes place when our reading the Word becomes no more than a verse or phrase here or there? What is lost?

E. What does Paul's language of the Ephesian banking industry applied to apostolic teaching say about the teaching? How does it compare to the idea of religious freedom?

G. What is the difference between viewing Scripture as being changing thoughts about God as opposed to being revelation from God? Why does it matter?

H. Some have come to believe that the Bible is a mystic mingling of both, and only a special group of people can interpret it. What happens to the church with that view? How are people and evangelism limited?

4. **Who Are We?**
    A. What historical understandings of "priest" within church history come to mind? How do they compare with the New Testament teaching?
    B. What are some examples (not necessarily religious ones) where the value of a "one another" commitment is clearly seen?
    C. In your experience what have been the best times for building oneness?
    D. What is the importance of "one baptism" in Ephesians 4? What should we understand from the New Testament teaching of baptism as an act of spiritual renewal?
    E. How does Paul describe the real spiritual power at work in Ephesus? What about our spiritual battle? How do we win?
    F. What is the spiritual danger associated with the politically neutral idea of religious freedom?
    G. What danger does religious mysticism hold to shaping our view of who we are?
    H. How do we go about applying 2 Corinthians 10:5 daily?

5. **Living as Children of Light.**
    A. What are some clues in Ephesians 4:17-6:9 that tell us Paul was dealing with pressure from Ephesian cults within the congregation?
    B. What does it appear that the early Christians were bringing with them from their previous faiths?
    C. How was first-century Ephesus similar to our present religious and social culture? How would that have influenced the early church in the city?
    D. How did Paul's view of a spiritual siege shape his view of his letters to Ephesus?
    E. What does the siege early Christians faced tell us about issues we face?
    F. How does the Ephesian letter guide us out of the darkness that surrounds us?

6. **Speaking in Song to One Another and to the Lord – Part 1.**
    A. How would you describe the background to Ephesians 5:18-21? What was threatening the Ephesian assemblies?
    B. How should we understand the parallel between exposing darkness and singing to the Lord? How does Christian music have a moral sense to it?
    C. How was Christian worship becoming debauchery? What does Paul mean?
    D. How are Christian congregational song and living as children of light related?
    E. What are some ways vocal music shows its importance beyond the religious sphere?
    F. How does the Spirit rescue people who have had their senses dulled by evil?

7. **Speaking in Song to One Another and to the Lord – Part 2.**
    A. How have some understood the Greek word *psallein* in "singing and making music?"
    B. How is Paul using *psallein*, and how does the phrase "singing and making music in your heart" parallel "speaking to one another?"
    C. What should we make of the contrast between the threat of "debauchery" and speaking in song?
    D. What is Paul teaching to be the value of vocal-only music for our assemblies? What does unified vocal music in congregational worship accomplish that instrumented music and/or separated out choirs/praise teams cannot?
    E. What steps can we take to better include/involve everyone in singing to one another and to the Lord?
    F. How can we specifically help children feel a part of the singing?

8. **Marriages and the Clash of Faiths and Rights.**
   A. How do you picture marriages in ancient Ephesus? What effect had the Asian cults likely had on marriages in the city and region?
   B. How have equal rights advocates understood Ephesians 5:21 and what have they meant by the idea of "mutual submission?" What does Paul's teaching about "headship" say?
   C. What are some common ways our society criticizes men and women? How does media and entertainment influence our views?
   D. What steps should we be taking to address the issue of broadly available pornography? What can husbands and wives do to heal spiritual and moral damage already done in their lives?
   E. How has feminism shaped marriage relationships in the past generation or more? What does our society understand by equal rights marriages?
   F. What does Paul mean by his command that husbands submit their headship to their wives' best interest? How is the relationship between the risen Christ and the church a model for such?

9 **Parents, Children, and the Spiritual Storm.**
   A. What are some ways that parents become deaf to the spiritual storms their children hear? How can parents become more sensitive to their children's spiritual fears?
   B. What catches your attention most in Paul's brief guidance in Ephesians 6:1-4?
   C. What are some of the spiritual dangers our children face?
   D. What are some ways boys and girls become frustrated with biblical teaching? How can we help children better know the Lord in ways they learn best?
   E. How can parents become more aware of non-Christian religious teaching that their children hear?

F. What are some ways we can better connect song in Bible classes with congregational worship assemblies so that children grow well in both settings?

10. Men, Women, and the Church's Worship and Work – Part 1.

A. What is the importance of apostolic teaching regarding the priesthood status of all Christians? What does Ephesians 2:6 say about the spiritual work of women?

B. What are some ways women help to build up others in the Lord as priests, even when public leadership of church worship assemblies is not in view?

C. How would you summarize the narrative of Mary and Martha in Luke 10:38-42? What was its importance for women in earliest Christianity?

D. What portrait of women believers does Luke paint in his Gospel and Acts? How are the Christian women of Macedonia described?

E. How should we understand the role of women evangelists from a reading of the Acts of the Apostles? How are women to be involved in spreading the Word?

F. What does 1 Corinthians 11:17 say about the context of 11:2-16? What situation was Paul addressing in verses 2-16?

11. Men, Women, and the Church's Worship and Work – Part 2.

A. What is Paul teaching in 1 Timothy 2:11-12?

B. What is the apostle teaching in 1 Timothy 2:13-14 that forms the foundation for verses 11-12?

C   Based on historical evidence, where were only women welcomed in teaching others about Christ in the first century? How does our time mirror the situation of 1900 years ago?

D. What work by women has been all but ignored by feminists? What does it suggest about a dark ruler's purposes? What steps can we take to better encourage teachers of children?

E. What do you envision would happen were women to immediately cease teaching young children about the Lord?

F. What are some steps churches can take to continue to reach out to women who need to hear the Gospel?

12. Church Elders Then and Now.

A. What is Paul generally teaching when he says "care for" in 1 Timothy 3:5?

B. How would you summarize Paul's description of an elder's qualities?

C. Numerous religious teachers have suggested that the NT represents a document that is limited by the culture of its time – a patriarchal society. Does this validly show the character of Scripture?

D. How did Ephesian religious culture challenge the notion of religious leadership only by men? How does it appear women were perceived within some of the native Asian religions? Would their leadership have been accepted in Ephesus?

E. What is Paul teaching about congregational elders/pastors in 1 Timothy 3:1-7?

F. How has the concept of congregations led by one pastor/elder misapplied Paul's teaching?

G. How is a priest of Christ (each Christian) different from a church elder? What has corruption of the word "priest" among some religious groups done to interfere with Christians' understanding of their spiritual status and role in heaven?

13. Glorious Bride, or Prostitute?

A. What spiritual dangers have come as a result of the decline of extended reading in our nation?

B. What are some ways churches can address the situation? What danger does a mystical approach to Christian faith hold?

C. What does Ephesians 5:25-27 say about Christ's love and authority?

D. What is the seductive trap of "prostitute" in the first century? Earlier times? What is the meaning of the symbolism?

E. What is the importance of the feminine images of the church for our time? Why spend time talking about the bride of the risen Christ or wife of the Lamb?

F. How can we help people see the spiritual deception associated with worship to Mary?

G. What are some ways the church can help people who are looking for near-term comfort, without giving up apostolic teaching or the spiritual character of Christian worship?

H. What do you see to be some key themes from Paul's letters to Ephesus that are important for others to hear? What are some ways we can personally help them hear the message?

Appendix B: Religious Feminism, Women's Studies, and Apostolic Teaching – A Brief Survey

Someone may ask, can a brief appendix on the subject of religious feminism, women's studies, and apostolic teaching in 1 Timothy 2:11-3:7 do justice to the subject? Given the large volume of books and articles that have been written, I certainly agree that this appendix runs the risk of being a waste of time and ink. However, I decided to make the attempt and then let the reader decide if it was worth a reading over a cup of coffee (or a glass of milk and some chocolate chip cookies).

If religious feminism and equal rights (i.e. egalitarianism) have represented a strong religious current in our day, then Ephesians 5:21-33 and 1 Timothy 2:11-3:7 have been seen as mainsail and jib. They have powered and helped steer the church – either with the current of equal rights or against it. Numerous religious writers have seen the teachings as important to how and where the ship of Christian faith and church life and leadership moves. Whatever people have felt about the teachings, it is clear that the majority has agreed that the words cannot be ignored.

Popular Religion and a World in Pain

One of the most telling measures of our society's health status of late has come in the form of the sheer volume of injustices and cruelty to women and children – and as well to men. The violence, oppression, selfishness, nights at the bar or in front of the TV, and physical and mental infidelity by many people have no defense. It has brought many wives and children to numbing tears and bitterness and greatly damaged a positive view of the word "father" for many children. The broad absence of male Christian love and leadership has represented one of America's darkest situations – perhaps rivaling the time of a divided nation 140 years ago.[1]

Similarly, another storm has threatened the nation as well. It is one thing to suffer. It is entirely another to suffer alone – without being able to seek help, an understanding heart, or justice. Whether the result of a violent, deceptive, or selfish spouse or a self-serving employer, many people in our day have known the depth of suffering that comes from a sense of isolation and powerlessness. Men may talk about it less; they hide it since it goes against their need and desire to show inner and outer strength. However, their suffering has often been just as great as that of women. However, in the absence of a solid spiritual foundation in Christ, men have allowed the evil that surrounds them to erode their spirits... and then wear away the lives of their wives and children.

The physical strength that some men have displayed with cruelty has reduced human oppression to what looks like one dimension. In truth, however, Satan has been destroying all – men, women, and children. Men, however, typically have made more visible the path of allowing the dark lord to have its way. But alternatives do exist. For example, I still recall my father's actions when he came to the end of his rope from the arrogance or selfishness by others at work. He would go out and wash a car or change the spark plugs (I am certain we had some of the cleanest cars and engines in Oklahoma). My father's positive example has prompted his son to find similar outlets (but cleaning the bathroom has not always been one of them – disappointingly for my wife).

The pain inside both men and women in the late twentieth and early twenty-first centuries often has oozed out like pus from a boil, affecting families, teachers, social workers, courts – and the list goes further. Nothing has served to destroy our nation faster. No terrorist threat; no political propaganda; no disease epidemic; no corporate deceit; no environmental negligence or indifference. No assault has been as deadly as that of men and women who have chosen a self-centered, godless life – consumed by their jobs, interests, drugs, or hidden relationships.

Ultimately, while the suffering is not confined to men, our society has sensed (correctly) that the greatest impact has been by men. That has been the correct – and biblical – signal of feminism. The recent popularity of Wiccan and New Age Spiritualism likely represents a reaction to the damage done to male-female relationships. The measurement is telling.

One spokesperson, for example, has shown how important emotional, social, and spiritual healing is for women in our time. Additionally, she has illustrated how the various characteristics of feminism and goddess culture are melding together in an attempt to address the need. Oprah Winfrey's sensitive and articulate blending of guidance for good health and emotional wellness have helped make her one of the most influential religious and social leaders in the country early in the new century. She has helped stir the American belief in self-help. Her media web of assistance has helped connect isolated people to others. Equally important her recommendations have caused book sales for recommended books to soar. Given a large viewing audience and a sizable treasury, it is clear that her message and actions have seemed like a fresh breeze to many people.

If Oprah Winfrey has represented one of the popular faces of feminism (even when she takes issue with some of its tenets), Mary Daly, Elisabeth Schüssler Fiorenza, Charlene Spretnak and Phyllis Trible have represented four of its most prominent religious scholars. Throughout the last thirty-five years, Mary Daly, the brilliant Catholic theologian turned feminist, has provided intelligent, articulate leadership to feminism. Her writings have assessed Christian doctrine with courage – asking tough and valid questions from her frame of reference of Catholicism and the science of biblical criticism. She and others have approached Scripture with different, but sometimes complementary, goals: 1) assessing how Scripture has affected and influenced women, 2) proposing how Scripture has been misinterpreted to oppress women, and 3) assessing more intently what Scripture has said about women. The conclusions have varied broadly. Some feminists have charged the Bible with what is essentially slander, looked more closely for messages about women, and/or proposed feminist interpretations.

Mary Daly's Assessment of the Bible

Mary Daly's 1973 book *Beyond God the Father* has carried significant feminist mind-share for over three decades. However, it is less valuable at this point for its portrait of the language of radical feminism of the 1970's and 80's. Its greater worth remains in its tough feminist assessment of Christian doctrine and biblical criticism. Mary Daly reveals in her assessment of Scripture a tension that is characteristic even of our time. On the one hand she wants to believe part of the message of Scripture; she embraces the hope-drenched message of a future coming of God. However, she considers the large majority of the Bible to be nothing more than male religious reflection (not revelation from God) – now being used as the instrument of oppression.[2]

Her book reveals a candid dismissal of Eve's fall. Mary Daly is no believer in Genesis 3 and the narrative of Eve's sin.[3] She also argues that neither are her colleagues (or she thinks virtually anyone else). As a result, she questions the biblical doctrine of evil's source and also of a redemptive plan. She proposes that both are nothing but the fabrication of a corrupt patriarchy.

Mary Daly's thorough training in biblical criticism and current Catholic doctrine has equipped her to apply tough thinking to both. Since nothing holds her back, she cuts into modern critical interpretation of Scripture as deeply as her rebellion can see. No Eve means no Jesus as savior. Further, if Jesus is no savior from sin, then Christianity disappears – and Galatians 3:28 with it. Mary

Daly, in actuality, hangs much modern biblical scholarship with its own rope. Taking her line of thinking to its conclusion, she writes that, "The idea of a unique male savior may be seen as one more legitimation of male superiority."[4] Daly adds to the theme with a bombastic recommendation:

> To put it rather bluntly, I propose that Christianity itself should be castrated by cutting away the products of supermale arrogance: the myths of sin and salvation that are simply two diverse symptoms of the same disease.[5]

She is not using hyperbole or exaggeration as shock therapy to make her point; she means every word she has written. In her recent book, *Amazon Grace: Re-calling the Courage to Sin Big*, she reveals the results of more than thirty years of thinking. *Amazon Grace* further fleshes out what it means to dismiss Genesis 3 and Scripture's teaching regarding the role of men and women. To Mary Daly "good" equates to a revolt by besieged women along with besieged animals.[6] It involves standing with Nature that is under attack from a patriarchal society. "Good" carries a responsibility to "sin" in our patriarchal culture by revolting against the evil, patriarchal power structures of Christianity, big business, and blind government.[7]

Amazon Grace and *Beyond God the Father* also reveal that in the middle of a valid critique of destruction of God's creation (cf. Hosea 4:1-3).[8] feminism has failed to see where it has contributed to or supported the destruction. As Mary Daly has written in *Beyond God the Father*,

> The woman who single-mindedly accepts the role of "housewife," for example, may to some extent avoid the experience of nothingness but she also avoids a fuller participation in being, which would be her only real security and source of community. Submerged in such a role, she cannot achieve a breakthrough to creativity.[9]

Ironically, what radical feminism typically has not seen is that stripping away the positive self-image of childbearing and childrearing has represented one more way humanity has pushed creation toward destruction. It has helped to make the next generation of (born and unborn) infants and children the first to go.[10]

Gladly, recent American publications about and for women have shown that Mary Daly's perspective regarding motherhood has withered under the summer heat of time and thought. People see more clearly in the early twenty-first century the self-defeating character of the thinking. As one example, *Self* magazine's ten most inspirational women of 2006 included two mothers at the top of the list.[11] While the word "religious" does not factor into the list, it does show that our nation has grown an increased appreciation for motherhood (and fatherhood). Western society is increasingly accepting responsibility for the care of creation – including the three-year-old in the bedroom down the hall.

Finally, Mary Daly shows the same stark inconsistency that other modern biblical scholars have shown relative to the Bible's message of hope. While willingly carving away Scripture that does not "fit" her time and society, her heart has been captivated by the unique messages of hope within the Bible. She may decide to dismiss the narrative of Eve's fall, but she fully embraces the biblical doctrine of the "second coming" – albeit with revision. It is not Christ's coming, but instead the coming of conquering feminism. As she writes,

> the awakening of women to our human potential through creative action would be envisaged as having the potentiality to bring about a manifestation of God which would be the second appearance of God incarnate, fulfilling the latent promise in the original revelation that male and female are made to the image of God.[12]

Mary Daly never explains how she has arrived at the idea of feminism representing a second coming of God. Also, she does not reveal how she has come to accept the biblical doctrine of male and female being made in the image of God. She just hopes for and declares such. So, while she dismisses much of what the Bible says, she embraces a part of Scripture that carries dreams and hope for all – male and female alike. Her beliefs and writing illustrate clearly what continues to draw people to the Bible, even those determined to "remake" the Bible. Ironically, her studies provide a further example of the power of the Scriptures, coming even from one in rebellion against much the Word has to say.

Elisabeth Schüssler Fiorenza's Assessment of the Bible

In *Bread Not Stone* and *But She Said,* Elisabeth Schüssler Fiorenza has penned a feminist assessment of Scripture that begins quite differently from Mary Daly's, but concludes with similar next steps. While she uses the language of the academy, her writings condense down to a few key points. The Bible must contain God's revelation since it has helped free humanity. As she writes "The Bible has inspired and continues to inspire countless women to speak out and to struggle against injustice, exploitation, and stereotyping."[13] In contrast, however, she suggests that,

> the litmus test for invoking Scripture as the Word of God must be whether or not biblical texts and traditions seek to end relations of domination and exploitation. In short, if we claim that oppressive patriarchal texts are the Word of God then we proclaim God as a God of oppression and dehumanization.[14]

It is clear that Elisabeth Schüssler Fiorenza believes in a loving Creator. However, she also believes that the language of God as "he" and apostolic teaching regarding submission by women (e.g. Eph. 5:22-33, 1 Ti. 2:11-12) represents a fallen world – not men supernaturally guided in their writing.

She insists that for feminism to succeed, women must carve out their own unique spiritual authority. The Scriptures must be subjected to this separate authority, given the male-bias in much of the Bible. As she writes, "a critical feminist historical reconstructive approach challenges dominant scholarship by insisting that history must be written not from the perspective of the "historical winners" but from that of the silenced or marginalized."[15] To summarize, what she proposes is not that we are misunderstanding the language and message of Scripture, but that we are seeing patriarchy-based evil that has slipped in and corrupted God's Word.

Building on this belief, Elisabeth Schüssler Fiorenza has suggested that apostolic teaching about male-female role relations has represented only a single historic point of human reflection, not God's Word for future ages. As she writes concerning her proposed handling of Scripture,

> In this feminist evaluative paradigm the Bible and biblical revelation no longer function as a timeless archetype but as a historical prototype open to feminist theological transformation. The Bible is not the controlling and defining "court of appeals" for contemporary biblical feminist theology and community but its formative root-model.[16]

Elisabeth Schüssler Fiorenza sees clearly the alternatives. Either Scripture carries authority over every culture or it is only a starting place for sociology.

Unlike some postmodernists, Schüssler Fiorenza believes we can and do understand the Bible. However, she believes the bigger question has been whether the Word has been limited by evil patriarchy. Has the Creator attempted to speak but been hindered by evil, corrupted patriarchs? Her writings have described clearly one of the most important questions – and proposed answers – of our time.

Ross Kraemer, herself a feminist scholar, has voiced a concern regarding Schüssler Fiorenza's handling of Scripture: "Where I would part company is with her argument that the earliest theology of Christianity is intentionally egalitarian and feminist."[17] Specifically, is Galatians 3:28 either? If so, is it the only true expression of early male-female role relations in Christian doctrine? Every other expression is influenced by (corrupting) patriarchy? Nowhere does Elisabeth Schüssler Fiorenza indicate how feminism itself can see clearly to filter (flawed) human reflection from spiritual truth. How does she know that feminism is itself not being corrupted in its approach to Scripture? She seems to embrace the belief that scholarship, sociology, and the war against oppression are enough to insulate against temptation and evil.

Interestingly, unlike Mary Daly's decision to face and discuss evil, but leave the origin of evil a mystery, Elisabeth Schüssler Fiorenza gives little attention to the mystery. She seems to believe that women have seen the face of evil in the oppression they have experienced and now social theory has helped them to see clearly how to address it. However, it is nowhere evident how feminism can determine what is religious, divinely-guided truth as opposed to itself becoming the oppressor of God's Word.

Throughout the writings of both Mary Daly and Elisabeth Schüssler Fiorenza, what appears most prominent is their willingness to reconstruct the Bible and Christian faith. They take both sailing on the winds of modern American sociology. As such they steer into the same dark storm the resurrection-is-myth theologians slipped in to some sixty years ago. They entrust their spiritual voyages to their own capabilities, judgments, and perspective of the world around them.

Ecofeminism's Assessment of the Bible

The last twenty years of American religious thought have also witnessed a combination of ecology with feminism. Known by terms such as ecofeminism, Gaia, Earth Spiritualism, and EarthBody, the pool of thought gathers together scientific data, mysticism, feminism, an ecological focus, and select Christian teaching.

The feminist and Catholic theologian Charlene Spretnak has represented one of the dominant voices of ecofeminism. Her writing swirls together feminism and mysticism into an inviting literary feast. She grapples with real issues related to a culture of illusion. And she sees clearly the social breaks and loneliness, ecological failures, financial stresses, and religious confusion in the West. She suggests that much Western religion has tarnished nature by the teaching that sin and total depravity have taken away good from anything material.

She is certain she has found the cure: let us unite around the mystical goddess.[18] She believes the only way to recover from the trap of modernity and the Bible is to be ecological and feminist.[19] It is the strength of ecofeminism that it catches hold of the wonder of a blue planet. It sees the astonishing complexity of life and the interdependence of God's creatures. Charlene Spretnak's wonder at the world around her is refreshing; it probably seems to many like a trickle of water touching a parched throat. However, the cool, renewing truth of a good creation sustained by a good God (Jer. 33:25-26) eludes she and others. Her only hope is in a "bursting forth of Gaian life stretched over hundreds of millions of years...."[20] She allows herself to be blinded to true hope in the person of the risen Lord and God's work to renew creation (2 Cor. 5:17). Her writings give no attention to the resurrection of Jesus.

Rosemary Radford Ruether's *Gaia & God* carries a similar message from one who claims ecofeminism and who indicates that she has believed in Jesus – in some way. She has suggested that Earth is under siege and one of its enemies is dualistic, patriarchal Christianity as expressed in the New Testament. She argues that Christianity must be revised to become both ecological and feminist – to counter the male-centered message in much of Scripture.[21]

The UK sociologist Frank Furedi has clarified much of the reason for ecofeminism's influence on churches. He suggests that some who claim belief in Christ have, in actuality, been in retreat from the teachings of Jesus and his apostles. Dominant expressions of Christianity in the early twenty-first century have been turning "green" as ecology replaces a focus on salvation and spiritual hope.[22]

Furedi's assessment strikes at the heart, not only of the ecology versus theology debate, but much more. He has written that by the 1980's, instead of influencing society, many churches began to yield to and internalize the attitudes of unbelievers. "Forced on to the defensive and sensitive to the charge of being out of touch with public concerns, Western religions have looked for new ways of rebuilding their authority."[23] One result is that Christ the Saviour is now becoming Christ the environmental activist.[24] Lost is the message of Christ's work as spiritually recreative – the reclaiming of humanity from sin. Some who claim belief in Christ seem to have become blind to the source of many ecological issues – the evil actions of humanity (IIos. 4:1-3).

Phyllis Trible's Assessment of the Bible

Phyllis Trible has represented a unique voice within feminism. Unlike Mary Daly or Elizabeth Schüssler Fiorenza, Phyllis Trible has approached the Bible both as a feminist and as one who loves the Scriptures. In reaction to some of feminism's radical conclusions about the Bible, Trible has noted two things about herself: "two things are beyond question for me: I am a Feminist, and I love the Bible."[25]

Her study entitled *God and the Rhetoric of Sexuality* provides a warm, informative look at the Lord's use of feminine imagery to describe divine compassion (e.g. Is. 46:3-4). She also presents an interpretation of Genesis 2-3 that announces patriarchy to be the consequence of sin. First, she suggests that the Hebrew word "adam" in Genesis 1:27 does not describe "Adam," but instead should be understood as the "earth creature." The word is a play on words with the Hebrew word for "earth."[26] She proposes that sexuality is not introduced until the "earth creature" meets the woman. As she writes, "the masculine gender of "the adam" does not signal sexuality in the narrative."[27] She sees no hierarchy associated with the "earth creature" being formed prior to the woman. Both male and female "arrive" as sexual beings at one and the same time. Equality without hierarchy existed in the beginning; no subordination of one to the other existed.[28]

She is certainly correct that the woman is revealed to be a companion, not an inferior helper.[29] Additionally, without question Genesis 2 describes a wondrous union. The man sees the woman as flesh of his flesh; she is like him. His words express wonder and intimacy.

However, Phyllis Trible's interpretation does not discuss and appears to have no answer for why the "earth creature" looks for a suitable partner (Gen. 2:20). The creature clearly perceives and feels isolation as "he" compares himself with the animals that the Lord brings to him. But why does he then feel alone? The narrative reveals that the Lord wants Adam to come to the conclusion that someone is missing.

Phyllis Trible's feminist starting place urges her to step over and avoid key questions. Her suggestion of an "asexual" earth creature prior to woman's creation makes no sense of the man's search or of his announcement. Ironically, where many incorrectly have seen the man's words as "controlling," Trible sees nothing of what the man's words say about the man. As man, he feels wonder at seeing woman! He knows her as "woman" because he knows she came from him – from man. Man existed before woman was made. "My bones" and "my flesh" complete the picture as he communicates his feeling of intimacy with her. Phyllis Trible's suggestion garbles the very heart of the narrative. It also dismisses Paul's teaching in 1 Timothy 2:13 of any supernatural guidance.

John Willis has provided greater clarity regarding this moment in the narrative:

> God determined to create a helper for man before he ever brought the animals to him that he might name them (vs. 18). But he does not make woman until man can appreciate her value in the fullest sense. So, first, he parades the animals before man that he might be convinced thoroughly that none of these could measure up to his aspirations or satisfy his needs. Clearly, the author's purpose is to extol the virtues of woman....[30]

Derek Kidner has drawn similar conclusions:

> The naming of the animals, a scene which portrays man as monarch of all he surveys, poignantly reveals him as a social being, made for fellowship, not power: he will not live until he loves, giving himself away (24) to another on his own level. So the woman is presented wholly as his partner and counterpart; nothing is yet said of her as childbearer. She is valued for herself alone.[31]

The Lord is revealing loving leadership with such perfection that it requires no announcement. It is enough that the man was made and that the woman was made as his companion. She was made from him and for him; she complements him. And he is filled with wonder when he sees her – almost a sense of speechlessness. He does not want to rule her; it does not even come to his mind. He wants to be with her. Walk with her; look in her eyes; feel her hands; see her smile; converse with her.

God and the Rhetoric of Sexuality is both powerful and disturbing. Unlike other feminist writing, Phyllis Trible's interpretation has penetrated deeply even into groups that have both affirmed apostolic authority and critiqued feminism. However, she has proposed a view of the creation of humanity that has undermined Paul's teaching to the Christians in Ephesus. In doing so she has laid the foundation for an equal rights (egalitarian) interpretation of Scripture and dismissed apostolic authority in places.

Disappointingly, some equal rights advocates have embraced Trible's interpretation seemingly without testing it with questions that have long been asked. A feminist or equal rights interpretation "fits" our time; we get comfortable with what most easily fits.

Richard Hess, for instance, has drawn a conclusion similar to Phyllis Trible's. As he writes, "the man and the woman were created sequentially in Genesis 2 in order to demonstrate the need they have for each other, not to justify an implicit hierarchy."[32] He dismisses Paul's statement in 1 Timothy 2:13 as being problematic as a basis for understanding a creation order. He never states positively what Paul is saying, but leaves the statement out of the discussion – apparently judging it to be irrelevant to the discussion.[33] Further, he adds that,

> There is neither explicit nor implicit mention of any authority or leadership role of the man over the woman, except as the sad result of their sin in the Fall and their ensuing judgments. Even then, such hierarchy is not presented as an ideal, but rather as a reality of human history like that of the weeds that spring from the earth.[34]

Similarly, Carroll Osburn and Rick Marrs have shown their acceptance of Phyllis Trible's conclusions regarding patriarchy:

> Gen. 1-2, then, teaches that originally man and woman shared an equality in a pristine world designed by God. The Fall in Gen. 3 shattered this equality and began a long history of gender conflict based upon male hierarchy. Patriarchy is an unfortunate result of the Fall, not something designed by God.[35]

Far beyond the influence of Mary Daly, Elisabeth Schüssler Fiorenza, or Charlene Spretnak, Phyllis Trible has made herself felt among those who have believed the authority of Scripture. Both Restorationists and Evangelicals have embraced her flawed conclusions and pushed them outward. Religious feminism's power in the early twenty-first century has represented much more than a "radical" perspective that has cast much of the Bible aside. If that summed up the situation, most would have moved beyond the discussion decades ago. However, in *God and the Rhetoric of Sexuality* we have seen one of religious feminism's most influential statements.

Women's Studies and a Better View of the New Testament World

In addition to bold challenges to Scripture, women's studies have also shed light on the Greco-Roman World and the prominence of women in ancient religions. Feminist scholars have carefully surveyed the evidence that includes a first century world. They have suggested that it looked a good deal different than the religious landscape imagined by some.[36]

Specifically, Sarah Pomeroy has written that even hundreds of years prior to Christ, religion among the Greeks was the major sphere of public life in which women participated.[37] During the Roman period, goddess worship of both Isis and Cybele afforded women considerable opportunities and status.[38] To emphasize, she references the prominence of a second century A.D. statement that Isis "made the power of women equal to that of men."[39] If women were not equal in civic affairs, they were certainly equal (or superior) in some of the goddess cults active in the first century. Some of the cults even exhibited all-women gatherings.[40]

Further, the studies by Barbara Goff and Ross Kraemer have carefully described the world of Dionysus religion and the opportunities for leadership it afforded women (see Appendix C for more information). As part of this focus, Barbara Goff has revealed the close association between women's responsibility for childrearing and women's religious status in much of the ancient world. The life giving and nurturing work of women was seen as carrying with it the responsibility for mediating for the family with the divine.[41] Women were seen as having great sensitivity to the supernatural and so were especially equipped to act as priests and other religious leaders.[42]

Conclusions About 1 Timothy 2:11-3:7

Recent women's studies have helped reveal a remarkable image of the Ephesus that Paul visited (see Appendix C). Perhaps surprisingly, some of the work of feminist scholars has clarified the religious background of 1 Timothy 2:11-

3:7. The work by Barbara Goff, Ross Kraemer, Sarah Pomeroy and others has helped filter the volumes of discussion over the last two decades.

Wayne Meeks has represented one extreme of the discussion. In his book *The First Urban Christians*, Meeks has argued that women held little prominence in civil government and families, but did hold some positions of leadership religiously. However, he suggests that even these were short-lived.[43] The glaring weakness of his work is that it gives little attention to Ephesus and the Artemis Ephesia religion. Less than one paragraph will do.[44] Indeed, beyond the minimal reference to Artemis, goddess religion receives little other attention, though he does mention a quote regarding Isis.[45] Further, Meek's study includes no discussion of the Dionysus cult.

At the opposite end of the spectrum, Catherine Clark Kroeger has proposed that the Artemis Ephesia cult had been instrumental in shaping a broad feminine religious influence in the city and the region. As she writes concerning 1 Timothy 2:13, "The concept of woman and her seed as first cause was in harmony with the religious views of Asia Minor and especially Ephesus, where the maternal principle reigned supreme."[46] Recent research in Ephesus suggests that she has overstated the situation. Inscriptions indicate that men occupied most of the priestly roles in the capital city during the Roman period.[47] Further, as Christine Thomas has highlighted, male heads of families made up the city's council that oversaw various religious festivals during the period.[48]

The Evangelical writer S. M. Baugh also has offered an assessment of Ephesus that carefully challenges any notion of a broad feminist society in the metropolis. The most he says is that evidence does exist that a few women held positions of high honor and patronage during the imperial period in Ephesus, Roman Asia, and elsewhere.[49] However, two weaknesses limit the value of his study. First, he gives little attention to influence from the Dionysus and Isis cults. Second, he does not acknowledge the influence of the council of both priests and priestesses of Artemis.[50] Recent evidence from Ephesian inscriptions signals that "priestess" was more than merely an honorary title associated with a husband's position. Some priestesses served separately from their husbands.[51]

Evidence for significant feminine influence in religious matters in Ephesus seems to be more than a matter of looking at the city through feminist lenses. Inscriptions discovered to date in the city indicate that during the Roman period more than a quarter of the city's priests were women.[52] Based on clues from Ephesians 4:17-5:33, the Dionysus cult, perhaps even more than the Artemis Ephesia cult, likely was responsible for strong feminine religious influence in the city and the province. 1 Timothy 2:11-3:7 could have been written to address issues that had surfaced regarding converts from the Dionysus and Isis religions as well as the Artemis cult.

Gregory Sterling draws a similar conclusion from his brief look at ancient Dionysus religion: "Religion now has a different function for women. In the ancient world, it frequently offered women a vehicle in which they could assert themselves; today it functions as the sphere which most restricts women. Why?"[53] The answer to his question is found in apostolic teaching to Ephesus. Sterling sees the answer, but elects to divide Paul's teaching into principle (e.g. Gal. 3:28) and practice (e.g. Eph. 5:22-24; 1 Ti. 2:11-15). He accepts the former, but rejects the latter as surpassed by an equal rights society.[54]

Certainly, equal rights advocates have misused a picture of Ephesus – suggesting that 1 Timothy 2:11-3:7 was written to address a unique problem of dominant women. However, the irony is that first-century Ephesus probably looked more like present Western religious culture than many have allowed. And even if our view of women's culture in the city and the region needs refinement in one or another direction, we need to recognize the supernatural character of Paul's letters. Apostolic teaching as the Spirit's counsel carries value and messages that every age and society needs to hear. In 1 Timothy 2:13-14 Paul appeals to Genesis 1-3 for a reason. By the Spirit's guidance his letter addresses a situation that is older than ancient Ephesus.

However we choose to translate or interpret the connective word Paul uses in 1 Timothy 2:13 ("for" Gk. *gar*), it is important to recognize that the apostle is placing 1 Timothy 2:11-12 on the foundation of what he writes in 1 Timothy 2:13-14. Further, 1 Timothy 3:1-7 extends the teaching into church leadership. For that reason views of 1 Timothy 2:13-14 have served as windows into peoples' conclusions regarding 1 Timothy 2:11-3:7. Listed below, for your reading, are quotes from studies of the text.

Ray Anderson writes that, "While the New Testament speaks with an emphatic voice concerning a restriction on the role of women in certain teaching and ministry situations, in other situations the emphasis is as clearly on the side of full participation and full parity. We only have to compare the insistent commands issued by the apostle Paul that women be "silent in the churches" (1 Corinthians 14:34) and not be permitted "to teach or to have authority over a man" (1 Timothy 2:11) with the rather matter-of-fact instruction that a woman who prophesies (in public worship) should keep her head covered (1 Corinthians 11:5)." (130-1) He writes further that, "while Paul adhered to the scriptural narrative so far as it was useful in evangelizing both Jews and Gentiles, and in pastoral care of the churches, he left several pointers to the narrative of the anointing of women for leadership in the church." (133) "While he [Paul] apparently restricted the role of women in the church at Ephesus (1 Timothy 2), he openly acknowledged the ministry of Lydia in the church at Philippi, of Phoebe as *diakonos* (Romans 16:1), and Julia, who was "prominent among the apostles" (Romans 16:7)." (134)[55]

Linda Bellville suggests of verse 13 that "first-then" language "does nothing more than define a sequence of events or ideas." Further, she writes that "The relationship between the sexes was not intended to involve female domination and male subordination. But neither was it intended to involve male domination and female subordination. Such thinking is native to a fallen creation order (Gen. 3:16)."[56]

Everett Ferguson writes that, "Verses 13-14 of 1 Timothy 2 introduce the reasons for the limitations in verses 11-12. The conjunction "for" (gar) has been interpreted as supplying illustrations, but this usage is rare, and the word should be given its normal significance of supplying a cause or reason. The basis is the man's priority in creation (1 Ti. 2:13), as in 1 Corinthians 11:8-9." Additionally he writes that "The unique female function of childbearing is obvious and is a matter of nature. Men's leadership in church is not something determined biologically, but 1 Timothy does seem to indicate that the instructions, which may appear to be arbitrary, are somehow founded on a distinction that goes back to creation and the natural order instituted by God."[57]

Susan Foh suggests that, "According to the Scriptures, the order of Creation is significant in two areas: marriage and the church. In both areas women are not to be the authority, the leader. To say this much is not to imply that all women are to be submissive to all men. In the church, the women are not told to submit themselves to all the men of the church, nor are all men given the right to teach and exercise authority (be elders) by virtue of their masculinity."[58]

George Knight, III writes that, "The first statement [verse 13] is that the order in which God created man and woman (Adam and Eve) expresses and determines the relationship God intended and the order of authority." Also, he writes that "The second statement [verse 14] is related to the Fall and the fact that Eve (woman) was beguiled. Paul does not expand and develop his argument, and we must be content with his brief statement of it."[59]

Margaret MacDonald agrees with those who suggest that 1 Timothy was written in the second century A.D. by someone claiming apostolic authority. Interestingly, she approaches the text with simplicity: "In this text, women are prohibited from teaching or leading prayer in public. They are called to emulate societal ideals of feminine modesty and virtue. Their subjection to the authority of men is justified by means of an appeal to the creation accounts in Genesis 1-3. The author stresses that Adam was formed first, then Eve."[60]

Carroll Osburn writes that, "Paul does not draw from Gen. 1-3 a universal principle from the historical Eve, but an ad hoc analogy from the later caricature of Eve in Jewish tradition. The point of similarity between v. 12 and v. 13 is that just as it is commonly remarked that Eve was deceived and led Adam astray, so certain women in the Ephesian church lack information and teach false information that leads people astray."[61] (Note: Carroll Osburn is suggesting a similarity between v. 12 and v. 14, not v. 12 and v. 13, at this point.)

Sarah Sumner suggests that egalitarians back away from 1 Timothy 2:13 and complementarians emphasize the verse (and then vice versa regarding the assessments of verse 14 that she lists). She does not offer a conclusion. Instead, she has written that each side of the discussion, championing one statement of Scripture over another, has convinced her "that this debate, underneath the surface, is not about 1 Timothy 2."[62]

Conclusion

1 Timothy 2:13-15 has been called a difficult text, which has made Sarah Sumner's study and suggestion a popular one. Her proposal has seemed to offer "a way out" of the issue for many, as has the conclusion of the "emerging church" movement. Each has allowed people to embrace both American equal rights and also belief in Jesus – eliminating a powerful tension. Building on the foundation of an "everyone should use their gifts" view of roles, some religious leaders have even taken the road that radical feminists before them have walked.[63] Mary Kassian, for one, has noted a pattern regarding people who have given up a commitment to apostolic authority after first embracing an equal rights approach to the Bible.[64]

The apostle's teaching, however, is not as difficult to grasp as some have suggested. It was written to a religious culture in many ways like our own. It is likely that Paul's words pressed against much of Asian religious and marital thought in the same way as it has pressed against Western equal rights.

As opposed to judging it as merely patriarchal or cultural, Paul's teachings should alert us to darkness in some of the religious thought of our day, just as was the case in first century Ephesus. An American equal rights starting point has carried its own form of spiritual deception. Life, freedom, and happiness are not "unalienable rights." They are gifts from the Lord. They are not ours to define as we wish. They are subject to his authority and his Word – as is the created order of male and female. While striving to appear true to Scripture, many have worked to adjust apostolic teaching to fit dominant American sociology and religious feminism.

In contrast, our need has been to let the Spirit speak through Paul as the apostle lays a foundation built on Genesis 1-3 – for all times and places. The apostle's teaching regarding the submission of women is grounded in Adam being formed first; the Lord's order of creation announces authority and submission within the family and the Church. But the apostle to the Gentiles emphasizes that leadership acts with the love of Christ. Ephesians 5:21 strikes no equal rights gong. It urges followers of Christ to submit themselves to the best interests of another. Men serving as church elders have a responsibility to act out Ephesians 5:21 within the family of God – submitting themselves to the best interests of the people placed in their spiritual care.

Appendix C: Visiting Ephesus and Three of its Religions

During the last three decades, students of the apostle Paul's letters have benefited from the results of extensive excavation and research in Ephesus (Gk. *Ephesos*) and throughout western Turkey. Work by the Austrian Archaeological Institute (*www.oeai.at*) and the Crisler Library at Ephesos (*www.crislerlibraryephesos.com*) continues to surface a wealth of information about the ancient city and the Roman province of Asia.

First-century Ephesus served as the influential trade center of Roman Asia. The city's location on the coast provided the inhabitants with a moderate climate and good conditions for growing both grapes and grains.[1] Surrounded by numerous estates that served as wheat farms, vineyards, and cattle ranches, the metropolis provided well-maintained highways for nearby landowners. In this way some of the most tasteful wine in the ancient world had easy access from the west coast of Asia Minor to all parts of the Mediterranean world. As a result the capital city had developed a strong popularity; ancient novels of the Roman period described it as bustling and glamorous.[2] Fertile, prosperous, and busy, Ephesus and the surrounding area possessed many of the attributes of the west coast of California.

Additionally, Ephesus was known for its healing arts and its rich legacy of religious strength. Tales of Amazon warrior-priestesses; Ephesian magic; the miracles of the patron goddess. Together, they likely propelled the metropolis to the status of legend. A two-hour pep rally in support of "Artemis of the Ephesians" (Acts 19:34) testifies to the influence of the Asian goddess cult. The religions of Dionysus and Isis also carry particular importance for this study. Both urged women's religious authority. Additionally, the Dionysus cult strongly promoted mysticism and music in its practices.

Artemis of the Ephesians

Was the supposed goddess Artemis a descendant of earlier mother goddess (Cybele) religion in the region? Evidence from ancient coins has illustrated that the goddess whose cult name was "Artemis Ephesia" was worshipped in Ephesus as early as 480 B.C. Ephesus' history appears to reach back to 1200 B.C. or earlier.[3] So, the question focuses on what happened during a span of 700 years or more. The answer is that historians can do no more than make educated guesses at present.

Richard Oster has suggested that the goddess cult reflected in some ways the geography of Ephesus. The supposed goddess probably mingled religious ideas flowing east and west together with local thought.[4] But the religious influence also worked in reverse. As numerous statuettes from the ancient world have announced, the strong tie to a seaport and metropolis also propelled Artemis Ephesia throughout much of the world of Paul's day.[5]

Richard Oster has also described how this composite cult developed a remarkable religious, civic, social, and economic sophistication in its ties with Ephesus. Inscriptions and other ancient writing provide a glimpse of this sophistication in the numerous titles applied to the supposed goddess:[6] Queen of the Universe, Lord, Saviour, Magistrate (Gk. *kosmeterai*),[7] "She Who is Robed in Gold" (Gk. *crusothoroi*),[8] "Theologian" (Gk. *theologoi*),[9] "She Who Concludes a Truce and Brings Peace" (Gk. *spondopoios*),[10] "Herald at the Sacrifice" (Gk. *hierokeirus*),[11] "Deliverer of Law" (Gk. *thesmodoi*),[12] "Protector" (Gk. *phulax*),[13] "Guardian of the Wild Beasts" (*theroskopos*).[14]

As her many roles announce, Artemis held preeminence in Ephesus and throughout the region. The majority of religious inscriptions discovered in the city to date have referred to her.[15] Some of the inscriptions have revealed how the goddess cult influenced family life, addressing matters ranging from cures for disease to citizenship decrees.[16] Others have shown a preoccupation with "Artem-" names in Ephesus, which indicate something of the devotion of families to the supposed goddess.[17] An inscription from nearby Pisidia announces a mingling of religious service with family lineage. A priest of Artemis named his daughter "Artemis" and she too became a mediator within the cult.[18]

The supposed goddess's sophistication was also seen in her statue at Ephesus. The image was covered with symbols representing the dramatic events of life and death.[19] The message may have been that the supposed goddess ruled over both. The Ephesians believed she presided over spirited city festivals and also acted as their protector in life-threatening moments. Individuals in need of protection could seek asylum in her temple.[20]

The belief in her power was self-fulfilling. Her cult owned and managed large estates of land and water.[21] Additionally, she was understood to own large herds of livestock outside the city – some of the estates/ranches sitting as far as twenty-five miles inland from Ephesus.[22] An additional source of income to the cult came in the form of taxation on various family events and business transactions in the city and the surrounding area. Port entry fees, for example, were used to sustain the cult.[23] Births in Ephesus were taxed, with the proceeds flowing into the temple.[24] Additionally, businesses, property leases, and the production of agriculture and industry also were taxed for the support of the religion and its sanctuary.[25]

The cult's massive assets insured that the temple could serve as the cornerstone of the financial and banking industry of the Asian metropolis. The temple lent money and required interest on the loan. It also received gifts of money from city residents – and foreigners – and safeguarded the deposits.[26] The goddess was also designated as an heiress in wills.[27]

Assigned the task of overseeing and maintaining the temple complex, the priests and priestesses of Artemis possessed a fame that was centuries old. While sensually inviting, the priestess role gave no sexual favors to arriving worshipers and tourists. S. M. Baugh's careful study of the priestly office has suggested that the priestesses of the goddess were not prostitutes, but were instead virgins.[28] They were likely young women who offered alluring beauty, fortune telling, and temple servitude as they captivated a city – especially during religious festivals.

Richard Oster has also provided an important overview of cult festivities and writes that "celebrations of Artemis in the month Artemision included games, festivals, banquets, sacred processions, and sacrifices.... Moreover it probably included Saturnalian elements such as the temporary freeing of slaves and dismissal of schools...."[29] The celebration was popular throughout the Greco-Roman world as a time when it was considered appropriate for a woman to seek out her husband[30] – something of an ancient version of Sadie Hawkins Day. Overlaying the festival were hundreds of years of tradition; tables of food illustrated generations of thought about human sensuality – expressed by the various aphrodisiacs laid out for the taking.

While we cannot know what cult practices prevailed during the time of Paul, we do have evidence that the roots of Ephesian worship grew deep. Even modern Turkish folk festivals continue to display strong sensuality and sexual symbolism.[31] Further, Near Eastern dervishes may mimic the dances of the ancient priestesses. It is likely that first-century Ephesus was well acquainted with sensational religion tied to Artemis Ephesia.

The Terraces Houses of Ephesus and the Cults of Dionysus and Isis

The Austrian Archaeological Institute is currently reconstructing some of the remarkable, ornate terrace houses (or slope houses) located in the city proper. The houses are filled with both artistry and engineering. Mosaic floors and nearby city streets of inlaid mosaics abound with color and intricacy. Frescoes decorate many of the walls and provide an ancient portrait of wealth and religious belief. Judging from photographs of the houses, only a little imagination is needed to see what the terrace house neighborhoods of Ephesus would have looked like on a bright day. Sunrays striking the frescoes and mosaics would have caused colors to dance around the entrances to the houses.

Additionally, the terrace houses illustrate the degree of sophisticated engineering that Ephesus was determined – and could afford – to provide in the first century. The houses received cold running water via a system of ceramic pipes that varied in diameter – something of an ancient water metering system. Ceramic pipes under the floor carried hot water, thereby warming the occupants on a brisk morning.

Did the houses represent family dwellings or were they instead meeting places for government affairs, trade guilds, or religious festivals and worship? Judging from the size of some of the rooms that have been restored to date, select houses could have served as a place for larger gatherings of people. In thinking about groups gathering in one of the houses, Luke's statement of "the lecture hall of Tyrannus" (Acts 19:9, NIV) comes to mind. The terrace houses excavated to date certainly had floor plans large enough to have accommodated a group of Christians meeting to worship (see Ro. 16:5; 1 Cor. 16:19; Col. 4:15; Philemon v. 2).

Of further interest to students of the Bible are the findings regarding religious belief and ritual that have surfaced from the excavations and restoration of the terrace houses. For example, Austrian archaeologist Maria Aurenhammer has noted that one of the terrace houses includes evidence pointing to Isis worship in the building.[32] A bronze statue of the supposed goddess suggests that the owners or occupants performed rites of some sort in her honor. Evidence in another terrace house suggests that the occupants were worshipers of the supposed god Dionysus:

> Inscriptions in Slope House 2 refer to the mountain-dwelling god. In an inscription in the peristyle court of luxurious apartment 6, the owner, C. Flavius Furius Aptus, presented himself as venerator of Dionysos Oreios Bakchios; he also set up a statuette of the god, which is now extant only in fragments.[33]

Further, both public and private buildings along Curetes Street, near the slope houses, contain numerous statues of Dionysus.[34]

The Austrian archaeologist has drawn an important conclusion from the recent findings: "Dionysus clearly dominated the male part of the Ephesian pantheon, even before Roman times."[35] Inscriptions about the religion and the presence of frescoes and statuettes of the supposed god within the terrace houses reveal that the cult penetrated urban as well as rural areas of Asia. One of the terrace houses may even have served as the site of cult rituals – complete with plenty of wine and evening music from flutes and drums.

Other archaeological evidence has added to the portrait of the Dionysus and Isis cults' influence in the city. Richard Oster has noted that inscriptions from the late Republic refer to the Dionysus priesthood and ceremonies associated with Dionysiac worship. Other inscriptions in the Ephesian *agora* (marketplace and political center) clearly show that people of the city celebrated the winter festival of Dionysus.[36] Further, evidence from coins dating from 39 B.C. announces the influence and veneration of Dionysus in Ephesus.[37] Finally, one inscription locates a Dionysiac guild, the *Technitai*, in Ephesus, at least during the reign of Antoninus Pius (138-161 A.D.).[38] The guild represented a collection of drama and music artisans who were devoted to the worship of the god of wine. David Magie's survey of Asian inscriptions and coins presents a similar portrait of the presence of the Isis cult in the metropolis in the Roman imperial period.[39] In summary, archaeological evidence testifies to the presence of the Dionysus and Isis religions in Ephesus in Paul's day.

Wine, Music and Obscenity

Historically paired with the Artemis cult, the Dionysus cult drank its way into each successive generation of Ephesian religion. The cult brought together wine, music and obscenity to a degree that rivaled any pagan religion in the Mediterranean world. As Dan Stanislawski has surveyed, the spread of wine-making in the Mediterranean region paralled a similar spread of the Dionysus cult.[40] Adding to the portrait, Ross Kraemer has observed that in addition to the well-known symbols of grapes and the ivy vine, Dionysus was associated with sexual symbolism. The god of wine was worshipped by means of parades during the *Phallophoria* festival (and perhaps others) that included villagers either carrying obscene images or pulling carts that included some form of suggestive symbolism.[41] These parades, together with other ritual events, appear to have taken place at night and to have involved frenzied dance – primarily by women initiates into the cult.[42]

One combined-cult all-night festival that was especially prominent for women was the *Haloa,* a midwinter festival featuring women feasting in honor of Dionysus and Cybele. The festival was famous for its large amounts of wine and intense sensuality – illustrated in part by the inclusion of foods that were in some way sexually suggestive.[43] Further, one ancient historian has noted that the cult festivals even included moments when priestesses whispered suggestions of marital infidelity into the ears of women.[44]

In describing women-led feasts in the Greco-Roman world, Joan Burton has emphasized the prominence that Dionysus cult ritual played especially for women. The worship of the god of wine extended beyond the private, ecstatic, all-night celebrations to include other settings as well – where women's influence could be more widely seen and felt.[45] Not only was the religion entwined with the economic success of the wine industry, it also afforded women opportunities for religious and social leadership and the mentoring of other women. For example, inscriptional evidence from third century B.C. Magnesia (sister city to Ephesus) shows that women were in charge of even mixed groups of worshipers of Dionysus.[46] Further, "in Menander's *Dyskolos* a city woman directs the sacrifice to Pan and the celebratory lunch, and if her son and his friends attend the lunch, they are there as guests."[47] Burton also notes that at the *Thesmophoria* feast "women elected female officials to preside, and wealthy women sponsored the feast (at their husbands' expense) for other women from the demes."[48]

While Dionysus worship, at times, included both male and female worshipers, only women could participate fully in the cult rituals.[49] Women dominated the cult.[50] The involvement of men appears to have been limited to public, versus secret, Dionysiac rituals. Further, even the public rituals clearly were led by women.[51] For example, "The epitaph of a priestess of Dionysus named Alcmeonis, daughter of Rhodius, supplements our knowledge of the cult at Miletus. She led the Bacchae of the city to the mountain, carrying unspecified sacred objects and implements."[52]

Female Dionysus worshipers, called *Maenads,* received legendary, even mythical, status in the ancient world. Their supposed trances presented enduring expressions of power that captivated people. Euripides' play *The Bacchae* described the *Maenads'* worship in stark detail: women who let their hair down to flow and wave as they moved; head flung back; eyes rolling;[1] limbs sensually moving during long periods of intense dance.[53]

It is certain that public Dionysiac religious assemblies carried much the same sensual weight as the secret gatherings. We underestimate the cult's power if we think of it as no more than a casual display of a bit of flute music, intoxication and some swaying. It was far more. The cult's sensual and sensational worship expressed itself in both the *Dithyramb* chorus to the supposed god and also the *Epilenion* – a type of high-energy composition found around rural winepresses.[54] An aphrodisiac in its public moments,[55] cult worship probably compared closely to the warm, welcoming music and movement of a comely, present-day female vocalist.

At the Heart of Dionysus Worship

But what prompted the cult rituals? Walter Otto has proposed an answer that makes startling sense of the ecstasy and frenzy of the rituals. The myths and religion arose out of the surge of new life. Cult ritual expressed both the trauma of childbirth and the bringing forth of a new human being.[56] At the same time the rituals bore a complex, powerful quality:

> All of his [Dionysus'] gifts and attendant phenomena give evidence
> of the sheer madness of his dual essence: prophecy, music, and fi-
> nally wine, the flamelike herald of the god, which has in it both bliss
> and brutality. At the height of ecstasy all of these paradoxes suddenly
> unmask themselves and reveal their names to be life and death.[57]

In this way the Dionysus cult rituals may actually, in a twisted view, look back to the very beginning of humanity – to the dramatic alternatives that lay before the first man and woman and the consequences of their sin.[58] However, in Dionysiac worship, the alternatives carry nothing of euphemism or God's graciousness even in recounting the Fall. Instead, the worship ritual illustrated the alternatives of life or death solely from the darkened perspective of chaos and suffering.

Isis Cult Leadership and Worship

The supposed Egyptian goddess Isis and her cult rituals were relative newcomers to Ephesus and Asia, but appear to have put down at least shallow roots by Paul's day. Similar to the cults of Artemis and Dionysus, "social pleasure and sensual gratification were among the rewards of the devotees of Isis."[59] Typically, the cult was closely associated with water – recalling its origin in the land of the Nile.[60] Holy water from the supposed goddess was sprinkled on cult members during rituals. Also the religion was closely tied to livelihoods such as fishing and sailing. Some mariners believed that Isis had invented the sail and that the supposed goddess protected them on their voyages.[61] One of the rituals of her cult included a procession of worshipers robed in white who walked to the edge of the sea and from there launched a sacred boat.[62] Daily rituals included washing her statue and singing morning and evening hymns to the supposed goddess.[63]

Especially important for understanding the background of Paul's letters to Ephesus was the prominence of female authority and leadership in the cult. Ross Kraemer has suggested that the Isis cult "sanctioned increased autonomy and authority for women at an explicit level not seen before (or after) in the religions of the Greco-Roman world."[64] Sarah Pomeroy's careful study of women's religious authority in the ancient world has provided a similar message regarding the Isis cult.[65] Both have emphasized that the famous statement from Oxyrhynchus Papyrus 1380 appears to have rung true in the Mediterranean world. In matters of religion, Isis had "made the power of women equal to that of men."[66] The church in Ephesus may have included women (and men) who previously had worshipped Isis and who were used to religious authority resting in the hands of women.

By Paul's day the Artemis and Dionysus religions represented the result of centuries of thought and action. Both religions, together with others such as the Isis cult, exerted the pressure of a dark lord in the city and region where Paul, Gaius, Aristarchus, Timothy, and others worked in spreading the Word in the first century.

Appendix D: Wiccan and New Age Spiritualism, the "Queen of Heaven," and "Emerging Churches" – A Brief Look at Present-Day Mysticism

The names of supposed ancient goddesses surface throughout the Internet in our day. Listed below are some of the websites that include the words: *Artemis Woman* – a line of women's cosmetics; *ArtemisGuide.com* – a guide to Women's studies at U.S. universities; *IsisForWomen.com* – performance outdoor clothing for women; *ArtemisRacing.com* – dedicated to the promotion of women's cycling; *Artemis Project* – Brown University's program to encourage women in the computer science field; *Isis Books* – New Age and Wiccan books and supplies; *ArtemisSingers.org* – the Chicago Lesbian Chorus; *MightyIsisClub.com* – dedicated to "helping young women find their mighty Isis within;" *ArtemisPress* – publisher of lesbian and feminist ebooks; *ArtemisCenter.org* – Center for Alternatives to Domestic Violence.

The catalog of websites associated with supposed goddesses may seem diverse, but it does have a common thread. All have to do with women and women's issues. In our day mysticism frequently gets tied to thought about or even belief in an ancient supernatural being having feminine qualities.[1] The websites parallel a current of thought urged by Carol Christ in her 1982 essay "Why Women Need the Goddess." She suggested that the emotional and spiritual needs of women could only be satisfied by leaning on, even worshiping, a female deity.[2] Similar to Charlene Spretnak's suggestion of Jesus plus the Goddess, other voices have taken the thought further. They have proposed that the inclusion of goddess spiritualism actually is more beneficial for everyone than all-male focused religion.

The Origin and Essence of Wicca

Wicca has represented one such expression of the "divine feminine." Numerous Wiccan worship groups (circles) have long taught that Wicca has a tradition dating back to antiquity. However, in the last decade Wiccans have revised this conclusion. Philip Davis's revealing study *Goddess Unmasked* has carefully linked Wicca to late nineteenth and early twentieth century European Romanticism.[3] Wiccans typically acknowledge now that Wicca represents a relatively new religion. However they also argue that it has an ancient, mystical element.

For example, Starhawk (the Wiccan name of Miriam Simos) has written numerous detailed rituals that she suggest create "sacred space." The space is expected to put a person in touch with supernatural power. For many this belief has bridged the various ancient cults with present Wicca. As Starhawk has commented, "We don't do what Witches did a hundred years ago, or five hundred years ago, or five thousand years ago...."[4] The view of many goddess worshipers is that ancient religion was seeking the same powers that modern neopaganism has called on. Typically, they refer to such power as an "inner goddess." The "inner goddess" is believed to awaken as a result of Wiccan rituals, similar to the belief of Buddhists that deity "awakens" in them. Miriam Simos and Hilary Valentine describe the belief with these words:

> And so in the center of our circle, we find deep within ourselves the Goddess of many faces, many genders, many colors, many ages. We find her in every human being, in every living thing, in every act and mood and nature. Her shape shifts and blurs in the firelight; she appears first in my face; in my voice, and then in yours. And so a kiss is passed around the circle: "Thou art Goddess, thou art God."[5]

What Miriam Simos and Hilary Valentine have revealed with warm, inviting language is that Wicca represents a powerful blend of individualism coupled with the friendship of a group. This is its most influential quality. It embraces religious freedom and eliminates isolation especially for women who have found themselves in need of a friend. Having built a bond of closeness, the worship of the Goddess then seeks to work outward to defend, support, and change others. As Judith Ochshorn has written, "If the Goddess is to liberate us, once we acknowledge her presence within and our worth as persons, she will turn our energies and talents outward to struggle with all forms of oppression...."[6]

Goddess Worship and the Source of Evil

Goddess worshipers frequently have been misrepresented as Satan worshipers. Wicca and witchcraft typically are not dedicated to Satan. Indeed, Wicca knows no individual who is responsible for the problem of evil; most Wiccans have no belief in Satan or a devil. So then who is responsible for evil?

Present-day goddess worship has suggested a unique answer to the question of evil. It has to do with the natural order of things. "Good" and "evil" are only a perception of the cycles of natural order – much as gentle rains compare to raging hurricanes. Everything is explained by the cycles of all that surrounds us. As such, "evil" represents no ethical conflict, but only what is painful for a season. Even death is perceived as only temporary pain – to be followed by renewal of some form, perhaps even reincarnation. As Cynthia Eller has summarized, "Nothing is lost in the goddess. What appears evil is incorporated into an organic cycle that is ultimately good and positive. Death does not overwhelm the goodness of life. It cannot even be said to be truly evil, for it is life's other side...."[7]

For all of their explanations of good and evil as the natural cycle of things, goddess worshipers continue to face one issue that takes them into the realm of ethics. Their writings express anger at the murder of thousands of so-called witches. But if death is merely part of a natural cycle, why do Wiccans respond with anger regarding the witch trials? In brief, this represents one of the most glaring inconsistencies of neopaganism. Wicca is intolerant of oppression and is justified in such – and so is a Christian. The witch trials had no justification. However, at the same time, Christians have a response that Wicca has not been able to grasp. The Trials were no expression of Christlikeness. They were, instead, the work of an insidious dark lord that used the word "Christianity" to mask evil. Unlike Wicca's puzzlement regarding evil, the Scriptures announce God's answer to the question of evil's source. They also describe the resolution to the challenge of evil (even when evil suggests it is a Christian act): "I saw Satan fall like lightning from Heaven." (Lk. 10:18, NIV).

Wicca and New Age Goddess religion serves as an inviting banquet in our day. It feeds individuals hungry for the compassion and nurture missing from much of Western society. The feminist Emily Culpepper has suggested that one of the motivations behind goddess worship has to do with the large number of women now in the U.S. workforce. Often they feel enslaved to cold, repetitive jobs and/or strained relationships. As some approach the twilight years, they want to make a difference and to do so "need more mythic, spiritual, and psychic resources."[8] At the same time the portraits of a good Creator's constant care and churches as families often get lost. As a result people end up looking elsewhere.

Similarly, some New Age answers have enticed people into a unique rebellion against apostolic teaching. For example, a growing number of people have sought to return to "real" (pre-Paul) Christianity. Frequently, during the past two decades that has translated into an embrace of second century

Gnosticism – with its goddess metaphors. Perhaps for that reason one of neo-Gnosticism's most influential voices has also been one of America's favorite storytellers: Marion Zimmer Bradley. Her bestselling 1982 novel *The Mists of Avalon* has illustrated the goddess versus "patriarchal Christianity" clash even as it has spawned a series of fantasy novels.

In looking at goddess religion, Charlotte Allen has noted a like "adjustment" to Christianity. As she writes,

> I am hardly the first to notice that Wicca bears a striking resemblance to another religion – one that also tells of a dying and rising god, that venerates a figure who is both virgin and mother, that keeps, in its own way, the seasonal "feasts of the Wheel," that uses chalices and candles and sacred poetry in its rituals. Practicing Wicca is a way to have Christianity without, well, the burdens of Christianity.[9]

Charlotte Allen has described not only the character of Wiccan mysticism, but also mingled religion in the form of veneration and worship to the "Mother of God." Similar to neo-Gnosticism, the roots of such extend deep, almost to the beginning of Christianity.

The Titles of Mary and the Evolving of Veneration

A portrait of goddess religion and veneration of Mary among early believers in Christ is sketchy and far from complete. Early evidence pointing to a possible connection comes from Asia Minor no more than 100 years after the apostolic age. British archaeologist William Ramsey has observed that "the earliest known trace of the veneration of the Virgin Mary in the Christian religion is in a Phrygian inscription of the second century...."[10] The inscription's location in the region long associated with worship of the "Great Mother" of Anatolia (Cybele) should catch our attention. A second piece of evidence in the form of a papyrus fragment comes from the (est.) mid-third century A.D. It contains a hymn to Mary known as *Beneath Your Compassion*. The hymn requests Mary's care.[11] Similarly, a fifth century A.D. inscription in Aphrodisias, a city 100 miles east of Ephesus, records the petition, "Mary, mother of God, help."[12]

While the evidence is limited, it is not difficult to see how worship of Cybele, Artemis, or Isis may have influenced early believers in Christ. Veneration or even worship of Mary may have represented one of the results of this influence.[13] It is naïve to believe that centuries of devotion in Asia Minor to supposed goddesses was something easily discarded.

Beyond early veneration of Mary, history has seen the mother of Jesus bestowed with other expressions and titles as well. Interestingly, these titles typically have brought together the two important characteristics of goddess religion: care and protection mated to power. Among the most prominent titles have been "Mother of the Church"[14] and "Queen of Heaven."[15] Not surprisingly, the title "Queen of Heaven" came to know a special prominence in the Middle Ages.[16]

Of late high leadership in Catholicism has explored the new title of "Coredemptrix" – one that declares Mary's role in humanity's spiritual redemption.[17] The word announces Mary's supposed work with Christ to bring about salvation. Catholicism has urged that the title "Coredemptrix" does not elevate Mary's status within Catholic doctrine and life. However, the semantics of the dogma matter little since the teaching further emphasizes her in peoples' minds. Indeed the discussion surrounding the new title for Mary has come to symbolize the tension about Mary within Catholicism of late.

The Rise of the "Queen of Heaven"

During the past twenty years, Catholicism has bubbled with thinking and writing permeated with a feminine emphasis. Similar to the Middle Ages, the title "Queen of Heaven" has known growing popularity in our day. The title has become a magnet for people from varying religious backgrounds – including feminism and goddess religions.[18] In contrast Catholic higher leadership has recognized the rising storm and reacted to it. For example, from Vatican II forward, the *Salve Regina* (*Hail Holy Queen*) prayer to Mary has been excluded from the Catholic Mass.[19]

In the last several years, the influential feminist and Catholic theologian Charlene Spretnak has brought greater pressure to bear on the relationship between veneration and worship of Mary, feminism, and goddess religion. In her book *Missing Mary*, she has suggested that "in Mary the extremely ancient female expression of the sacred has been kept alive in the West...."[20] She proposes that early Christians did not stumble into honoring Mary simply because they lived among forms of goddess spiritualism. Instead, she believes they saw what Christianity needed. It needed a Mary with goddess-like powers. Otherwise, she suggests that Christianity would not have survived much longer than the ancient cult of Mithras.[21]

For Charlene Spretnak, Mary is more than human, and the title "Queen of Heaven" fully justified. As she writes,

> Surely it is likely that Mary's experience of growing God-the-Son in her body, from her body, as part of her body, *changed* her. Though never officially acknowledged in Church doctrine, it has seemed entirely plausible to most Catholics that the Mother of God-the-Son would partake of a semi-divine status.[22]

The unique feature of this pressure in Catholicism of late is that feminists have tapped the historical, orthodox, and popular mystic role that Mary has played in Catholic teaching. They have emphasized the 1854 papal declaration of Mary's "immaculate conception" – suggesting that Mary no longer needs to be "saved."[23] They have also highlighted the papal announcement of 2002 which appears to suggest that Mary (and the Rosary) stands at the center of contemplating the story of Jesus.[24] As a result feminists have left Catholic leadership to grapple with a dilemma: how to focus on the Father, Son, and Spirit while accepting the mystical focus on Mary.

In his September 13, 1995 General Audience address, Karol Wojtyla (John Paul II) delivered a message entitled "Mary is the Virgin Mother of God."[25] At first look the address seems to have been no more than a blending of the existing doctrines and titles of "Blessed Virgin," "Mother of God," and "Mother of the Church." However, during the address Karol Wojtyla appears to have made a subtle revision to Catholic doctrine about Mary. Vatican II came closest when it described Mary's relation to the Church with the words "the Mother of God is a model of the Church in the matter of faith, charity, and perfect union with Christ."[26] Karol Wojtyla, however, declared that the title "Virgin Mother" has to do with more than Mary's role in the birth of Jesus. He announced that her maternal role also "involves the birth and growth of the Church."[27]

Karol Wojtyla's statement may seem to represent no more than a restatement of existing teaching, until it is compared with Catholic medieval mysticism – what Charlene Spretnak highlights in *Missing Mary*. Interestingly, the language of the 1995 address looks much like the language used by Juliana of Norwich, the fourteenth century Catholic mystic:

> For in that same time that God knitted Himself to our body in the Virgin's womb, He took our Sensual soul in which taking He, us

all having enclosed in Him, oned it to our Substance: in which one-ing He was perfect Man. For Christ having knit in Him each man that shall be saved, is perfect Man. Thus our Lady is our Mother in whom we are all enclosed and of her born, in Christ: (for she that is Mother of our Saviour is Mother of all that shall be saved in our Saviour;) and our Saviour is our Very Mother in whom we be end-lessly borne, and never shall come out of Him.[28]

Both Juliana of Norwich's *Revelations of Divine Love* and Karol Wo-jtyla's message illustrate how Catholicism's focus on Mary has swung like a pendulum between two distinct roles: Mary as the mother of Jesus and also in some way the "Mother" of the saved.

150 years after the announcement of Mary's "immaculate conception," the mother of Jesus has become for many people a goddess. Similar to Char-lene Spretnak's suggestion, many envision a supernatural "She" who stands alongside "He." Queen of Heaven; Mother of God; Coredemptrix; Eu-charistic woman;[29] Our Lady of Guadalupe.[30] Each accents the mystical image of Mary. Indeed, the Latin American visualization of "Our Lady of Guadalupe" blends together imagery from the Revelation to John (Rev. 12:1) with visual elements associated with ancient goddesses.[31]

Equally remarkable in our time the suggestion of Mary as a supernatural goddess even extends beyond Catholicism. For example, the bestselling novel *The Secret Life of Bees* introduces people to a vastly powerful and nurturing Mary (the "Black Madonna") – with no mention of Jesus. Sue Monk Kidd directs the matriarch of her story to speak of Catholicism with the addition of other ingredients – that fits her faith in the Goddess.[32] She portrays Mary as everywhere: "Inside rocks and trees and even people...."[33] She is a deity in the image of those worshiping her. As Sue Monk Kidd writes, "everybody needs a God who looks like them...."[34]

Can the Creator be the Goddess?

Since the Creator is spirit (Jn. 4:24), what issue exists in talking about "She?" Should Christianity indeed change to focus on Jesus and the God-dess? Does a balance of male and female deity enrich Christian faith? These appear to be the questions being raised by a growing number of voices, not only in Catholicism, but in the "Emerging Church" movement as well. For example an Internet forum for women in the "Emerging Church" movement reveals that an increasing number of people are willing to talk about a supernatural being as "She," as the Goddess.

Brian McLaren's *A Generous Orthodoxy* approaches the "divine feminine" as he discusses Catholic veneration of Mary. While he does not urge worship of Mary, what he does write lines up closely with Charlene Spretnak's long-standing proposal. Both urge that the focus of Christianity change. After meditating in a garden area dedicated to Mary, McLaren writes, "I realized how impoverished my Protestant faith was with its exclusively male focus."[35] He talks about a statue of Mary in the garden where he sat as if he were in her presence: "I found myself sitting on a bench with Mary towering over me, looking down on me with a kind face, her arms extended." [36] So how does Mary tower over Brian McLaren? And do eyes fixed on Jesus (Heb. 12:1-2) indeed impoverish faith?

William Young, Wayne Jacobsen, and Brad Cummings's novel *The Shack* paints a similar portrait, urging faith in a Creator that is "She" as well as "He." Indeed, the novel's popularity appears to reveal much about the religious thought of the nation early in the twenty-first century. The story tells of the Creator who is there when we hurt and who has the wisdom and power to rescue us from brokenness. That is its strength. It paints the portrait of a supernatural being who urges forgiveness, kindness, and giving up "rights." Young, Jacobsen, and Cummings emphasize the new commandment of Jesus that we love as Jesus loved (Jn. 13:34-35).

The Shack also unveils a bold portrait of the Father and Spirit – perhaps more than William Young originally envisioned in his story. The Father is revealed by the name "Elousia" – in the image of an African-American woman. The Spirit, in the image of a smaller Asian woman, embraces the name "Sarayu." Both visit the main character, Mack, along with Jesus. All three come to the shack to help Mack emotionally and spiritually heal. Young, Jacobsen, and Cummings describe a God who is approachable. They suggest that we can imagine the Creator in ways that are comfortable to us – avoiding the struggles and scars that are part of our past.

Are William Young, Wayne Jacobsen, and Brad Cummings right? Is the New Testament message about a heavenly Father no more than cultural convention? Are the authors merely scraping away the crusty residue of centuries of language that does not fit our day? Is *The Shack* actually nothing more – or less – than a restatement of the Gospel for our day? A new Gospel of Jesus for a new century?

Setting the novel alongside the Gospel of John and Paul's letters to Ephesus reveals far more than questions about gender language and imagery. Other important questions surface as well. Accepting for a moment a (post)modern novel about Jesus appearing in our time, why does Jesus not come to the shack by himself? Would Jesus' appearance alone have been insufficient for Mack? Should we conclude that first-century Judea, Galilee, and Samaria knew no evil, selfish men? No abuse of women and children? No scars left by fathers? Would it have been better if a divine Mother, Son, and Spirit had appeared to first-century society? Similar to Judas Iscariot's query in the 1971 rock opera *Jesus Christ Superstar*, can we chastise God for appearing when (or how) he did?

The Shack embraces a view of the Creator that ignores one of the dominant themes of the Gospel of John. Young, Jacobsen, and Cummings allow humanity complete freedom to name the Creator; they offer Elousia and Sarayu. In contrast the fourth Gospel unveils Jesus as the Creator made human (Jn. 1:1, 14). He is the Gate of Heaven; he tells Nathaniel that he will see angels ascending and descending on the Son of Man (Jn. 1:51; cf. Gen. 28:10-22). He is the God of the Hebrews (Jn. 8:58). Strikingly, Jesus says simply, "Anyone who has seen me has seen the Father." (Jn. 14:9, NIV) While Young, Jacobsen, and Cummings show us that they believe "Papa" (Elousia) and Jesus are one and the same,[37] their novel severs what the Gospel of John binds together.

The Creator has revealed himself in human form through Jesus alone. The Son of Man and King of Kings has clothed the Creator with flesh, bone, and stem cells for all peoples and all time. The fourth Gospel paints a portrait that the risen Lord urges us to imprint on our minds. The King of Kings counsels us to follow every brush stroke, note every nuance of color. We are to fix our eyes on Jesus (Heb. 12:1-2), not proposed feminine images of the Father and Spirit. To talk of the Creator as "She" reveals something other than the Gospel translated for a given culture. Eventually, it reveals that people have lost sight of Jesus Christ. The risen Jesus reveals himself as the "King of Kings and Lord of Lords" (Rev. 19:16, NIV) to Asia Minor – a land that had been drenched in goddess religion for centuries. The portrait of the King was intended as well for every age and every people.

William Young, Wayne Jacobsen, and Brad Cummings clearly are in tune with dominant currents of social and religious thought in our day. As a result *The Shack* is more than a comfortable portrait of God. It is also a labyrinth of peril. The authors both depend on the Bible and dismiss or misstate part of the risen Lord's teaching. While they talk about the love of Jesus, they also conceal the Jesus who defines love as obedience to apostolic teaching – the result of the Spirit's guidance (Jn. 14:15-21; 16:5-15). As a result their understanding of the church seems blind to apostolic teaching and the importance of Christians meeting together (Heb. 10:19-25).[38]

Additionally, the authors raise key questions about sin and about Scripture. They cannot see or choose to avoid the staggering impact of humanity's sin on the relationship of the Father, Son, and Spirit. They do not believe the cross forced the Father to forsake his Son.[39] They also seem to have less regard for Scripture than Jesus reveals as he talks with teachers of the Law in his Father's house (Lk. 2:45-49). For Young, Jacobsen, and Cummings, the Scriptures appear to be, at times, powerless – God confined to paper.[40] In place of (supposed) powerless Scripture, the authors seem comfortable in speaking for God. Much of *The Shack* is written as if the authors' filtering of apostolic teaching is coming from the mouth of the Creator.

Passionately Seeking the Creator in a Spiritual Siege

In addition to emphasis on "the divine feminine," other expressions of Christian faith have surfaced of late that bear resemblance to New Age spiritualism. For example, an article by Mike Perschon in *Youth Specialties* magazine includes an example of spiritual contemplation that resembles counsel in the Wiccan guidebook *The Twelve Wild Swans*:

> I built myself a prayer room—a tiny sanctuary in a basement closet filled with books on spiritual disciplines, contemplative prayer, and Christian mysticism. In that space I lit candles, burned incense, hung rosaries, and listened to tapes of Benedictine monks. I meditated for hours on words, images, and sounds.[41]

As Mike Perschon's comments illustrate, mysticism often focuses on "me."[42] It highlights the inviting character of personal, tangible interaction with the supernatural. Experience shapes popular religion to such a degree that at least one "Emerging Church" voice has even described indifference of late to reading the printed Word of God.[43]

Another of America's favorite storytellers, Max Lucado, further illustrates popular religion's emphasis on "me." In *The Great House of God*, the capable storyteller passionately distances Christian faith from mysticism as he

222

describes the importance of reading the Word.[44] However, he also misses Paul's message in Ephesians 4:15; he becomes ensnared in seeking God speaking to each of us where Paul's purpose is quite different.[45]

The apostle talks about each of us acting to benefit someone else. Is the Ephesian letter talking about individuals "finding God's will?" No, it is the apostle to the Gentiles urging Christians to build up one another – God's will for all collectively. An inside-to-out spiritual goal, not outside-to-in. Paul's focus is not on the individual in Ephesians 4:15, but on a church, a group. He says nothing in the teaching to indicate that we will hear a personal message from God in our one-another conversations.

Max Lucado struggles to hear what Ephesians 4:15 is saying, similar to many. He is not deaf to the sounds of a spiritual siege. However, he seems to believe the threat is far enough distant that we can shape Scripture to say what we wish. He is mistaken. Paul is preparing us collectively for the staggering winds and debris of a dark storm. In a time when isolation can slip up on us, Paul urges us to think of "we" versus "me."

Brian McLaren's approach to Christian teaching and history walks a path similar to that of Max Lucado. He too believes that spiritual threat is somewhat distant. As one example of his struggle, he hears part of the message and meaning of baptism "in Jesus day,"[46] but is willing to leave the original teaching buried. The seal of God; God's action to wash away sins; the event of immersion and rising out of water as a powerful participation in Jesus' death and resurrection. All of the teaching is almost within Brian McLaren's grasp. However, at that point he allows his eyes to stray from the risen Lord. After seeing the difference between baptism "in Jesus' day" and many present-day beliefs, he concludes by beginning with three short words: "but my sense...."[47] He lets a mystical approach to church history and apostolic teaching filter his listening to the Spirit of God. He silences a crucial message about Christ and from Christ. The "secret message" about baptism stays concealed from his readers in *The Secret Message of Jesus*.

He approaches Christian faith and doctrine as he does because he believes that among the earliest Christians, "having a right attitude toward Jesus (i.e. confidence or trust in him) was about all it took."[48] *A Generous Orthodoxy* sees a dark, raging storm and naïvely suggests that it will not touch us. His assessment offers false confidence. So, we can see clearly to embrace some teachings and discard others? Brian McLaren does not see that the love he talks about frequently is itself defined by the teaching and life of

Jesus. Christ-like love is itself part of "the truth" – the doctrine he appears to reduce to being a practice.[49]

Further, he suggests that church history represents Christians "continually being led and taught and guided by the Spirit into new truth."[50] As a result, he suggests that teaching about God should be "*conversational* (never attempting to be the last word, and thus silence other voices, but rather inviting ongoing dialogue in the search for truth)."[51] However, apostolic teaching itself raises challenges to what he has strongly suggested. For example did the Ephesian Christians' involvement with myths actually represent the Spirit's guidance into new truth (and Paul was blind to the situation; 1 Ti. 1:3)? The path Brian McLaren takes ignores the spiritual deception that has been the work of a dark lord in every generation.

He also urges us to see other religions "whenever possible, as dialogue partners and even collaborators."[52] To highlight how far he takes the thought, he goes to Jesus' parable of wheat and weeds (Mt. 13:24-30) and suggests that Christians should not "seek to root up all the bad weeds in the world's religions (including our own), but rather seek to encourage the growth of good wheat in all religions including our own, leaving it for God to sort out as only God can do."[53] He believes the various religions of the world (with the exception of radical Islam) have much to offer Christianity. For example, he suggests that Christians can benefit from learning more about and embracing the meditative practices of Eastern religions.[54]

The Catholic theologian Bede Griffith provides a powerful reminder that such thinking is not confined to a postmodern time. Over forty years ago he wrote, "We cannot look upon the Hindu, the Buddhist or the Muslim as outside the covenant of grace.... There is already a 'presence' of Christ and therefore of the Church in all genuine religion, however hidden it may be."[55]

Brian McLaren's view of other religions and of Christian teaching also meet in his assessment of earliest Christianity. He suggests that Christianity better discovered what it was about by dialogue with Judaism and Greco-Roman religions in the first centuries of the church. As he writes, "Without non-Christian dialogue partners, there would be no Christian theology as we know it."[56] So, it was good for other religions to challenge Christian faith and confuse people? Brian McLaren seems blind to the powerful siege affecting children of light in Ephesus and beyond (Eph. 4:17-5:20). Non-Christian dialogue was not with "partners" in first-century Ephesus; the Asian cults were the tools of a dark lord – a powerful, insidious enemy of the risen King.

Brian McLaren fails to see the successes of a dark lord in challenging Christian teaching and lifestyle in every age. In his effort to forge a "generous" view of religious truth, he allows himself to be blinded to the efforts of "the ruler of the kingdom of the air" (Eph. 2:2, NIV). As a result he loses his grip on Paul's teaching about the authority of the risen Lord (Eph. 1:19-22).[57] He permits a blindfold to the desperate situation of God's people and all of humanity at any given moment.

In contrast Scripture unceasingly reveals such desperate situations and how the Lord counsels people. The Son of God tells Peter, "Get behind me, Satan!" (Lk. 8:33, NIV). He shows us the "lifestyle shock" of a rich young ruler. He unveils the "doctrinal shock" of Saul of Tarsus. Our spiritual struggles often become just as desperate; we are enticed to minimize the shock by our own efforts. Sometimes in response we say or think, "I feel that...," instead of listening to the Scriptures. The deceptions that plagued the earliest Christians in Ephesus have surfaced again in our day.

Conclusion

Recalling the strong imagery in ancient myths; Wicca; prayer to Mary; *The Shack*. All announce a common longing for spiritual life – with conditions. A mystical approach to the supernatural has represented one of the most powerful enticements to people. Ephesus felt the pressures of a dark lord who used numerous religions and strong human desire to confuse. While ritual has changed, mysticism has remained inviting. In some ways our day echoes the 1960's and 70's and the "Age of Aquarius."

We revisit a time of "Jesus, yes; the Church, no." Why? Much of the answer likely is rooted in healthy desires for clarity versus religious confusion and peace in the middle of a nation engaged in war. Also, many long to shape (or reshape) worship to Christ to be more a renewing gathering of family.

In the balance we face a threat we cannot elude. We experience a dangerous spiritual siege; a dark lord remains close. His goal is to wear away thoughts of refreshing, exuberant faith and worship and as well urge us away from the counsel and love of the risen Jesus. We are enticed to think in terms of stark distinctions. Experience versus Scripture. Vibrant gatherings versus institutional churches. He suggests we avoid putting faces to the word "institution" or taking time to bind together Scripture with the experience of living like Jesus. A dark lord works to surround us with a slippery blackness, a weathered cavern that challenges our footing and lays siege to our ankles. Walking together can seem close to impossible.

Of late the threat has transformed into servings of the four Gospels, but only crumbs of teaching from apostolic letters. In a world conditioned to short bursts of speech and writing, catching hold of Jesus' words may seem enough of a challenge. So did the risen Lord not guide his ambassadors? We do not have time for apostolic letters? We do not face the same issues? In a day when reading much of Scripture has seemed "out" and stories, experience, meditation, and relationships "in," people often keep the "ins" and "outs" from mingling. Churches reading Scripture together often comes in short bursts.

In response we need to ask ourselves simple questions about lasting relationships. How close will we get to family or friends if our efforts are composed of clearing our mind and thinking about a word or brief phrase they have spoken to us? Will our five year old understand? Our teenage daughter? A close friend? We have learned (or should have learned) that spending extended time listening to others is crucial to understanding them.

Similarly, we need to hear the Word of God with patience and at length. Whether listening to Scripture or meditating on creation (Ps. 104:34; Ro. 1:20), we need to allow time for more than a text-message from God. And we need to grasp the overarching question that hangs suspended over six billion people: Is Jesus risen? And closely related, did the risen Lord guide and speak through his apostles? If so, then Paul's letters to Ephesus and Roman Asia are worth hearing and reading together with the Gospels. We need to hear both.

Appendix E: Simple Spiritual Disciplines

Individuals who talk about the value of meditation certainly are correct that people need to "slow" inwardly – something especially needed in our work, shop, or play-until-we-drop society. A good bit of discussion in our day has focused on medieval contemplation. However, the simple practice of memorizing Scripture has been less a part of the discussion. The irony is that the practice wove through the monastic practices called the *Rule of Benedict.* Speaking, praying, and singing the Psalms made up a large part of medieval meditation.

The roots of such are not difficult to find. Jesus' teaching abounds with dependence on the Scriptures. In time of weariness and temptation he sought Psalm 91. Paul counseled Timothy to publicly read the Word – helping people to remember. (1 Ti. 4:13) Similarly, the simple practices in childrens' Bible classes of memory verses and singing songs from Scripture represent powerful "spiritual disciplines." By neglecting such simple practices in teen and adult studies, we invite a pressuring evil that threatens to suffocate Christian understanding. We end up trying to catch our breath on little more than the still, humid air of an equatorial Summer.

So, what do we do? We have a need to sit quietly and read Scripture – perhaps a Psalm. And reread it. Then take time to memorize a verse. Then two. I speak from experience; memorizing Psalm 104 was not as difficult as I expected it to be. It simply took time and discipline in the presence of the risen Lord. With time, verses connected together in my thought. They surfaced as I lived and worked in the created world. The words of Psalm 104 have renewed me during laborious Houston freeway travel, hiking trips, and times of spiritual trial. Taking time to commit Scripture to memory helps fuel prayer, song, acts of help to others, teaching others, and imagination that is shaped by the Word.

Of similar value mingling together prayer, Scripture readings, and songs into a common theme in worship assemblies can help people better focus on the subject. In a time when attention spans and Bible reading have declined, spending extended time together singing Scripture and listening to Scripture read will help churches grow. No guesswork is involved in knowing how effective such simple practices will be. The Lord will bless us as we meditate on his Word. By doing such he will prepare us to help and teach others.

Abbreviations

AJA
American Journal of Archaeology

Bacchae
Euripides, *The Bacchae,* trans. Philip Vellacott (New York: Penguin Putnam, 1973)

BDAG
Walter Bauer, William F. Arndt, F. Wilbur Gingrich, and Frederick W. Danker, *A Greek-English Lexicon of the New Testament and Other Early Christian Literature*, 3rd ed. (Chicago: University of Chicago Press, 2000)

DBE
Discovering Biblical Equality: Complementarity Without Hierarchy, 2nd ed., ed. Ronald W. Pierce, Rebecca Merrill Groothuis, Gordon D. Fee (Downers Grove, IL: InterVarsity Press, 2005)

Ephesos
Ephesos, Metropolis of Asia, An Interdisciplinary Approach to its Archaeology, Religion, and Culture, ed. Helmut Koester (Cambridge. Harvard University Press, 2004)

ESV
English Standard Version of the Bible

EWEC
Essays on Women in Earliest Christianity, 2 vols., ed. Carroll D. Osburn (Joplin, MO: College Press, 1993-95)

Exhortation
Clement of Alexandria, *Exhortation to the Greeks*, Loeb Classical Library, trans. G. W. Butterworth (Cambridge: Harvard University Press, 1960)

HTR
The Harvard Theological Review

IAph2007
Joyce Reynolds, Charlotte Roueché, and Gabriel Bodard, *Inscriptions of Aphrodisias* (2007). Available at *http://insaph.kcl.ac.uk/iaph2007*

IEph
Die Inschriften von Ephesos, ed. H. Wankel et. al., 8 vols. in 11 (Bonn: Habelt, 1979-84)

JRS
The Journal of Roman Studies

KJV
King James Version of the Bible

LSJ
Henry George Liddell, Robert Scott, Henry Stuart Jones, and Roderick McKenzie, *A Greek-English Lexicon*, 9th ed. (Oxford: Clarendon Press, 1968)

NASB
New American Standard Version of the Bible

NEA
Near Eastern Archaeology

NIV
New International Version of the Bible

NT
New Testament

SEG
Supplementum Epigraphicum Graecum

TDNT   *Theological Dictionary of the New Testament,* 10 vols., ed. Gerhard Kittel and Gerhard Friedrich, trans. and ed. G. W. Bromiley (Grand Rapids: William B. Eerdmans Pub. Co., 1972)

WC   *Women in the Church: An Analysis and Application of 1 Timothy 2:9-15,* 2nd ed., ed. Andreas J. Köstenberger and Thomas R. Schreiner (Grand Rapids: Baker Academic, 2005)

WCO   *Women and Christian Origins,* ed. Ross Shepard Kraemer and Mary Rose D'Angelo (New York: Oxford University Press, 1999)

WGT   *Women and Goddess Traditions in Antiquity and Today,* ed. Karen L. King (Minneapolis: Fortress Press, 1997)

Notes

Introduction

1.   Michael I. Rostovzeff, *The Social and Economic History of the Roman Empire*, 2nd ed., rev. P.M. Fraser (New York: Oxford University Press, 1998), 570, note. 2: An edict of Paulus Fabius Persicus (A.D. 44), proconsul of Asia (Ephesus), announces "affectionate solicitude for the province and a deep sense of duty...."[3] It is likely that the expression of care by the proconsul was influenced by the many positive aspects of the city – not the least of which were its capacity for managing a key trade route and for generating taxes.

2.   The KJV translators rendered the Greek name/word "Artemis" (Gk. *Artemis*) as the Roman "Diana" in Acts 19:24, 27-28, 34-35. Luke records the population of Ephesus using the Greek name "Artemis." This book will use the Greek titles "Artemis" and "Artemis Ephesia" (the cult title) when referring to the supposed goddess.

3.   While we cannot know which sculptures had endured to the first century, we do know that the supposed goddess had been honored with numerous works of art. See, for example, Karl L. H. Lehmann-Hartleben, "The Amazon Group," *Parnassus* 8 (April 1936): 9: "The fact remains certain, that there existed four statues of Amazons in the famous sanctuary of Artemis at Ephesos, moreover that they were works of Phidias, Polykleitos, Kresilas, and Phradmon, dedicated there by unknown persons or communities in the same period, i.e., the second half of the Fifth century B.C."

4.   Aelius Aristides, *On Harmony, to the Cities* 24: (Gk. *tameion te koinon Asias*; "the common bank of Asia"). See also Dio Chrysostom 31.54: The deposits in the *Artemisium* were officially recorded.

5.   Pausanias, *Description of Greece* 7.5.4. Pausanias observed that the Artemision's preeminence was associated, not only with its immense size, but also with its vast wealth.

6.   Rostovzeff, *The Social and Economic History of the Roman Empire*, 739, note. 17.

7.   Pliny, *Natural History* 36.21.

8.   Beate Dignas, *Economy of the Sacred in Hellenistic and Roman Asia Minor* (New York: Oxford University Press, 2002), 192. Beate Dignas suggests that the "bankers" of the Artemis cult were the priests and priestesses of the cult or a subgroup assigned to serve as the financial ministers. See also

G. H. R. Horsley, "The Inscriptions of Ephesos and the New Testament," *Novum Testamentum* 34 (Apr., 1992): 143. Horsley draws the same conclusion; he suggests that the *synedrion* (council of priests) of the Artemis cult was "responsible to oversee the maintenance of the temple and its sacrifices and festivals." BDAG, 967: *synedrion* indicates a "council." The word is used in the New Testament only to refer to the Sanhedrin or to a civic council.

9. See, for example, *IAph2007* inscription no. 1.186, *Honours for Aurelia Apphia daughter of Epiktetos*, and no. 12.609, *Posthumous honours for Apphia daughter of Theodoros*. The third and fifth century A.D. inscriptions indicate that priestesses of Artemis existed into the Roman period and further.

10. Richard Oster, "The Ephesian Artemis as an Opponent of Early Christianity," *Jahrbuch für Antike und Christentum* 19 (1976): 33: "The frequency of loans made by the financial ministers of Artemis is reflected by the reference to sacred loans and related matters in an Ephesian debtor's law."

11. David Magie, *Roman Rule in Asia Minor* (Princeton, NJ: Princeton University Press, 1950), 166: The Artemis Ephesia cult received revenues (probably from fishing-rights) from the lakes near Ephesus.

12. Dignas, *Economy of the Sacred in Hellenistic and Roman Asia Minor*, 238. See also the wrenching article about child abandonment (ancient "exposure") by W. V. Harris, "Child-Exposure in the Roman Empire," *JRS* 84 (1994): 1-22.

13. *IAph2007* from inscription no. 12.533. *Honours for Aelia Laevilla*: "High Priestess and Magistrate of Artemis Ephesia" (Gk. *archiereian kai kosmeteiran tes Ephesias Artemidos*; second-third centuries A.D.; translation by the author). LSJ, 984 translates *kosmeteira* as "a female magistrate." *Corpus Inscriptionum Graecarum*, vol.2, ed. Augustus Boeckhius (New York: Georg Olms Verlag, 1977), 2823 records the use of *kosmeteira* in association with the Artemis cult in Ephesus. See also *SEG* 40, no. 1197: the high priestess of Asia appears to generally have served as a position focused on religious rituals. The office "is a matter of wealth and public 'ritual' rather than of (power) politics."

14. Dieter Knibbe, "Via Sacra Ephesiaca: New Aspects of the Cult of Artemis Ephesia," *Ephesos*, 148: Even today the plain where the remains of the Artemisium is located can become a shallow lagoon during heavy rains. Archaeological work has discovered that early in the Imperial period, the Ephesians constructed a road between the city and the temple that was made of plaster and small stones. However, the road continued to experience

flooding and degradation until a later road of large limestone blocks and masonry was built.

15. Oster, 41: "By the very fact that the zodiacal signs were so prominently depicted on the goddess one can be confident that all who came to the goddess for assurance about the safety of the future went away comforted." See also Lilian Portefaix, "The Image of Artemis Ephesia – A Symbolic Configuration Related to Her Mysteries?" in *100 Jahre Österreichische Forschungen in Ephesos, Akten des Symposions, Wien, 1995*, ed. H. Friesinger and F. Krinzinger (Vienna: Verlag der Österreichischen Akademie der Wissenchaften, 1999), 614-6.

16. Christine M. Thomas, "At Home in the City of Artemis: Religion in Ephesos in the Literary Imagination of the Roman Period," *Ephesos*, 81-4. She writes that "these novels are a compelling snapshot of the religious imagination of the eastern Roman Empire; religion forms an inextricable part of their fabric." (82)

17. See, for example, Lynn LiDonnici's "Women's Religions and Religious Lives in the Greco-Roman City," *WCO*, 80: "Almost every aspect of life, from sports to shopping to taking a bath, from eating to cleaning the house, was made part of a whole system of hopes, practices, and beliefs that involved divine forces (the gods and goddesses) with the minute details of everyday activity."

18. Richard Oster, "The Ephesian Artemis "Whom all Asia and the World Worship" (Acts 19:27): Respresentative Epigraphical Testimony to ʻΑΡΤΕΜΙΣ ΕΦΕΣΙΑ Outside Ephesos," in *Transmission and Reception: New Testament Text-Critical and Exegetical Studies*, Texts and Studies Third Series 4, ed. J. W. Childers and D. C. Parker (Piscataway, NJ: Gorgias Press, 2006). Richard Oster surveys the evidence of Ephesians and their religion abroad. For example, inscriptions honoring Ephesians who died abroad have been discovered in Attica, Rome, Chios, Laconia, Ostia, Puteoli, on Nisyros, and on Rhodes. (224) Additionally, he suggests that the competitive games hosted in Ephesus would have brought to the city numerous athletes, musicians, and gladiators, who could have adopted belief in Artemis and taken it with them as they left for another contest. (225) See also Robert Turcan, *The Cults of the Roman Empire*, trans. Antonia Nevill (Cambridge: Blackwell Pub., 1996), 255-6: "Replicas and variants, whole or fragmentary, of the many-breasted Artemis have been found at Salonae, Athens, Cos, Caesarea of Palestine, in Cyrenaica, Tripolitania, but above all in Italy: in the port of Aquileia,

where Greeks from Asia Minor worked, at Verona, Liternum, Ostia and Rome, which alone has yielded around fifteen examples."

19. Ephesus minted a coin during the period 198-202 A.D. which pictured two boys playing Knucklebones (Gk. *Astragali*) at the temple's foundation.

20. S. M. Baugh, "Cult Prostitution in New Testament Ephesus: A Reappraisal," *Journal of the Evangelical Theological Society* 42 (September 1999): 443-60. Ephesian inscriptions mention priestesses as daughters, not wives. (456) Four of the inscriptions mention the gift of 5,000 denarii as a donation to the Artemis cult by the priestess for the privilege of serving. Given the size of the gift, it is likely that only the aristocracy could have served in this role. (457) Finally, the idea of "pure" or "purity" is mentioned prominently in two Ephesian inscriptions. Based on theis evidence, Baugh believes it unlikely that the priestesses were prostitutes; instead, they were probably the virgin daughters of prominent Ephesians. (457) See also Oster, 28, who suggests that the priestesses of Artemis were sexually pure – not prostitutes.

21. See, for example, Maya Vassileva, "Further Considerations on the Cult of Kybele," *Anatolian Studies* 51 (2001): 56: "the rites of the Great Mother-Goddess were closely associated with those of Dionysos both in Thrace and in Phrygia." It is likely the association extended south of Thrace as well – to the worship of another "Kybele," Artemis Ephesia. The name given to the supposed god of wine, the Asian mountain god, is never found in Scripture. "Dionysus" represented the name given by the Greeks. "Bacchus" or "Liber" represented the names given by the Romans. This book will use the Greek (and Asian) name for the supposed god since that name represents the oldest tradition.

22. Ross S. Kraemer, "Ecstasy and Possession: The Attraction of Women to the Cult of Dionysus," *HTR* 72 (Jan., 1979): 72. See also Livy, *History of Rome*, 39.15.

23. Walter F. Otto, *Dionysus: Myth and Cult*, trans. Robert B. Palmer (Bloomington, IN: Indiana University Press, 1965), 141: "The fullness of life and the violence of death are both equally terrible in Dionysus." Additionally, he writes, "We should never forget that the Dionysiac world is, above all, a world of women.... The terrible trauma of childbirth, the wildness which belongs to motherliness in its primal form, a wildness which can break loose in an alarming way not only in animals – all these reveal the innermost nature of the Dionysiac madness: the churning up of the essence of life surrounded by the storm of death." (142)

24.   *Bacchae* 53-55, 302.

25.   Everett Ferguson, *Backgrounds of Early Christianity*, 3rd ed. (Grand Rapids: William B. Eerdmans Pub. Co., 2003), 83: "Mediterranean cities were built around a marketplace (Gk. *agora*, Lat. *forum*). In those cities influenced by Hellenistic town planning the marketplace was a large open area, rectangular in shape, given over to public monuments and statues. It was surrounded by a covered porch (*stoa*), which had shops and offices behind. Life then, as now, in Mediterranean countries was lived mostly outdoors, and the town marketplace was the center of life – a marketplace of conversation and ideas as well as of economic activities (cf. Acts 17:17)."

26.   While the historical connection between honey-wine prophecy and Artemis Ephesia is uncertain, evidence exists which points to a close association between mother-goddess religion and bees/honey. See, for example, Susan Scheinberg, "The Bee Maidens of the Homeric Hymn to Hermes," *Harvard Studies in Classical Philology* 83 (1979): 1-28. Scheinberg suggests a connection between belief that the bee maidens (Gk. *Melissa*) had the power of soothsaying and belief that an intoxicating liquid made from honey bestowed this power. (16-17) "Linguistic evidence, too, helps confirm the hypothesis that the earliest speakers of Greek knew or partook of an intoxicating honey drink." (19) Additionally, see G. W. Elderkin, "The Bee of Artemis," *The American Journal of Philology* 60 (1939): 203: "The early association of the bee with the cult of Artemis is attested by varied evidence. It appears not only upon the strange polymastoid statue of the Ephesian goddess but upon the earliest coins of her city." A connection between bees/honey and goddess religion surfaces even beyond Asia Minor. See Amihai Mazar and Nava Panitz-Cohen, "It is the Land of Honey: Beekeeping at Tel Rehov," *NEA* 70 (Dec., 2007): 202-19. One cult object found in the *circa* ninth century B.C. apiary was a clay altar with four horns and two goddess figures flanking a tree on its facade. (212)

27.   Homer, Iliad 21, 511. Homer uses the Greek word *keladeine* in reference to the goddess. LSJ, 936 suggests a translation of "noisy," but notes that Homer uses the word as an epithet for Artemis/Diana. See also Otto, *Dionysus: Myth and Cult*, 92. He proposes a translation of "Lady of Clamours." However, I will suggest that "Queen of Clamors" better captures Artemis' position in Asian thought and religion. At least one other word within the "kela-" group refers to Artemis/Diana: *keladodromos*. LSJ, 936: "rushing amid the noise of the chase."

28.   Otto, *Dionysus: Myth and Cult*, 93.

29.   Ferguson, *Backgrounds of Early Christianity*, 261: "A period of fasting preceded the winter festival. Weakened by the fasting, the devotees in wild ecstatic dance to the accompaniment of the *aulos* [flute] worked themselves into a delirium." Additionally, see *Exhortation*, 45 and *Bacchae* 58 and 155: "sing of Dionysus, beneath the heavy beat of drums." See also Ovid, *Metamorphoses* 4.1, Aristophanes, *Lysistrata* 1-3 and Livy, *History of Rome* 39.8, who mention the noise of flutes, tambourines, cymbals and drums as part of Bacchic/Dionysiac ritual. Further, see Veronica Doubleday, "The Frame Drum in the Middle East: Women, Musical Instruments and Power," *Ethnomusicology* 43 (Winter, 1999): 108: "Frame drums were also used in the cult of Cybele, the Phrygian mother-goddess." Given the known syncretism in the cult of Artemis of the Ephesians, it is possible that the frame drum was even heard at her temple in Ephesus.

30.   I appreciate the following Christian men and women thinking with me about the various occupations and domestic roles that likely were part of Roman Ephesus: Casi Kenyon, Erin Davenport, Julian Firman, Danielle Morton, Janelle Franklin, Luke Guthridge, Amy Manchester, Catherine McMenamy, Brandi Moody, Ryan Moody, Aaron Morton, Lauren Morton, Stephen Morton, Kelli Morton, Marcus Riley, Natalie Stephen, Jordan Tanner, Jeremy Townsend, and Sarita Williams.

31.   Paul's letter to the Ephesians may have been written to a broader audience as well: churches throughout the Roman province of Asia. Some New Testament manuscripts exclude the phrase "in Ephesus" in Ephesians 1:1. Additionally, the letter is unique in its absence of specific greetings to individuals.

32.   See, for example, *www.religion.ucsb.edu/faculty/thomas/ephesos/index.html* for an overview of the current Ephesus Harbor Project. In addition to excavations at Ephesus, work at Pergamon, Aphrodisias, and 200 miles east of Ephesus at Çatalhöyük has raised great interest as well. See the website *www.catalhoyuk.com* for information about the site.

33.   See, for example, the Internet website of the Austrian Archaeological Institute (*www.oeai.at*).

Chapter 1. Adopted by God and the Blessing of Hope, Wealth, and Power

1.   Kirbyjon Caldwell and Mark Seal, *The Gospel of Good Success: A Road Map to Spiritual, Emotional, and Financial Wholeness* (New York: Simon & Schuster, 1999).

2.   John Turtle Wood, *Discoveries at Ephesus; Including the Site and Remains of the Great Temple of Diana* (London: Longmans, Green, 1877; reprint ed. New York: Georg Olms Verlag, 1975), Appendix: An inscription from the site of the Temple of Artemis includes the words "the first and greatest metropolis of Asia...." See also *IAph2007* inscription no. 12.719, *Decree of honours for Kallikrates son of Diogenes, pancratiast* which includes a reference to "the metropolis of Asia, Ephesus." Inscription no. 5.214, *Honours for Aurelius Achilles*, includes a reference to "the most splendid city of the Ephesians...."

3.   Luke's use of (Gk.) *dialegomai* gives us a glimpse of Paul's work in spreading the Gospel in Ephesus. The word can indicate a lecture (e.g. Acts 20:7) or discussion, as it does in Mark 9:34 and Acts 24:12. BDAG suggests that in Acts 19.8, 9 *dialegomai* should be understood as an "instructional discourse that frequently includes exchange of opinions...." (232)

4.   See Clinton E. Arnold, *Powers of Darkness: Principalities & Powers in Paul's Letters* (Downers Grove, IL: InterVarsity Press, 1992), 186: "In the New Testament world it was common for people to believe the agency of an evil spirit causes sickness (a belief that is also characteristic of many contemporary non-Western cultures)." Magic was perceived as a means to address or prevent illness. The Gospels reveal some illness to be the result of Satan's activity. Paul may have been referencing a like situation in his life (2 Cor. 12:7-10).

5.   *Bacchae* 10.

6.   Ibid., 140: "The earth flows with milk, flows with wine, flows with the nectar of bees...."

7.   Dana F. Sutton, *Papyrological Studies in Dionysiac Literature* (Oak Park, IL: Bolchazy-Carducci Pub., 1987). Dana Sutton provides a translation and a review of a Greek hymn to Dionysus (*Papyri russischer und georgischer Sammlungen I.11*) that sings of a supposed miracle by the mountain god. To prove who he is to King Lycurgus, Dionysus reduces the earth around Lycurgus to barrenness: "[Neither by the elm] did the spring flow, nor were there watering-holes. [There were no paths, no] hedges, no trees – all had vanished." (105)

8.   *Bacchae* 155: "Sing to the rattle of thunderous drums." While the evidence is limited, the drums may have recalled images of his Bacchanals, his initiates, as his army. (see also *Bacchae* 50)

9.   "Adoption" (Gk. *hyiothesia*) is used five times in the New Testament (Ro. 8:15, 23; 9:4; Gal. 4:5; Eph. 1:5). The opposite situation was once

described by the Greek word *orphanos*, the root of our English word "orphan." Eduard Schweizer, "*hyiothesia*," *TDNT*, 8:398: Typically, adoption was linked closely with acquiring an heir to an estate; "the legal process of adoption was often combined with making a will."

10.   I appreciate John Cannon, minister to the East Fifth Street Church of Christ, Katy, Texas, highlighting this important contrast between ancient Ephesian thinking and the blessing from God.

11.   Otto Betz, "*stigma*," *TDNT*, 7:658-60: "In Ethiopia children were dedicated to Apollo by a mark on the knee-cap...." (660) "The Syrians consecrated themselves to the gods Hadad and Atargatis by signs branded on the wrist or neck...." (660) See also C. P. Jones, "Stigma: Tattooing and Branding in Graeco-Roman Antiquity," *JRS* 77 (1987). "Marks" (Gk. *stigma*; *sphragis*; *character*) took the form of "absorbed letters" (tattoos) or scars inflicted by cutting or burning the skin. The large majority of marks on people were tattoos or skin cuts, not brands. (140-2) The branding of people was a rare practice. (141) Most tattoos and skin cuts were applied to the forehead, ear, neck, arm, wrist, hand, or ankle. (142-52) See also Leviticus 19:28.

12.   Reinier Schippers, "Seal," in *The New International Dictionary of New Testament Theology*, 3:497, ed. Colin Brown (Grand Rapids: Zondervan, 1978).

13.   Plutarch, *De Adulatore et Amico*, 12. Gottfried Fitzer, "*sphragis, sphragizo, katasphragizo*," *TDNT*, 7:943: "In the mysteries, esp. the Dionysus cult, the seal has again a part to play. Worshipers of Dionysus had the sign of the god, the ivy leaf kissofullon [*kissophyllon*] burned on them...." See also LSJ, 954: "ivy-crowned [*kissostephanos*], of Dionysus." See also 3 Maccabees 2:29. Clement of Alexandria refers to the cult seal as he uses imagery from the Dionysus cult to describe the truth of Christian faith: "O truly sacred mysteries! O pure light! In the blaze of the torches I have a vision of heaven and of God. I become holy by initiation. The Lord reveals the mysteries; He marks the worshipper with His seal...." *Exhortation*, 257.

14.   G. R. Beasley-Murray, *Baptism in the New Testament* (Grand Rapids: William B. Eerdmans Pub. Co., 1973), 174.

15.   T. W. Brents, *The Gospel Plan of Salvation* (Nashville: McQuiddy Printing Co., 1874; reprint ed. Gospel Advocate Co., 1973), 642.

16.   Marcus Barth, *Ephesians 1-3*, The Anchor Bible (Garden City, NY: Doubleday & Co., 1974), 137-8.

17.   Edward C. Wharton, *The Church of Christ* (West Monroe, LA: Howard Book House, 1987). The phrase "into the name" often signified

possession in the ancient world. (45-6) See also Hans Bietenhard, *"onoma,"* *TDNT*, 5:245.

18.   Rudolf Bultmann, *"elpis, elpizo,"* *TDNT*, 2:531.(144)

19.   Ferguson, *Backgrounds of Early Christianity*, 131: "The collection of magical spells and charms represented in the magical papyri may be comparable to the books the practitioners of magical arts burned in Ephesus in Acts 19:19. Ephesus was in fact considered one of the centers for the practice of magic." See also H. J. Rose, *Religion in Greece and Rome* (New York: Harper & Row, 1959), 121: "when about some dangerous business [e.g. childbirth], many, especially many women, commonly wore amulets." The word "amulet" [Latin *amuletum* – charm] was used to describe a device/object used to protect a person from trouble or evil spirits. (see Isaiah 3:18-23) See also Ferguson, 176: "Although moderns distinguish magic from the spirit of religion, the ancients did not do so. Superstition, sorcery, use of amulets, the magical powers of statues, formulas for healing and cursing, and private divination were all on the increase in late antiquity." Many of the ancient Greek incantations had to do either with love or cursing. The phrase *Ephesia Grammata* ("Ephesian Writings") was commonly used in the ancient world for documents containing magic spells (Clement of Alexandria, *Stromateis* 242.45.2). I appreciate Edward Wharton alerting me to this aspect of Ephesian religious culture.

20.   *Elegy and Iambus With the Anacreontea*, Loeb Classical Library, 1:231, ed. and trans. J. M. Edmonds (Cambridge: Harvard University Press, 1961): One ancient prayer to Artemis announced, "give Thou ear unto my prayer, and ward off the Spirits of Ill, a thing small, O Goddess, for Thee, but great for me."

21.   Dignas, *Economy of the Sacred in Hellenistic and Roman Asia Minor*, 246: "many sacred laws were not composed for what we would call religious purposes but were simply measures that would guarantee sacred income and thereby the smooth running of cult activities."

22.   Paul uses three words in the letters to Ephesus to spell out the idea of supernatural power and activity. The volume of his use of the first two words is unique within the New Testament. (Gk. *energeia*) in Ephesians: 1:19, 3:7, 4:16. (Gk. *energein*) in Ephesians: 1:11, 20, 2:2, 3:20. Georg Bertram, *"energeo, energeia, energema, energes,"* *TDNT*, 2:652: "used almost exclusively for the work of divine or demonic powers." (Gk. *dynamis*) in Ephesians: 1:19, 21; 3:7, 16, 20; 1 Ti. 1:5; 2 Ti. 1:7, 11; 2:9.

23.   When Paul refers to "powers" in Ephesians 6:12, he uses a word (Gk. *kosmokrator*) that is found only once in the New Testament. It carries the sense of "lord of the world" (LSJ, 984) and parallels the phrase "the spiritual forces of evil in the heavenly realm." (Eph. 6:12)

24.   Werner Foerster, "*eusebes, eusebeia, eusebeo*," *TDNT*, 7:183-84.

25.   The word (Gk.) *ektrepomai* (turn to or from) occurs only in the letters to Timothy (1 Ti. 1:6, 5:15, 6:20; 2 Ti. 4:4) and in Hebrews 12:13. In the letters to Timothy the word is associated with (turning to or from) empty, godless speech, Satan, and myths/fables.

26.   L. Michael White, "Urban Development and Social Change in Imperial Ephesos," *Ephesos*, 42-3. "Recent archaeological work suggests a wider geographical distribution of the population at Ephesus including outlying village districts in the Kaystros Valley." White judges the population of Roman Ephesus to have been between 180,000 and 225,000.

27.   Rudolf Bultmann, *Jesus Christ and Mythology* (New York: Charles Scribner's Sons, 1958), 36. He believed that the cause-effect order of the universe precluded the possibility of supernatural activity. (61-62)

28.   Rudolf Bultmann, "New Testament and Mythology," in *Kerygma and Myth*, 1:38, 2nd ed., ed. Hans Werner Bartsch, trans. Reginald Fuller (London: SPCK, 1964). Bultmann suggests that the New Testament writers attempt to convey the cosmic significance of Jesus' death through the use of mythological imagery (the resurrection).

29.   Bultmann, *Jesus Christ and Mythology*, 71-72. Further, he suggested that faith in God could offer no perspective that corrected science. (65) See also Bultmann, "New Testament and Mythology," 41: He suggests that, "faith in the resurrection is really the same thing as faith in the saving efficacy of the cross, faith in the cross as the cross of Christ."

30.   Kenneth F. W. Prior, *The Gospel in a Pagan Society* (Downers Grove, IL: InterVarsity Press, 1975). Kenneth Prior makes an insightful – and crucial – observation from the New Testament. He notes that the early Christians did not attempt to establish the truth of Christian faith by appealing to what God had done in their lives. Paul certainly talks about Christ living in him, but never does he use his life as the foundation for urging belief. Instead, he points people to the resurrection of Jesus. (51)

Chapter 2. Our Glorious Father, the Eternal, Immortal, Invisible King

1.   The National Coalition For Child Support Options reveals how far non-custodial parents have morally fallen in making little or no effort to

help their children economically, not to mention spiritually and emotionally. The enacting of the Passport Denial Program and the development of services such as the National Child Support Enforcement Association (*www.ncsea.org*) indicate the progress and hope that many custodial parents and their children are now experiencing in an effort to collect part of the huge national debt owed to children (not to mention financial help to many custodial mothers and fathers).

2.   See *fathersandhusbands.org* for reviews of marketing that has used male bashing. The good news here is that the U.S. as a whole is becoming more savvy to and intolerant of the actions by large advertising firms in their use of unkindness (toward both females and males), sarcasm, and cynicism to sell products.

3.   Sue Monk Kidd, *The Dance of the Dissident Daughter: A Woman's Journey From Christian Tradition to the Sacred Feminine* (San Francisco, CA: HarperSanFrancisco, 1996), 7.

4.   See *www.genderneutralbibles.com* for an overview.

5.   Barth, *Ephesians 1-3*, 382-3. Barth provides a thorough discussion of the historical interpretations of Paul's teaching regarding every family in heaven and earth deriving its name from God the Father. Two of the interpretations are 1) "God is the archetype of a father, the creator of all fatherhood; and, he bears the name "Father" in an exemplary way...." and 2) The name "Father" in reference to God declares the adoption of even the Gentiles into God's house, and the submission of all principalities and powers to him (Eph. 1:19-23).

6.   See, for example, Aida Besançon Spencer, Donna F. G. Hailson, Catherine Clark Kroeger, and William David Spencer, *The Goddess Revival* (Grand Rapids: Baker Books, 1995), 113-29. The authors seek to focus on the God revealed in the Bible as they counsel religious feminism. However, they end up not describing clearly how we should address the Creator. Further, they never quote or focus attention on Jesus' words recorded in John 14:9 or see the import of God's revelation as Father in Paul's Ephesian letter.

7.   Gottlob Schrenk, "*patria*," *TDNT*, 5:1017: "But for the true Father who precedes all such naming, one could not speak of any πατριαι [*patriai*; families]. The reference is to the origin and orientation of every such patria, which by its very name is referred back to the Father and forward to the goal."

8.   See M. A. Murray, "Female Fertility Figures," *Journal of the Royal Anthropological Institute of Great Britain and Ireland* 64 (1934): 93-100.

Murray observes that goddess images fall into one of three groups: 1) the mother image (e.g. Egyptian Isis), 2) the divine woman (e.g. Ishtar), or 3) the birthing image (a woman seated in the birthing position).

9.   See, for example, Brian D. McLaren, *A Generous Orthodoxy* (Grand Rapids: Zondervan, 2004), 75: "The masculine biblical imagery of "Father" and "Son" also contributes to the patriarchalism or chauvinism that has too often characterized Christianity...." See also Elisabeth Schüssler Fiorenza, *Bread Not Stone* (Boston: Beacon Press, 1984), xi: "The Bible is not only written in the words of men but also serves to legitimate patriarchal power and oppression insofar as it "renders God" male and determines ultimate reality in male terms, which makes woman invisible or marginal."

10.   Charlene Spretnak, *The Resurgence of the Real: Body, Nature, and Place in a Hypermodern World* (New York: Addison-Wesley Pub. Co., 1997), 73. Charlene Spretnak suggests that for most people "God the Father" is a phrase that has been associated with a (rationalist) view of the universe as a machine and of related "fixed" spiritual truth. Throw out a mechanistic universe as has happened in our day and she argues that "fixed" truth and God's Fatherhood necessarily follow.

11.   See *www.herchurch.org* for one example of the suggestion.

12.   See, for example, *www.sociologyguide.com* for a summary view of Auguste Comte's thought and contributions to modern education and commerce.

13.   Mary Daly, *Beyond God the Father: Toward a Philosophy of Women's Liberation* (Boston: Beacon Press, 1973), 13. Additionally, see the chapter entitled "After the Death of God the Father" (13-43). See Appendix B for further discussion of Mary Daly's writing.

14.   Kidd, *The Dance of the Dissident Daughter*, 141.

15.   Ibid. For example, she describes how she accepted a speaking/teaching role at a Christian women's seminar only to use the seminar as a forum for attacking Christian teaching and promoting goddess religion. (126) Further, she seems oblivious to her actions as an illustration of feminist oppression of others!

16.   Ibid., 20.

17.   Julie Clawson, "Welcoming the Awakened Woman," *Next-Wave Ezine* (Oct., 2007). Available at *www.the-next-wave.org*.

18.   Sue Monk Kidd, *The Secret Life of Bees* (New York: Viking, 2002). In the novel the African-American sisters who take in the main character, Lily, center their worship on Mary by means of a "Black Madonna" statue. The three sisters call Mary "Our Lady of Chains." (90) In addition to

her proposal of goddess religion, Sue Monk Kidd also provides brief glimpses of her conclusions about the God revealed in the Bible. Worship of him by churches seems ineffective in people's lives. (3) His followers allow women little say in things. (58)

19.   Charlene Spretnak, *Missing Mary: The Queen of Heaven and Her Re-Emergence in the Modern Church* (New York: Palgrave Macmillan, 2004). "As the grand convergence of religions, cultures, and time, Mary is a "Co-Redeemer" in ways that extend beyond the Christian sense of sin and fallenness." (21-2) She suggests that Mary is part of a mystical, cosmic tradition that includes supernatural powers worshipped also as Quan Yin, Tara, Yemaya, Durga, and White Buffalo (Calf) Woman. (109) In summary she proposes that Christian faith must be revised to become a focus on Jesus plus the Goddess. As she writes, "She [Mary] is the mother of spiritual salvation in the West, not only bringing forth the Incarnation but also embodying the correction to so much that is otherwise unbalanced, incomplete, and ill conceived – not the least of which is all-male religion." (53)

20.   Mary Daly, *Amazon Grace: Re-calling the Courage to Sin Big* (New York: Palgrave Macmillan, 2006). Throughout the book Daly gives significant attention to the oppression of women and of Nature (that are indeed oppressed by evil). However, her only two comments regarding the oppression of children have to do with the deaths that have resulted from polluted water (59) and the suffering of Iraqi women and children during recent war (101). Nor does Mary Daly equate the killing (aborting) of unborn infants with the oppression of creation. Children get all but left out of her polemic.

21.   Spencer, Hailson, Kroeger, and Spencer, *The Goddess Revival*, 131. See also Judith Ochshorn, "Reclaiming Our Past," in *Women's Spirit Bonding*, ed. Janet Kalven and Mary I. Buckley (New York: Pilgrim Press, 1984), 290-91: "In this time of global ecological crisis, it is important that human beings abandon a paradigm of the divine as above nature, existing eternally whether the natural universe lives or dies; rather let us return to the earlier reverence for all nature as sacred."

22.   See Jack Cottrell, "The Gender of Jesus and the Incarnation: A Case Study in Feminist Hermeneutics," *Stone-Campbell Journal* 3 (Fall 2000): 171-94. Jack Cottrell provides a thorough look at the discussions by some feminists regarding Jesus' gender.

Chapter 3. Guarding the Deposit: Hearing and Teaching the Lord's Word

1.   The word commonly translated "deposit" (ESV, NIV, KJV; Gk. *paratheke*) is found three times in the New Testament, all in Paul's letters to Timothy (1 Ti. 6:20, 2 Ti. 1:12, 14). BDAG, 764: "property entrusted to another, deposit". Christian Maurer, "*paratithemi, paratheke*," *TDNT*, 8:162: Both the Attic and Hellenistic forms of the verb mean "deposit," i.e., "goods placed in trust" or "agreement in respect of entrusted goods," "a trust agreement"...." "In the ancient Gk. and Jewish sphere, as well as the ancient Roman, one finds the legal device whereby an object can be entrusted to another's keeping for a specific period." He notes that the verb form (Gk. *paratithemi*) is a "commercial term." (8:163) It is found in Luke 12:48, Acts 14:23, 20:32, and 1 Timothy 1:18 and 2:2.

2.   See Herodotus 9.45. The use of the word "pattern" (Gk. *hypotyposis*) appears to have been rare in the ancient world, and is also infrequent in the New Testament – occurring only twice in Paul's letters. It carries with it the idea of example, pattern, or soundness and health. While some have challenged the idea of "pattern theology" in the New Testament, ironically postmodernism and feminism also apply a "pattern" in their interpretation of the Scriptures.

3.   J. N. D. Kelly, *A Commentary on the Pastoral Epistles; I Timothy, II Timothy, Titus.* Harper's New Testament Commentaries (New York: Harper & Row, 1963), 150.

4.   Monster Cookie Recipe (as shared by Leona Bailey, Conway, Missouri – Christian, precious mother-in-law, and nice lady): 12 eggs; 2 lbs of brown sugar; 4 cups of sugar; 1 tablespoon of vanilla; 1 tablespoon of white corn syrup; 8 teaspoons of baking soda; 1 lb of margarine; 3 lbs of peanut butter; 14 cups of quick-cook oatmeal; 1/2 lb of chocolate chips; 1/2 lb of M&Ms ®. Drop by spoonfuls on a cookie sheet and bake 10-12 minutes at 350 degrees Fahrenheit. Note: I would appreciate folks not sharing (at least for awhile) the suggestion that the recipe is the best part of the book. Please feel free to tell my family, but leave me in the dark for now.

5.   See *www.sec.gov* for information about current backdating/et.al. reviews by the U. S. Securities and Exchange Commission. A good overview of the practice of both illegal and legal stock option backdating is available at *www.biz.uiowa.edu*.

6.   See, for example, "Undercover Marketing Uncovered," *60 Minutes*, 25 July 2004, for a brief review of the practice of undercover marketing (also called "stealth marketing").

7.   The Sarbanes-Oxley Act of 2002. See the *cpcaf.aicpa.org* (Center For Public Company Audit Firms) for information.

8.   L. Michael White, *From Jesus to Christianity: How Four Generations of Visionaries and Storytellers Created the New Testament and Christian Faith* (San Francisco: HarperSanFrancisco, 2004). Concerning Jesus' life and work, Whites suggests that, "There are no court records, official diaries, or newspaper accounts that might provide firsthand information. Nor are there any eyewitnesses whose reports were preserved unvarnished." (3-4) His book includes numerous other similar statements as well.

9.   Ibid., 266.

10.   White, *Ephesos*, 36: "Using Acts uncritically as evidence for the social and religious situation in Ephesos during the midfirst century will prove misleading at the very least."

11.   Arthur Darby Nock, *St. Paul* (New York: Harper and Row, 1963), 230-31.

12.   See Donald J. Guthrie, *New Testament Introduction* (Downers Grove, IL: InterVarsity Press, 1970) for information regarding arguments for and against authorship by Paul – and the conclusion that Paul indeed penned Ephesians and 1 and 2 Timothy.

13.   Ibid. Neil R. Lightfoot, *How We Got the Bible*, 3rd ed. (New York: Fine Communications, 2003). John A. T. Robinson, *Redating the New Testament* (Philadelphia: The Westminster Press, 1976), 63.

14.   Thorsten Moritz, *A Profound Mystery: The Use of the Old Testament in Ephesians*, Supplements to Novum Testamentum; 85 (New York: E. J. Brill, 1996), 1.

15.   *Exhortation*, 19. He also references Ephesians 2:12 as having been written by "the Apostle." (47)

16.   Polycarp, *Letter to the Philippians*, 3. See also Kenneth Berding, "Polycarp of Smyrna's View of the Authorship of 1 and 2 Timothy," *Vigiliae Christianae* 53 (Nov., 1999): 349-360. Berding provides a helpful summary of the quotations from 1 and 2 Timothy in Polycarp's letter and observes that Polycarp, writing in the early second century, indeed believes Paul to be the author of the letters. See *Exhortation*, 191 and 193 for further examples of quotes from 1 and 2 Timothy.

17.   White, *From Jesus to Christianity*, 6. In contrast with White's announcement, the Gospels announce that Jesus' earliest followers included others in addition to Jews (e.g. Jn. 4:39; Lk. 7:1-10).

18.   Ibid., 55. Nothing in the Gospels or in apostolic teaching suggests that Jesus used such formulas.

19.   In *From Jesus to Christianity*, Michael White talks little about Jesus, his death, and his resurrection in his chapter "The Historical Figure of Jesus." The large majority of attention is given to his proposal regarding how the Gospels were composed. White makes an important announcement in the chapter's conclusion: "Ultimately, the Gospels are stories about the growth of belief in Jesus." (116) However, later he does state that "Paul had some sort of visionary experience of the resurrected Jesus...." (155)

20.   Schüssler Fiorenza, *Bread Not Stone*, 140.

21.   See Paul Trebilco, *The Early Christians in Ephesus from Paul to Ignatius*, Wissenschaftliche Untersuchungen zum Neuen Testamentum; 166 (Tübingen: Mohr Siebeck, 2004) for a further suggestion of "diversity" in apostolic teaching. Paul Trebilco concludes that earliest Christianity in Ephesus saw different groups of Christians with somewhat different beliefs. He believes some lined up with the apostle Paul, others with the apostle John.

22.   Lucetta Mowry, "Feminism and the Bible," *Christian Science Monitor* (3 September 1982). Available at *www.csmonitor.com*.

23.   Ibid.

24.   Robertson McQuilkin and Bradford Mullen, "The Impact of Postmodern Thinking on Evangelical Hermeneutics," *Journal of the Evangelical Theological Society* 40 (March 1997): 75: "If we do not do interpretation on the premise that God has spoken and that he can be understood, that truth about him can be communicated accurately in words, we run the danger of ending up where postmodern thinking has taken some proponents: speaking nonsense. That is, they use words in an attempt to communicate their own thought about how impossible communication with words is." (75) Additionally, see Phil Sanders, "Postmodernism," *The Spiritual Sword* 33 (April 2002): 26: "Postmodernism as a world view seeks to destroy the foundational beliefs and moral values of the dominant structures in our society, especially Christianity. It denies absolute truth and absolute morals."

25.   See, for example, Ray S. Anderson, *An Emergent Theology For Emerging Churches* (Downers Grove, IL: InterVarsity Press, 2006). Anderson urges that "emerging churches" challenge postmodernist relative ethics and lean on Jesus' new command and all that flows from the command (144-55).

26. McLaren, *A Generous Orthodoxy*, 164.

27. Ibid., 165: "And we have languished and wandered when we have used the Bible as a weapon to threaten others, as a tool to intimidate others and prove them wrong, as a shortcut to being know-it-alls who believe the Bible gives us all the answers, as a defense of the status quo – none of these being the use Paul the apostle wanted Timothy, his protégé, to make of the Scriptures." See also Greg Taylor, "Changing Signs and Signs of Change in a Tulsa Congregation," *Christian Standard* (Nov. 16, 2008): "No, we don't express our faith in the same way as Pentecostals or Catholics, but we reject the notion that we ought to spend energies to "correct" them. We believe they are intelligent enough to read the Bible and come to faithful conclusions just as we believe we can." Available at *www.christianstandard.com*.

28. Mark Love, Douglas A. Foster, and Randall J. Harris. *Seeking a Lasting City: The Church's Journey in the Story of God* (Abilene, TX: ACU Press, 2005), 1-14, 188-9.

29. Ibid., 187. The authors write that, "the increasing biblical illiteracy in our churches stands out as a serious problem that needs to be addressed. In our desire to make the Christian story approachable, we've sometimes de-emphasized knowledge and placed a greater premium on engaging, up-lifting classes and services."

30. Ibid., 12: "Another problem with a static view of the church is that it leads Christians to misunderstand the gospel in a fundamental way – to see it as a set of propositions to be believed or a set of forms to be erected rather than a call to action in the world." Additionally, they look at Matthew 7:24-27 and conclude that, "The emphasis here is not on understanding, but doing. In the final analysis, the faithfulness of the church is determined not by what we claim to believe, but how we embody God's mission in the world." (12) However, in pages 75-77 the authors essentially overturn their earlier statement and describe how belief/doctrine lays for the foundation for mission. They draw the same conclusion as they review Gnosticism and other second century corruptions of Christianity. They highlight that "it was crucial for the church to eliminate these teachings not simply because they were factually wrong – intellectually off base – but because they distorted the church's understanding of Christ and therefore of itself and its mission, drawing it away from its journey toward the lasting city." (109) Interestingly, as the authors look at the second century, they recognize that beliefs/doctrine and mission are intertwined; false beliefs lead to failed mission. Both determine the church's faithfulness.

31.   I appreciate Cecil Hutson highlighting this challenge facing the church in a postmodern society. He has observed that some of the preaching in a previous generation was unkind and that we are probably seeing a reaction to such in the "emerging church" movement.

Chapter 4. Who Are We?

1.   Paul uses the phrase "heavenly realm" (NIV) "heavenly places" (KJV) "heavenly places" (ESV) (Gk. *epouranios*) more in the Ephesian letter than in any other letter (Eph. 1:3, 20; 2:6; 3:10; 6:12). BDAG, 388: "associated with a locale for transcendent things and beings," LSJ, 677: "heavenly." Paul's other use of the word in his letters to Ephesus occurs in his second letter to Timothy – where it is used as an adjective describing "kingdom" (2 Ti. 4:18). Helmut Traub, "*epouranios*," *TDNT*, 5:540, suggests the phrase "in the heavenlies" was part of the vocabulary of pagan cults.

2.   *The Documents of Vatican II*, ed. Walter M. Abbott, S.J. (Chicago: Association Press, 1966), 27: "Though they differ from one another in essence and not only in degree, the common priesthood of the faithful and the ministerial or hierarchical priesthood are nonetheless interrelated. Each of them in its own special way is a participation in the one priesthood of Christ. The ministerial priest, by the sacred power he enjoys, molds and rules the priestly people. Acting in the person of Christ, he brings about the Eucharistic Sacrifice, and offers it to God in the name of all the people."

3.   Hugh B. Brown, *Mormonism* (Salt Lake City, UT: Deseret Book Co., 1962), 13: "The presiding authority of the Church is the First Presidency, consisting of three high priests, a president and his two counselors." Contrast this with Hebrews 8:1-10:18 and Jesus' identity as our High Priest.

4.   Robert E. Webber, *Ancient-Future Faith, Rethinking Evangelicalism for a Postmodern World* (Grand Rapids: Baker Books, 1999). "Baptism was a physical sign and seal of conversion, of turning away from a wrong way of life, of trusting in Jesus. It was no empty symbol, but an act that was a *necessary* aspect of conversion." (147) "Baptism implies repentance and renunciation; its form symbolizes the main facts of the gospel; its content signifies an entrance into the new community and a mark of the reception of the Spirit." (147) "Postmodern people learn through images. Because baptism is the image of an identification with Christ (knowledge) and a pattern for living (spiritual wisdom), the classical approach to evangelism and education around the image of baptism will capture the imagination of the postmodern mind (see table L). " (162)

5.   LSJ, 1430. See also Heinrich Seesemann, *TDNT*, "*poikilos*," 6:484-5.

6.   J. Armitage Robinson, *St. Paul's Epistle to the Ephesians* (London: James Clarke & Co., 1904), 170. See also Ulrich Wilckens, *TDNT*, "*sophia, sophos, sophizo*," 7:524. The word *polupoikilos* is found in many Near Eastern and Hellenistic texts, particularly in designation of the supposed goddess Isis.

7.   Sherri Coale, *The Sooner Blog Spot*, 14 January 2007.

8.   Schüssler Fiorenza, *Bread Not Stone*, 82: "Jesus' call to service in the gospels is addressed to those in power, to those who are first in the community, not to those who are least."

9.   *SEG* 43, no. 1197: (sheep) knucklebones were used for "games; gambling; divination."

10.   Ernest E. Blanche, "Lotteries Yesterday, Today, and Tomorrow," *Annals of the American Academy of Political and Social Science* 269, Gambling (May, 1950): 71-6. Ernest Blanche's survey, which includes the ancient world, provides a rare portrait of the social and spiritual roots of gambling. He concludes that, "lotteries change the very pattern of living, distort the sense of values, and incubate the eggs of crime. Examine the sociological and economic implications of the lottery, and you will behold a Frankenstein monster capable of consuming both those who run the lotteries and those who play them. The financial returns, insignificant in proportion to the national income or the Federal expenditures, are like the thirty pieces of silver paid for the betrayal." (76)

11.   See, for example, Charlene Spretnak, *States of Grace: The Recovery of Meaning in the Postmodern Age* (San Francisco: HarperSanFrancisco, 1991), 33-155.

12.   LSJ, 305-6: "dip, plunge... dipping in water, immersion." Albrecht Oepke, *TDNT*, "*bapto, baptizo*," 1:540: "To baptism as a mere rite or realistically developed symbol no such comparable efficacy could be ascribed in the NT world of thought." Baptize (Gk. *baptizein*) has "the sense of "to immerse" (trans.) from the time of Hippocrates, in Plato and esp. in later writers." (1:530) "Sacral baths are found in the Eleusinian and similar cults, in Bacchic [Dionysiac] consecrations, in Egyptian religion and the worship of Isis outside of Egypt...." (1:530) The word is used of Jewish ritual washings (in an immersion pool) in Mark 7:4. Regarding immersion pools, see Herbert Danby, *The Mishnah* (Oxford: Oxford University Press, 1933;

reprint ed., 1983), 732: "pools in which men and vessels suffering certain kinds of uncleanness must be totally immersed."

13.   Oepke, *TDNT*, "*bapto, baptizo*," 1:540: "Though mediated by men, baptism is the action of God or Christ (Eph. 5:26)." See also Ro. 6:3-4; Col. 2:11-12; Gal. 3:26-27. See also S. R. Llewelyn, "Baptism and Salvation," *New Documents Illustrating Early Christianity: A Review of the Greek Inscriptions and Papyri Published 1984-85*, 8:176-79. ed. S. R. Llewelyn (Grand Rapids: William B. Eerdmans Pub. Co., 1998). S. R. Llewelyn documents the following inscription from the third century A.D., written at the death of Nikandros: "until the glad day of resurrection comes, pure since desirously he has attained divine washing." Concerning divine washing (cf. Titus 3:5), Llewelyn notes that "Baptism was preeminently the rite which absolved the individual from his sins." (177) Additionally, Jack P. Lewis, "Baptismal Practices of the Second and Third Century Church," *Restoration Quarterly* 26 (First Quarter 1983): 1-2: "That baptism conveys the remission of sins can be traced through a series of writers beginning with Barnabas, who, in a passage in which typology is abundant, complains that Israel will not receive "baptism that brings remission of sins."

14.   Nils Alstrup Dahl, David Hellholm, Vemund Blomkvist, and Tord Fornberg, *Studies in Ephesians: Introductory Questions, Text- & Edition-Critical Issues, Interpretation of Texts and Themes*, Wissenschaftliche Untersuchungen zum Neuen Testamentum; 131 (Tübingen: Mohr Siebeck, 2000), 421: "The view of baptism as a making holy and as a purification was common in early Christianity. What is unique with Ephesians' presentation is basically to be seen in the idea that Christ wants to make the church holy through baptism's purification by washing. The personification of the church is connected with the depiction of Christ's love taken as an example of a husband's love for his wife. The words about baptism are formed so as to apply to Christ and his bride. The washing with water is the bridal bath." See also G. R. Beasley-Murray, "Baptism," in *The New International Dictionary of New Testament Theology*, 1:153: "Eph. 5:26 may allude to the ceremonial bath taken by a bride in preparation for marriage. For the bride of Christ, the counterpart to this bath is baptism, in which the members of the body are cleansed "by the washing of water by the Word."

15.   Paul uses the Greek word *syndesmos* in describing the character of peace in bringing about the unity of the Spirit. Gottfried Fitzer, *TDNT*, "*syndesmos*," 7:856: "link, joint, means of binding;" the word was also used to describe the unifying force of a state or society (857).

16.   Donald Kagan, "The Dates of the Earliest Coins," *AJA* 86 (Jul., 1982): 343-360. D. Kagan surveys the evidence from excavations of the Temple of Artemis at Ephesus in order to date Ephesian coinage as early as the Seventh century B.C. – making them among the earliest coins (or the earliest coins). "Hogarth reported that the earliest level of the temple included a foundation deposit made up of about one thousand small precious objects of gold, silver, ivory, amber, etc., among them twenty-four electrum coins." (343). See *http://online.mq.edu.au/pub/ACANSCAE/index.htm* for an overview of the coinage of Ephesus.

17.   Arnold, *Powers of Darkness*, 154.

18.   Stephen Brunet, "Olympic Hopefuls from Ephesos," *Journal of Sport History* 30 (Summer, 2003): 220: Inscriptions unearthed at Ephesus "provide a unique insight into the issues athletes faced in terms of training and the decisions they needed to make in order to promote their careers. More than anything else these case studies show that the road to Olympia was not an easy one and that good planning may have been nearly as important as sheer talent in becoming an Olympic victor."

19.   See, for example, *www.angelfire.com/ar/armorofgod* and *www.thearmorofgod.com.*

20.   Herodotus, *Histories*, 7.226.

21.   Portefaix, "The Image of Artemis Ephesia – A Symbolic Configuration Related to Her Mysteries?" 614-6.

22.   James S. Ruebel, "Politics and Folktale in the Classical World," *Asian Folklore Studies* 50 (1991). Myths incorporated elements that were intended to assimilate a new deity into society. (7) For example, the cult of Dionysus became urbanized in Athens by the creation of a festival and the inclusion of a new type of theatrical performance – tragedy. In this way the god became identified with an important part of social activity. The two became entwined as people acted out their emotions. (10)

Chapter 5. Living as Children of Light

1.   Carroll D. Osburn, *Women in the Church: Reclaiming the Ideal* (Abilene, TX: ACU Press, 2001), 155-6. See also Neil R. Lightfoot, "Exegesis of Ephesians 5:19 and Colossians 3:16," *Abilene Christian University Lectures, 1988*: "Be filled with the Spirit" is the leading thought of verses 19-21. The main ideas of these verses may be represented as follows:
Be filled with the Spirit
Speaking to one another in psalms, hymns, and spiritual songs

Singing and
Making melody to the Lord with all your heart
Giving thanks to God in the name of Christ
Submitting to one another in reverence to Christ.

The structure shows that five present participles amplify the imperative, "be filled with the Spirit."

2.   James MacKnight, *MacKnight on the Epistles* (London, 1821; reprint ed., Grand Rapids: Baker Book House, 1969), 339-40: "Here the apostle condemns the Bacchanalian rites of which the heathens were immoderately fond."

3.   Michael Weed, *The Letters of Paul to the Ephesians, the Colossians, and Philemon,* The Living Word Commentary, ed. Everett Ferguson (Austin, TX: R. B. Sweet Co., 1971), 177: Ephesians 5:18 "is not the abrupt change of subject that it might at first appear to be. Many ancient religions (e.g. the cult of Dionysus) used wine, dancing, and music in wild rites designed to produce a frenzied intoxication which was believed to facilitate escape from the limitations of mortality, enabling communication with deity." See also Jimmy Jividen, *Worship in Song* (Fort Worth, TX: Star Bible Pub., 1987), 17: "The Dionysus mystery cult was perhaps in the background of this exhortation." Additionally, see Marcus Barth, *Ephesians 4-6,* The Anchor Bible (Garden City, NY: Doubleday & Co., 1974), 580: "The text of Ephesians contains nothing that would permit a choice between secular and religious alcoholism. Perhaps misuse of alcohol is in itself an attempt to bridge the gap between the secular and the religious. Bacchus festivals have both dimensions." Further, see Cleon L. Rogers, "The Dionysian Background of Ephesians 5:18," *Bibliotheca Sacra* 136 (1979): 249-57. Finally, see Moritz, *A Profound Mystery: The Use of the Old Testament in Ephesians,* 94-5.

4.   Harold W. Hoehner, *Ephesians, An Exegetical Commentary* (Grand Rapids: Baker Academic, 2002). Harold Hoehner sees the possibility of Dionysus-like conduct referenced in Ephesians 5:12 and 18-20, but argues that Paul does not specify such in 5:12 (681) or specifically mention it as the Ephesian religious practice in 5:18-20 (701). Interestingly, he gives important attention to 5:19-20 as related to worship assemblies and suggests that the "main point is the verbalizing of praise through singing." (712) However, he does not apply this setting backwards to 5:18. See also Robinson, *St. Paul's Epistle to the Ephesians,* who suggests that public worship is not in view, but instead that the setting is a common meal accompanied by a sacred song. He also suggests the setting represented a Christian alternative to

"idolatrous rites with which such banquets were associated." (122) So, while he attempts to distance Paul's teaching from Christian assemblies, he concludes that cult pressure was in view and was shaping Christian activity – whether called a worship assembly or a "charity supper." (122)

5.   Rogers, "The Dionysian Background of Ephesians 5:18," 257.

6.   Barbara Goff, *Citizen Bacchae: Women's Ritual Practice in Ancient Greece* (Berkeley, CA: University of California Press, 2004). Barbara Goff has carefully described the power of the Dionysus cult in crafting women's freedom – especially in religious matters. She has noted that the Dionysus cult essentially carved out a women's city-within-a-city. (6) "The various festivals for adult women can be seen to equip them to perform their roles and duties in a variety of ways. At an elementary level, such festivals allow them a respite from domestic life in which to recreate, and so return refreshed." (144) See also Livy, *History of Rome*, 39.15 and *IEph* 275.

7.   Larry J. Kreitzer, "'Crude Language' and 'Shameful Things Done in Secret' (Ephesians 5.4, 12): Allusions to the Cult of Demeter/Cybele in Hierapolis?" *Journal for the Study of the New Testament* 71 (September 1998): 51-77. While Kreitzer's suggestion of an author other than Paul misguides, his look at the language used to describe the ancient cults bears fruit. He cites the comment in the margin of the ancient writer Lucian's *Dialogues of the Courtesans* 7.4. The margin note describes one aspect of a women-only festival to Dionysus (and Cybele): "it not only mentions women saying shameful things to one another, but also tells of priestesses secretly whispering suggestions for marital indiscretion into the ears of women...." (63)

8.   Ibid, 73: Kreitzer observes that excesses of wine associated with Dionysiac rites "were legendary in the ancient world and may explain the exhortation against drunkenness contained in Eph. 5:18."

9.   Turcan, *The Cults of the Roman Empire*, 294.

10.   Weed, 128.

11.   Gottfried Fitzer, *TDNT*, "*sphragis, sphragizo, katasphragizo*," 7:943: The cult signing was called (Gk.) *sphragizein*, the same word Paul uses in Ephesians 1:13 and 4:30. *Sphragizein* could also carry the meaning of "bearing the impression of the seal of the Lemnian priestess of Artemis...." (LSJ, 1742) See also, Chapter 1, notes 11-13.

12.   *Exhortation*, 73: "For if it were not to Dionysus that they held solemn procession and sang the phallic hymn, they would be acting most shamefully," says Heracleitus; "and Hades is the same as Dionysus, in whose honor they go mad and keep the Lenaean feast," not so much, I think, for the sake of bod-

ily intoxication as for the shameful display of licentiousness." In the text the word translated by "licentiousness" is the Greek word *aselgeia*. LSJ, 255: "licentiousness, wanton violence, outrageous acts" as in excessive sexual desires. The NIV translates Paul's use of *aselgeia* in Ephesians 4:19 as "sensuality." This is the only use of the word by Paul in his letters to Ephesus. He also uses the word in one other letter to Asia Minor – in Galatians 5:19.

13.   Kraemer, "Ecstasy and Possession: The Attraction of Women to the Cult of Dionysus," *HTR*, 60-61. See also *Exhortation*, 45: "Formerly night, which drew a veil over the pleasures of temperate men, was a time for silence. But now, when night is for those who are being initiated a temptation to licentiousness, talk abounds, and the torch-fires convict unbridled passions."

14.   Richard Oster, "Ephesus as a Religious Center under the Principate, I. Paganism before Constantine," *Aufstieg und Niedergang der römischen Welt*, 2.18.3: 1661-1728 (Berlin: de Gruyter, 1990). Inscriptions indicate that the cult of Dionysus revealed its energy and prominence in Ephesus even late into the period of Roman rule. The *Katagogia* festival to Dionysus is mentioned in inscriptions from the city (1674), as is the *Thesmophoria* festival. (1671) Finally, the Ephesian calendar included a month that designated and honored Dionysus. (1673) See also Ferguson, *Backgrounds of Early Christianity*, 259: the popular cult of Dionysus possessed broad influence throughout Asia Minor. "Despite opposition in some circles, Bacchus was very popular and held a strong place in the imagination of the people. Thousands of images in all sizes and every artistic medium have been found from all over the Roman influenced world." (262)

15.   Paul's "keep your head" in 2 Timothy 4:5 (NIV) includes a Greek word (Gk. *nephein*) that typically carries either of two senses: 1) literally "be sober," or 2) figuratively "be self-controlled." See Otto Bauernfeind, *TDNT*, "*nepho*," 4:938: "It had often happened that states of Dionysiac inspiration, whether cultic or non-cultic, had been affirmed, that they had been described in terms of intoxication, and yet an attempt had been made to express their soberness...." Certainly, the apostle was using the word in the sense of "keep your head," but may also have been making a subtle reference to a specific myth (Dionysus), given his warning regarding "myths" in 2 Timothy 4:4.

16.   Aristophanes' *The Clouds* 654 references a cursing gesture that in our day is known by multiple names ("the finger" or "the bird"). Similar to the ancient use, the gesture continues to express a sexual curse. The fact that Aristophanes refers to the gesture in passing illustrates its common use in fifth century B.C. Greece and likely its far deeper historical roots (as "black

magic"). In addition to the general reference, Aristophanes also mentions similar sexual (phallus) symbolism in his play *The Acharnians* as being closely associated with Dionysus (260-73). The playwright observes that the phallus is a comrade of Dionysus. Additionally, see *Greek Lyric V: The New School of Poetry and Anonymous Songs and Hymns*, Loeb Classical Library, ed. and trans. David A. Campbell (Cambridge: Harvard University Press, 1993). Athenaeus' *Scholars at Dinner* contains the record of an announcement made by a procession of phallus-bearers honoring Dionysus: "Stand back, make plenty of room for the god! For the god, erect and at bursting-point, wishes to pass through your midst." (239) See also Otto, *Dionysus: Myth and Cult*, 164-5: "We see that the phallus enjoyed a high position as the attendant and announcer of the god." Additionally, see Chapter 7, note 11 and Appendix C, note 57.

17.   See, for example, *www.popstarsplus.com* for a report of phallus symbolism used by the Rolling Stones.

18.   See *www.deitch.com* for an article about Mariko Mori's November 8-December 22, 2007 New York City art exhibit, "Tom Na H-iu." "Tom Na H-iu is an ancient Celtic site of spiritual transmigration." The exhibit features a large light-up standing stone/phallus.

19.   See *www.irishmegaliths.org.uk* for a survey of the many phallic standing stones in Ireland.

20.   I appreciate Edward Wharton highlighting this parallel.

21.   See *www.rosslyntemplars.org.uk* for one overview of the historic connection between the Green Man of Celtic myth and Dionysus. Images of the Green Man (likely the supposed god of wine) saturate the British Isles.

22.   Robert Jordan, *The Eye of the World* (New York: Tom Doherty Associates, L.L.C., 1990), 739ff.

23.   Mikey Goralnik, "Seemingly Stupid 'ATL' Successfully Surprises," *The Tufts Daily* (Sept. 6, 2006). Available at *www.tuftsdaily.com*.

24.   *www.dionysusrecords.com*.

25.   Aristophanes *The Acharnians* 729ff. provides an example of just how much dishonor of human sexuality permeated worship to the god of wine. In the Dionysiac chorus/play, the playwright uses a Greek word that has the double meaning of "young pig" and "female external sexual organs" (Gk. *choiros*). He uses the double meaning to produce a word play intended as coarse, dishonoring humor (773). See also LSJ, 1996.

26.   See, for example, *www.collegehumor.com* and *www.thetoque.com*. The *Urban Dictionary* includes the meanings behind the various coded

words used by many people. "Sausage" refers to one of the sex organs of a man and "sausage party" indicates an all-men (or mostly-men) gathering. Similarly, the phrase "bearded clams" is used as a coded term for women, referring to a woman's external sex organs (vulva). Some (or many) campus bachelorette and bachelor parties have featured like sexual innuendos and symbolism. See, for example, Jeanie Lerche Davis, "Bachelorette Party: Sexual Expression?" *WebMD Health News* (Aug. 29, 2003). Available at *women.webmd.com*.

27.   Osburn, *Women in the Church*, 171: "It is vital to understand that neither Paul nor Jesus before him called for the radical overthrow of hierarchalism. Both had ideals along egalitarian lines, yet both worked within the cultural systems of the day – whether regarding slavery or gender roles – and taught Christians to "walk wisely" given certain cultural constraints. Paul's admonition for mutual submission [Eph. 5:21] is still valid for twenty-first century Christians." See also I. Howard Marshall, "Mutual Love and Submission in Marriage, Colossians 3:18-19 and Ephesians 5:21-33," *DBE*, 199: "Submission would be naturally expected in this relationship in the ancient world, especially as the wife could have been as much as twelve to fifteen years younger than her husband and the marriage would have been arranged. Consequently, in the first century context submission can be seen as appropriate, but the element of authority is not inherent for all time."

28.   See, for example, David L. Balch, "Household Codes," in *Greco-Roman Literature and the New Testament: Selected Forms and Genres*," ed. David E. Aune (Atlanta: Scholars Press, 1988): 25-50.

29.   Marshall, "Mutual Love and Submission in Marriage, Colossians 3:18-19 and Ephesians 5:21-33," *DBE*, 204: "Paul wrote as he did about marriage because in his world he did not know any other form than the patriarchal. As he did with other relationships, he worked within the structures of his time and gave directions for Christian behavior within them." See also Gordon D. Fee, "Hermeneutics and the Gender Debate," *DBE*, 374: "Paul thus assumes a Greco-Roman patriarchal culture when he instructs Christians on how to live within it in Ephesians 5:21-6:9, but he does not thereby bless the culture itself nor explicitly instruct men to exercise authority over their wives."

30.   See, for example, Christine M. Thomas, "Greek Heritage in Roman Corinth and Ephesos: Hybrid Identities and Strategies of Display in the Archaeology of Traditional Mediterranean Religion," UCSB Interdisciplinary Humanities Center, *The Ancient Borderlands Research Focus*

Group, Core Graduate Seminar (Jan. 11, 2008), 15: "The display of names from prominent [Ephesian] families could have performed a number of different functions: it indicated their survival and flourishing as a class, their continued ability to act as sponsors, and their financial support for traditional Ephesian identity."

31.   David Kinnaman and Gabe Lyons, *UnChristian: What a New Generation Really Thinks About Christianity... and Why it Matters* (Grand Rapids: Baker Books, 2007). Kinnaman and Lyons performed an extensive survey to determine how a new generation perceives Christians. The view of a large portion of the nation is not comforting or encouraging to Christians. Many in the age group 16-29 are especially averse to Christians and Christian teaching. However, the research is important for understanding the struggle between light and darkness in early twenty-first century America. It will take a careful, prayerful mingling of truth and love to reach many who are hurt or afraid.

Chapter 6. Speaking in Song to One Another and to the Lord – Part 1

1.   Werner Foerster, *TDNT*, "*asotos, asotia*," 1:507. Concerning the New Testament use of (Gk.) *asotia*, Foerster writes that, "In all these passages the word signifies wild and disorderly rather than extravagant or voluptuous living." The classical use of the word carried the meaning of "one who by his manner of life, esp. by dissipation, destroys himself...." (506) *SEG* 36, no. 132: *asotia* is used to describe the conduct of a husband whose actions are considered "wastefulness."

2.   Aristophanes, *The Clouds* 333. Specifically, Aristophanes uses the Greek word *asmatokamptes* to convey his stinging critique of Dionysiac cult music (specifically the Dithyramb). LSJ, 258: "twisters of song."

3.   Aristophanes, *The Frogs* 1304ff. represents one example of the close association of debauchery with the Dithyramb.

4.   Scholion, Aristophanes, *The Clouds* 333d: *oi palaioi diaphthoran mousikes egounto einai tous dithyrambous.* Author's translation: "The ancients believed that the Dithyramb caused the corruption of music." Concerning (Gk.) *diaphthora* see LSJ, 418: "in moral sense, *corruption, seduction.*" See also J. C. Franklin, "Dithyramb and the 'Demise of Music,'" in *Song Culture and Social Change: The Contexts of Dithyramb*, ed. B. Kowalzig and P. Wilson, International Colloquium, Oxford, 11-13 July 2004. Franklin suggests that *diaphthoran mousikes* ought to be understood as the "ruin of music." (1)

5.　　Franklin, "Dithyramb and the 'Demise of Music,'" 12. Additionally, the demise of music (among composers of the New Music) represented "melodic/musical movement in which there is not even an identifiable *harmonia* from which one is departing, and all point of 'harmonic' reference is lost." (9)

6.　　*Greek Lyric V: The New School of Poetry and Anonymous Songs and Hymns*, 3-5.

7.　　Henry van Dyke, *Joyful, Joyful, We Adore Thee* (1907).

8.　　Stephen R. Guthrie, "Singing, in the Body and in the Spirit," *Journal of the Evangelical Theological Society* 46 (December 2003): 639.

9.　　Ibid.

10.　　Ibid., 641.

11.　　Ibid., 641-2.

12.　　Everett Ferguson, "The Art of Praise, Philo and Philodemus on Music," in *Early Christianity and Classical Culture, Comparative Studies in Honor of Abraham J. Malherbe*, Supplements to Novum Testamentum; 110, ed. John T. Fitzgerald, Thomas H. Olbricht, and L. Michael White (New York: E. J. Brill, 2003), 426.

13.　　Ibid.

14.　　Joan Russell is the Director of Music Education, McGill University. See Chapter seven for more information.

15.　　Wendy Moore, "Good Vibrations," *The Observer* (February 11, 2001). Available at *www.guardian.co.uk*. I appreciate Kevin Cain making me aware of the article.

16.　　"Folkestone Seminar Explains How Choral Singing Boosts Health And Well Being, Folkestone, UK," *Medical News Today* (April 7, 2008). Available at *www.medicalnewstoday.com*.

17.　　*Exhortation*, 9.

18.　　David Lipscomb, Elisha Granville Sewell, and M. C. Kurfees, *Questions Answered, Being a Compilation of Queries with Answers by D. Lipscomb and E. G. Sewell, Covering a Period of Forty Years of Their Joint Editorial Labors on the Gospel Advocate* (Nashville: Gospel Advocate Co., 1921; reprint ed., Gospel Advocate Co., 1974). D. Lipscomb and E. G. Sewell provide a succinct observation from a previous century's experience: "Christians are to teach and admonish one another in song, and sometimes the singing of a good song may cause even lifeless members to repent and turn to the Lord and do their first works." (608)

Chapter 7. Speaking in Song to One Another and to the Lord – Part 2

1. Barth, *Ephesians 4-6*, 583-84. He suggests that "sing" and "make music" may represent a hendiadys (figure of speech that substitutes conjunction for subordination). In this case "make music" refers to vocal music. However, he thinks this is outweighed by the practice in Jewish temple worship.

2. Everett Ferguson, "Lifting Our Voices," *Gospel Advocate* (Feb., 2000): 13: "Worship is grounded in our relation to God, as creature to the Creator. That means we must come before God on His terms. The gifts we offer are those he appoints. Instrumental music was an act of worship and not an aid in the Old Testament. It was a separate act. Playing an instrument is doing something different from singing. To offer mechanical music would require explicit authorization from God."

3. Jack P. Lewis, "New Testament Authority for Music in Worship," in *The Instrumental Music Issue*, ed. Bill Flatt (Nashville: Gospel Advocate Co., 1987), 37-38: "one may argue that here in Ephesians the dative phrase *te kardia humon* (in your heart) is also instrumental. The singing and making melody is to be done with the heart."

4. William Woodson, "Music in the Early Church," *The Spiritual Sword* 21 (July 1990): 10: "It is obvious from the New Testament that no authority was given for the introduction or use of such instrumentation in the worship of the church. It is also evident that instrumental music was not introduced into church worship until hundreds of years after the close of the New Testament."

5. A pattern perspective is common to any approach to Scripture, but is often critiqued when it characterizes a directness at getting to apostolic teaching and the question that has always faced Christian faith: Is there a collection of Christian truth (orthodoxy) whereby to judge other teaching? The answer Paul gives throughout his letters is "yes" (e.g. 1 Cor. 11:2; 14:36-38; 2 Thes. 3:4; 2 Ti. 1:13-14).

6. LSJ, 2018: "pluck, pull, twitch... mostly of the strings of musical instruments."

7. Paul's *ado-psallo* construct follows the pattern that is found in three Septuagint texts: Psalm 26:6b (Gk. *asomai kai psallo to kurio* = "I will sing and make music to the Lord." Psalm 27:6b, NIV); Psalm 56:8b-9a (Gk. *asomai kai psallo*, which clearly parallels and refers to "awake, harp and lyre" in the text = "I will sing and make music. Awake my soul! Awake, harp and lyre!" Psalm 57:7b-8a); Psalm 107:2b-3a (Gk. *asomai kai psallo en te doxe mou* which parallels "Awake, harp and lyre!" in the text = "I will sing and

make music with all my soul. Awake, harp and lyre!" Psalm 108:1b-2a, NIV). All Greek texts are from the *Septuaginta*, ed. Alfred Rahlfs (Stuttgart: Deutsche Bibelgesellschaft Stuttgart, 1935).

8.	F. LaGard Smith, *The Cultural Church* (Nashville: 20th Century Christian, 1992), 202.

9.	Herbert Preisker, *TDNT*, "*methe, methuo, methusos, methusko-mai,*" 4:548.

10.	William A. Johnson, "Musical Evenings in the Early Empire: New Evidence from a Greek Papyrus with Musical Notation," *The Journal of Hellenic Studies* 120 (2000): 59: Johnson notes that the ancient Greeks equated a plunge into low tones with the event of possession by supernatural forces.

11.	Historically, the Greek "*phall-*" word group announced the sexual symbolism and decadence of the Dionysus cult. For example: *phallephoria,* "festival of Bacchus where a phallus was carried in procession" (LSJ, 1914); *phallobates,* "one who mounts on a phallus-shaped pillar, phallic priest" (LSJ, 1914); *phallikos,* "the phallic song" (LSJ, 1914). See also *Aristophanes,* 3 vols., Loeb Classical Library, trans. Benjamin Bickley Rogers (Cambridge: Harvard University Press, 1924; reprint ed., 1950), regarding his use of *phallikos* in *The Acharnians* 259-61: "O Xanthias, walk behind the basket-bearer, Holding, you two, the phallus-pole erect. And I'll bring up the rear, and sing the hymn [*phallikos*]...." Martin P. Nilsson, "The Bacchic Mysteries of the Roman Age," *HTR* 46 (Oct., 1953): 191: Sexual symbolism was "the peculiar characteristic of the cult of Dionysos." See also *Exhortation,* 73: "In fulfilment of the vow to his lover Dionysus hastens to the tomb and indulges his unnatural lust. Cutting off a branch from a fig-tree which was at hand, he shaped it into the likeness of a phallos, and then made a show of fulfilling his promise to the dead man. As a mystic memorial of this passion phalloi are set up to Dionysus in cities." See also Chapter 5, note 16 and Appendix C, note 57.

12.	Friedrich Hauck, *TDNT*, "*akathartos, akatharsia,*" 3:429: "Young Christianity regards the sexual immorality of the Hellenistic world as ungodly akaqarsia [*akatharsia*; impurity]...."

13.	*Exhortation,* 255. Clement specifies "Bacchic revelry" later in Chapter Twelve (257) but sees no need initially. He may even be using generality as one way to catch peoples' attention.

14.	Ibid.

15.	"American Unity Through Music," *Music Educators Journal* 27 (March-April, 1941): 10.

16.   Joan Russell, "A "Place" for Every Voice: The Role of Culture in the Development of Singing Expertise," *Journal of Aesthetic Education* 31 (Winter, 1997): 106.

17.   Ibid., 100. Additionally, she writes about her experience, "All around me the congregation is singing in harmony. The unanimity of the phrasing, the balance between the voices, the seemingly perfect intonation, and the resonance of the sound as the chords unfold raise goose bumps on my skin. For a brief moment I think I am hearing an organ. Then I think that the sound is surely amplified by speakers, and I am disappointed. But there is no organ, no electrical power here. Just the sounds of men, women, and children singing as they do every Sunday morning." (95)

18.   *Elegy and Iambus With the Anacreontea*, 2:153.

19.   Guthrie, 642. He also suggests that "There is an analogy of form between the sound of people singing together and the unity to which the church aspires, and for this reason music is a particularly apt vehicle for worship." (644) See also Daryl L. Tippens, *That's Why We Sing: Reclaiming the Wonder of Congregational Singing* (Abilene, TX: Leafwood Pub., 2007). Singing "is one of the church's primary means to inspire and build community." (13)

20.   *Goshen College Bulletin* (March 2000).

21.   Dan Kimball, *The Emerging Church* (Grand Rapids: Zondervan, 2003), 138.

22.   Love, Foster, and Harris, *Seeking a Lasting City*, 199.

23.   Joan Borysenko, *A Woman's Journey to God, Finding the Feminine Path* (New York: Riverhead Books, 1999), 48.

24.   *Millard's & Badger's Hymns* (1849).

Chapter 8. Marriages and the Clash of Faiths and Rights

1.   Robinson, *St. Paul's Epistle to the Ephesians*, 123: "Having struck the key-note of subordination – the recognition of the sacred principles of authority and obedience – the Apostle proceeds to give a series of positive precepts for the regulation of social life, which is divinely founded on the unchanging institution of the family."

2.   Brooks & Dunn, *My Maria* (Arista Records, 1996).

3.   See, for example, Berkeley and Alvera Mickelsen, "What Does *Kephale* Mean in the New Testament?" in *Women, Authority & the Bible*, ed. Alvera Mickelsen (Downers Grove, IL: InterVarsity Press, 1986), 105: "When Christ is spoken of as the head of the church, it may refer to him as

the church's source of life, as its top or crown, as its exalted originator and completer. These rich meanings are lost when "authority" or "superior rank" is considered the only meaning for head."

4.   LSJ, 945: "head of man or beast;" "of things, *extremity*;" "source of a river."

5.   Wm. Paul Young, Wayne Jacobsen, and Brad Cummings, *The Shack* (Los Angeles: Windblown Media, 2007), 121-24.

6.   Gordon D. Fee, "Praying and Prophesying in the Assemblies, 1 Corinthians 11:2-16," *DBE*, 154. In Ephesians 1:10 he concludes that authority is in view; in Ephesians 4:15 source of life is meant. In Ephesians 5:23 Paul is again using *kephale* with the meaning of the one who sustains, similar to Ephesians 4:15.

7.   See, for example the use of "head" (Gk. *kephale*) in the Septuagint in Judges 10:18, 11:8-9, and Isaiah 7:8-9.

8.   James W. Thompson, "Creation, Shame, and Nature in 1 Cor 11:2-16, The Background and Coherence of Paul's Argument," in *Early Christianity and Classical Culture, Comparative Studies in Honor of Abraham J. Malherbe*, Supplements to Novum Testamentum; 110, ed. John T. Fitzgerald, Thomas H. Olbricht, and L. Michael White (New York: E. J. Brill, 2003), 257.

9.   Marshall, "Mutual Love and Submission in Marriage, Colossians 3:18-19 and Ephesians 5:21-33," *DBE*, 199-200.

10.   Ibid. Paul Jewett made a similar argument in 1975. See *Man as Male and Female* (Grand Rapids: William B. Eerdmans Pub. Co., 1975). See also Osburn, *Women in the Church*, 171: "It is vital to understand that neither Paul nor Jesus before him called for the radical overthrow of hierarchalism. Both had ideals along egalitarian lines, yet both worked within the cultural systems of the day – whether regarding slavery or gender roles – and taught Christians to "walk wisely" given certain cultural constraints. Paul's admonition for mutual submission is still valid for twenty-first century Christians." See also Gregory E. Sterling, "Women in the Hellenistic and Roman Worlds (323 BCE-138 CE)," *EWEC*, 1:92: "There are indeed NT texts which impose restrictions on certain women. Yet there are also texts which affirm the equality of women with men within the NT. This same tension characterizes a number of the philosophical texts we noted, especially those of Plato and the Stoics. Like them, the issue we face is whether to emphasize principle or practice. NT texts which accentuate convention or practice did so within the cultural context of patriarchy. Since we no longer live in

such a context, we must ask whether we should maintain the same convictions. The issue is not whether we should dismiss the NT; we should not. The issue is, how can we be true to it? I, for one, think that loyalty to the NT requires us to give priority to principle rather than to practice." Contrast this with Russ Dudrey, "Submit Yourselves to One Another": A Socio-Historical Look at the Household Code of Ephesians 5:15-6:9," *Restoration Quarterly* 41 (First Quarter, 1999): 40: "I am convinced that the primary purpose of the household passages of the NT is not to repress the socially downtrodden, but to transform spiritually all who are in Christ – husbands, fathers, and masters included. This in turn transforms all their relationships. Rather than deconstructing the submission of Christian wives to their husbands, we should pay renewed attention to the construct of mutual submission and reciprocal self-sacrifice that is the major force of the household codes." See the similar conclusion by Kenneth V. Neller, "Submission" in Eph. 5:21-33," *EWEC*, 1:260: "the emphasis in "headship" is not on gender superiority, but on role."

11.   Marshall, "Mutual Love and Submission in Marriage, Colossians 3:18-19 and Ephesians 5:21-33," *DBE*, 194.

12.   See also Osburn, *Women in the Church*, 166-69 where he summarizes the linguistic evidence that points to submission in the teaching being a voluntary submission. Contrast this with Jack Cottrell, *Headship, Submission & the Bible: Gender Roles in the Home* (Joplin, MO: College Press Pub. Co., 2008), 20: "For egalitarians the distinction between voluntary and compulsory subordination is important because it suggests that Christian submission, especially that of wives to husbands, is not an obligation based upon a God-established order of things but is something a wife chooses to do simply because as a Christian she *wants* to do it." Further, he writes that, "whatever the nature of the submission in Eph 5:21 and elsewhere, the act of submitting is no more voluntary and no less mandatory than any other act of obedience to the will of God. Middle voice or not, it is still a command of God; and those to whom it applies have an absolute obligation to obey it." (21)

13.   F. LaGard Smith, *Male Spiritual Leadership* (Nashville: 21st Century Christian, 1998), 236.

14.   See, for example, Cottrell, *Headship, Submission & the Bible: Gender Roles in the Home.* Jack Cottrell summarizes that, "egalitarianism is the belief that men and women should be equal in every way, to the point that all role distinctions based on gender should be abolished." (10)

15. Cynthia Dianne Guy, *What About the Women? A Study of New Testament Scriptures Concerning Women* (Nashville: Gospel Advocate Co., 2005), 37.

16. Jordan, *The Eye of the World*, 131.

17. *www.click2houston.com/newsarchive/10111309/detail.html.*

Chapter 9. Parents, Children, and the Spiritual Storm

1. See *www.bacchusgamma.org*. "BACCHUS" is an acronym for "Boosting Alcohol Consciousness Concerning the Health of University Students."

2. Gk. *parorgizein*. BDAG, 780: "make angry." Robinson, *St. Paul's Epistle to the Ephesians*, 192: "the state of feeling provocation, wrath."

3. Gk. *paideia*. BDAG, 748: "the act of providing guidance for responsible living, upbringing, training, instruction, in our lit. chiefly as it is attained by discipline and correction...."

4. Eugene F. Klug, "Parenthood," in *Baker's Dictionary of Christian Ethics*, ed. Carl F. H. Henry (Grand Rapids: Baker Book House, 1973), 487.

5. Ferguson, *Backgrounds of Early Christianity*, 109.

6. Spretnak, *The Resurgence of the Real*, 114-5. Spretnak offers a pointed observation regarding the loss of a foundation for education: "So many nonreaders are graduated from our high schools today that between a fifth and a quarter of the U.S. population is functionally illiterate, or partially so." (114) Spretnak's suggestion to address the issue: do what she did for her daughter; shut down significant chunks of TV. (115) My addition: add Bible reading. Read at random moments when questions surface.

7. Daniel Mendelsohn, "Συγκεραυνοω: Dithyrambic Language and Dionysiac Cult," *The Classical Journal* 87 (Dec., 1991 – Jan. 1992): 111: "In the Pratinas fragment, the speaker complains that dithyrambic performance leads to street brawls of young drunkards." See also *SEG* 43, no. 1291: evidence exists to indicate that children were initiated into the Dionysus cult at an early age. As a result children had ample opportunity to learn and practice the rituals prior to the teen and young adult years.

8. Spretnak, *The Resurgence of the Real*, 120.

9. Ibid.

10. G. Lloyd Carr, *The Song of Solomon: An Introduction and Commentary* (Downers Grove, IL: InterVarsity Press, 1984), 95.

11. C. S. Lewis, *The Screwtape Letters* (San Francisco: HarperSanFrancisco, 2001), 117.

12.   E. Lovett, "The Ancient and Modern Game of Astragals," *Folklore* 12 (Sept., 1901): 280-293. Among the ancient Greeks and Romans, different numerical values were attributed to the four sides of the knucklebones, or Astragalis. Similar to dice, the various throws carried varying levels of value. The highest level of value was called a "Venus." Other throws carried the names of other gods, well-known men, women, and heroes. *SEG* 43, no. 1197: (sheep) knucklebones were used for "games; gambling; divination."

13.   Guy Bar-Oz, "An Inscribed Astragalus with a Dedication to Hermes," *NEA* 64 (Dec., 2001): 215-217.

14.   Christina Hoff Sommers, *The War Against Boys* (New York: Simon & Schuster, 2000), 95.

15.   Derek Kidner, *Psalms 73-150: An Introduction and Commentary* (Downers Grove, IL: InterVarsity Press, 1975), 442.

Chapter 10. Men, Women, and the Church's Worship and Work – Part 1

1.   Osburn, *Women in the Church*, 265. See also Rebecca Merrill Groothuis, "Equal in Being, Unequal in Role: Exploring the Logic of Woman's Subordination," *DBE*, 333.

2.   Ibid., 267: "Finally, though many are bothered by questions about the "role" of women in the church, we must remember that reservations about the "role" of women in worship and leadership are not really the main issue. Instead, the principal concern should be the recovery of the egalitarian view of women that God had in mind in the creation."

3.   Tertullian, *De Cultu Feminarum*, section I.I, part 2 (trans. C.W. Marx): "Do you not know that you are Eve? The judgment of God upon this sex lives on in this age; therefore, necessarily the guilt should live on also. You are the gateway of the devil; you are the one who unseals the curse of that tree, and you are the first one to turn your back on the divine law; you are the one who persuaded him whom the devil was not capable of corrupting; you easily destroyed the image of God, Adam. Because of what you deserve, that is, death, even the Son of God had to die." Author's note: It is disappointing that someone did not tell Tertullian at this point to please keep quiet and go read Luke 8:1-3.

4.   Augustine, *De Trinitate* 12.7.10.

5.   Edgar Hennecke, *New Testament Apocrypha*, ed. Wilhelm Schneemelcher, trans. and ed. R. McL. Wilson, 1:299 (Philadelphia: The Westminster Press, 1963).

6.   When discussing with my wife, Sharon, how the ancient priestly role had often changed to a secular one in our time, she shifted into playful gear and asked, "So, it has changed into a jelly roll or a cinnamon roll?" (breaking me away from this stuff for a bit) I responded that in honor of her breaking my train of thought, I would add her question to an endnote for all to read and enjoy!

7.   Mary Rose D'Angelo, "Women in Luke-Acts: A Redactional View," *Journal of Biblical Literature* 109 (Autumn, 1990): 441-61. Mary Rose D'Angelo has provided an important overview of recent research by feminists in Luke and Acts as part of the article.

8.   See, for example, the careful review by Allen Black, "Women in Luke," *EWEC*, 1:468: "Luke's interest in the fulfillment of the prophecies concerning the restored people of God provides a theological explanation for his inclusion of many women and men-women parallels in Luke-Acts. Through both volumes of his work, Luke demonstrates that men and women are healed, hear Jesus' teaching, become disciples, bear witness, receive the Spirit, prophesy, and receive salvation. For Luke, this is not a matter of being pro- or anti-feminist, or of seeking to relieve women from oppression within a patriarchal framework, but rather demonstrating how God has kept his promises to Israel and to the nations."

9.   Turid Karlsen Seim, *The Double Message: Patterns of Gender in Luke-Acts* (Edinburgh: T & T Clark, 1994), 102-3: "Women needed also to have a certain knowledge of the Law, in order to observe the prohibitions and the rules that affected them. This knowledge was transmitted from mother to daughter. But mainly it was a woman's task in connection with studies of the Law to give support on the domestic side, so that her husband could devote himself to his studies as much as possible. In the light of this, it is not only noteworthy that Mary is given the position of a student: it also gives a perspective on the conflict dealt with in the narrative, between domestic obligations and the supreme right to listen to the word of the Lord."

10.   D'Angelo, "Women in Luke-Acts," 461.

11.   Mary Rose D'Angelo, "(Re)Presentations of Women in the Gospel of Matthew and Luke-Acts," *WCO*. She suggests that "Luke is concerned not with changing the status of women, but with the appropriate deployment of gender." (187)

12.   Ibid., 191.

13.   Seim, 259.

14.   Osburn, *Women in the Church*, 188: "According to 11:2-16, women in the Corinthian church are praying and prophesying in the public worship. In 14:34-36, certain women are also speaking in the public worship in an instructional setting, but doing so in a disruptive way. The commonality shared by 11:2-16 and 14:34-36 is not "women speaking in public," but women showing disrespect for others, for decorum, and for propriety – and thus contributing to chaos, disruption, and disunity in the congregation." See also Gary Selby, "Women and Prophecy in the Corinthian Church," *EWEC*, 2:302: "Most importantly, the evidence of 1 Cor 11 clearly indicates that this prophetic activity was carried out publicly by women in the Christian assemblies at Corinth. The practice itself is not at issue. What is at issue is the manner in which the Corinthian prophetesses were engaged in that practice."

15.   See, for example, Osburn, *Women in the Church*, 252. "Put simply, any female who has sufficient and accurate information may teach that information in a gentle spirit to whomever in whatever situation they may be." See also Linda L. Bellville, "Teaching and Usurping Authority, 1 Timothy 2:11-15," *DBE*, 223: "Paul would then be prohibiting teaching that tries to get the upper hand – not teaching per se."

16.   See Bart Ehrman, *Misquoting Jesus: The Story Behind Who Changed the Bible and Why* (San Francisco: HarperSanFrancisco, 2005), 183-6 for a recent example of the proposal that 1) 1 Corinthians 14:33b-36 was a scribal addition to Paul's letter and 2) 1 Timothy 2:11-15 was not written by Paul. Bart Ehrman believes that Christian scribes who lived after Paul suppressed the apostle's directive that permitted women to prophesy/teach in church assemblies.

17.   Bruce M. Metzger, *A Textual Commentary on the Greek New Testament* (New York: United Bible Societies, 1971), 565: "Several wit nesses, chiefly Western, transpose verses 34-35 to follow ver. 40.... Such scribal alterations represent attempts to find a more appropriate location in the context for Paul's directive concerning women."

18.   1 Corinthians 14:33b-36 carries far less breadth than numerous writers have proposed. See, for example, Craig S. Keener, "Learning in the Assemblies, 1 Corinthians 14:34-35," *DBE*, 161: "Very few churches today take 1 Corinthians 14:34-35 to mean all that it could possibly mean." Instead, Paul's teaching to "keep silent" in the text refers specifically to prophesy or tongue speech. The context has to do with those specific speeches (1 Cor. 14:27-39), and Paul's two other uses of "keep silent" (Gk. *sigao*) in the

context (1 Cor. 14:28, 30) refer specifically to this kind of speech. So also does his use in 1 Corinthians 14:34.

19.　Everett Ferguson, *Women in the Church* (Chickasha, OK: Yeomen Press, 2003), 25-6. See also F. W. Grosheide, *Commentary on the First Epistle to the Corinthians*, The New International Commentary on the New Testament (Grand Rapids: William B. Eerdmans Pub. Co., 1953), 252: "Paul in ch. 11 speaks of praying and prophesying (of women) in public rather than in the meetings of the congregation. This interpretation has in its favor that it avoids a conflict with the absolute language of 14:34; it makes clear why Paul in this chapter argues from the divine ordinance of creation, as he points out that a Christian woman shares in the blessings of Christ (vs. 11), but does not touch upon the conditions in the congregation...." Mark Black discusses this suggestion in his "1 Cor. 11:2-16 – A Re-Investigation," *EWEC*, 1:191-218. He concludes that Grosheide is pointing to "an informal gathering or a separate assembly for women only." (193) He correctly asks why Paul would be so concerned with head coverings in such informal settings. (193) However, he misses what Grosheide has suggested. Grosheide proposes that Paul is dealing with propriety in a public setting, not an informal one. He is addressing public prophetic speech beyond a religious sanctuary, such as was common among Dionysus worshipers. See Gregory Sterling, *EWEC*, 1:87: "Not all prophetesses were connected with specific sanctuaries. The most famous prophetesses who were not were the sibyls, old women whose prophecies were mostly of future calamities."

20.　Pausanias, *Description of Greece* 2.11.6. (*www.Perseus.Tufts.edu*): "There is a similar image of Health; this, too, one cannot see easily because it is so surrounded with the locks of women, who cut them off and offer them to the goddess, and with strips of Babylonian raiment."

21.　Dan Stanislawski, "Dionysus Westward: Early Religion and the Economic Geography of Wine," *Geographical Review* 65 (Oct., 1975): 443: Concerning Greece he writes that "Corinth was the place of the earliest and greatest development of the Dionysian choruses and dithyrambs." See also Oscar Broneer, "Paul and the Pagan Cults at Isthmia," *HTR* 64 (April-July, 1971): 182. Broneer cites archaeological evidence of the cult's presence in Corinth as early as the fourth century B.C.

22.　*Bacchae* 299: "And this god is a prophet; the Bacchic ecstasy and frenzy hold a strong prophetic element. When he fills irresistibly a human body he gives those so possessed power to foretell the future." See also Livy, *History of Rome*, 39.13.

23. Goff, *Citizen Bacchae: Women's Ritual Practice in Ancient Greece*, 157: The cult prostitutes of Corinth mimicked the familial roles of respectable women when they undertook the task of intercession. Further, Goff cites Athenaeus' comment that prostitutes and respectable women celebrated separate festivals of Aphrodite.

24. See Carroll D. Osburn, "1 Cor 11:2-16 – Public or Private?" *EWEC*, 2:307-16. Carroll Osburn provides a careful survey of the reasons for seeing 1 Corinthians 11:2-16 as addressing public versus private settings. See also Grosheide, 253: "We feel justified in maintaining that Paul refers to a public action and fail to understand what objection Paul could have against a married woman performing certain functions in her own house, i.e. in the presence of her husband and children, with her head unveiled...."

25. Paul's later statement regarding Christian men of the province of Asia is equally striking (2 Ti. 1:15). Aside from the examples of Onesiphorus, Tychicus, and Trophimus (Acts 20:4; 2 Ti. 1:16-18; 4:12, 20) we read little that is positive about Christians in the region.

26. Gk. *parabiazomai*. BDAG, 759: "urge strongly, prevail upon."

27. Ross Shepard Kraemer, *Her Share of the Blessings: Women's Religions Among Pagans, Jews, and Christians in the Greco-Roman World* (New York: Oxford University Press, 1992), 41, 77.

28. See, for example, Kraemer, *Her Share of the Blessings*. Phoebe is the recipient of a description in Ro. 16:2 ("great help", NIV) that "clearly connotes status, prestige, and authority." (182) Linda L. Bellville, "Women Leaders in the Bible," *DBE*, 120: "Euodia and Syntyche are singled out as leaders of the Philippian church." "Under Roman Law, Nympha had legal responsibility for and hence authority over the church that met in her house (Col. 4:15)." (124)

Chapter 11. Men, Women, and the Church's Worship and Work – Part 2

1. Alan Padgett, "Wealthy Women at Ephesus: 1 Timothy 2:8-15 in Social Context," *Interpretation* 41 (Jan., 1987): 19-31. He believes a particular group of women were the subject of 1 Timothy 2:8-15 – women who were wealthy enough to expect positions of prominence and bold enough to seek them.

2. Doug Heidebrecht, "Reading 1 Timothy 2:9-15 in its Literary Context," *Direction* 33 (2004): 181-2.

3. Osburn, *Women in the Church*, 251: "It may be concluded, then, that 1 Ti. 2:9-15 was directed to a specific group of troublesome women in

a particular place in the early church. Their particular problem was specifically that of being misinformed and domineering teachers."

4.   Bellville, "Teaching and Usurping Authority, 1 Timothy 2:11-15," *DBE*, 219: "Why were the Ephesian women doing this? One explanation is that they were influenced by the cult of Artemis, in which the female was exalted and considered superior to the male." She suggests in summary that "The women at Ephesus (perhaps encouraged by the false teachers) were trying to gain an advantage over the men in the congregation by teaching in a dictatorial fashion. The men in response became angry and disputed what the women were doing." (223)

5.   Carroll Osburn's extensive research has led those who have suggested a translation of "domineer." Carroll D. Osburn, "Αυθεντεω (1 Ti. 2:12)," *Restoration Quarterly* 25 (First Quarter 1982): 1-12. See also Osburn, *Women in the Church*, 246: "The term *authentein* is taken by some to mean "exercise authority" [RSV, NIV], but stronger reasons exist for taking it to mean "domineer." Instead of "domineering over a man," they are encouraged to be "deferential" (2:11). Instead, they should evidence an attitude of "peaceableness/ quietude." See also *LSJ*, 275: "to have full power or authority over." Concerning (Gk.) *authentes*: "an absolute master, autocrat, commander, one who has power and can delegate it."

6.   Osburn, *Women in the Church*, 246.

7.   Ibid.

8.   Neil R. Lightfoot, *The Role of Women: New Testament Perspectives* (Memphis, TN: Student Association Press, 1978), 32.

9.   Gk. *manthano*. BDAG, 615: "to gain knowledge or skill by instruction, learn." The word is used five times by Paul in his letters to Timothy: 1 Ti. 2:11; 5:4, 13; 2 Ti. 3:7, 14.

10.   Guy, *What About the Women? A Study of New Testament Scriptures Concerning Women*, 79.

11.   Dorothy Kelley Patterson, "What Should a Woman Do in the Church?" *WC*, 150.

12.   C. R. Nichol, *God's Woman* (Abilene, TX: Abilene Christian University Bookstore, 1938), 153: "If a woman teaches a Sunday School class, at the solicitation of the elders in the church of Christ, she does not usurp authority over man." Nichol's interpretation of 1 Timothy 2:12 illustrates the misunderstanding of Paul's teaching that is associated with "usurp authority" (1 Ti. 2:12, KJV).

13.   Osburn, *Women in the Church*, 249. See also 248-49: "Well, Paul is certainly not engaging in exegesis of Gen. 1-3. Rather, he is using a common Jewish analogy in which Eve was caricatured as a deceived and bumbling fool who constantly led Adam into trouble." Further, Osburn writes, "The point of similarity between v. 12 and v. 13 is that just as it is commonly remarked that Eve was deceived and led Adam astray, so certain women in the Ephesian church lack information and teach false information that leads people astray." (249) In contrast see, for example, Douglas Moo, "What Does it Mean Not to Teach or Have Authority Over Men? (1 Timothy 2:11-15)," in *Recovering Biblical Manhood and Womanhood*, ed. John Piper and Wayne Grudem (Wheaton: Crossway Books, 1991), 185: "by citing creation rather than a local situation or cultural circumstance as his basis for the prohibitions, Paul makes it clear that, while these local or cultural issues may have provided the context of the issue, they do not provide the reason for his advice."

14.   Roger Nicole, "Biblical Hermeneutics: Basic Principles and Questions of Gender," *DBE*, 357: "Paul's descriptive analogy between Adam's priority in creation and Eve's priority in sin in 1 Timothy 2:13-14 – even though it is used to support the ad hoc prescription in 1 Timothy 2:12 – seems to fall far short of being theologically prescriptive or determinative." Nicole describes the Bible from a prescriptive versus descriptive perspective – mere history being told without moral statement versus moral/spiritual imperative from God. This, however, misses the mark in the case of 1 Timothy 2:13-14. Paul's "description" in 1 Timothy 2:13-14 lays the foundation for "prescription" in 1 Timothy 2:11-12.

15.   One of the best surveys is by Thomas R. Schreiner, "An Interpretation of 1 Timothy 2:9-15: A Dialogue With Scholarship," *WC*, 115-20.

16.   Bellville, "Teaching and Usurping Authority, 1 Timothy 2:11-15," *DBE*, 219: "they [Christian women in Ephesus] need not look to Artemis as the protector of women as did other Ephesian women who turned to her for safe travel through the childbearing process." See also C. F. D. Moule, *An Idiom-Book of New Testament Greek* (Cambridge: Cambridge University Press, 1953), 56. Additionally, see Pausanias, *Description of Greece* 4.30.5. Artemis was "feared" in childbirth – in reference to the belief that she fiercely defended women and children.

17.   Schreiner, "An Interpretation of 1 Timothy 2:9-15: A Dialogue With Scholarship," *WC*, 118-20.

18.   See Ross S. Kraemer, *Maenads, Martyrs, Matrons, Monastics* (Philadelphia: Fortress Press, 1988), 221: An epitaph from third century

A.D. Asia Minor attests to a woman elder in region: "Diogas the bishop to Ammion (fem.) the elder, in memory." As one explanation, Kraemer suggests that she was a Montanist. The Montanists were a second century movement in Asia Minor known for their acceptance of women as church leaders.

19. Sarah Pomeroy, *Goddesses, Whores, Wives, and Slaves* (New York: Schocken Books, 1995), 176: "Roman women, in contrast to Athenian, were not sequestered, and it is not difficult to believe that the affairs of state were of interest to them. Moreover, they were accustomed to all-female gatherings for religious purposes."

20. Goff, *Citizen Bacchae: Women's Ritual Practice in Ancient Greece*, 216-18. Dionysian events actually carved out for women something of a "city of women," a religious "city" where they held complete sway. An epitaph from second or third century B.C. Miletos honors a Dionysus cult priestess as "citizen Bakchai" – a title denoting political authority in Miletus. It is likely that worship to the goddess Cybele and the goddess Isis further demonstrated itself in women-only gatherings as well, both as spiritual retreats and as times of socializing between women. (215)

21. Ibid., 136: One historical account describes how a man, Battos of Cyrene, who pressed his way in to see what went on at the *Thesmophoria* festival, was attacked by the women at the festival and castrated using the sacrificial tools.

22. As one example see Anna M. Griffith, "A Mustard Seed Kind of Faith," in *Trusting Women*, ed. Billie Silvey (Orange, CA: New Leaf Books, 2002), 61-72. She summarized her efforts to reach out to others in an AIDS treatment facility where she served cookies for six weeks. She writes that after three months "someone finally asked my name. Of course, by that time it was a moot question, because everyone just called me "Cookie Lady." If someone has AIDS, building trust with them is a tedious, time-consuming, patience-challenging process." (67)

23. Marguerite Lena, "A Creative Difference: Educating Women," in *Women in Christ, Toward a New Feminism*, ed. Michelle M. Schumacher (Grand Rapids: William B. Eerdmans Pub. Co., 2004), 316-18. See also Borysenko, *A Woman's Journey to God*. Joan Borysenko's *Gathering of Women* retreats have surfaced similar conclusions. She comments that a survey of 3.746 women reveals the common thread of time-pressure and the resulting need among many women, especially women in pain, to reach out and converse with other women as a key step to healing. (7-8)

24. Debbie Bumbalough and Dwina Willis, editors, *Woman to Woman, A Guide to Teaching and Leading Women* (Nashville: Gospel Advocate Co., 2007). See also Susan Hunt and Peggy Hutcheson, *Leadership For Women in the Church* (Grand Rapids: Zondervan, 1991).

25. See Miriam Therese Winter, Adair T. Lummis, and Allison Stokes, *Defecting in Place: Women Claiming Responsibility for Their Own Spiritual Lives* (New York: Crossroad Pub. Co., 1994). The study provides an important overview of religious "defection" by women in the late twentieth century.

26. Borysenko, *A Woman's Journey to God,* 250.

27. Ibid., 268-72. She also quotes a doctor who observed from a visit to the United States that women were so busy and isolated that he believed the country would not survive the decimation of its women. (135)

28. Ibid., 128. She embraces all of the world's religions – provided women are able to secure places of prominence and by such positions craft helpful new rituals within those religions. (238-58)

29. Ibid., 238-58.

30. Ibid., 7.

31. Joan Borysenko does mention the resurrection of Jesus twice: 1) in connection with the story of Mary Magdalene and 2) in connection with the beliefs by some in Easter ritual. (214, 248) However, in neither place does she discuss whether the resurrection actually took place. Her focus is solely on Mary Magdalene in the first instance.

32. Eusebius provides a glimpse of the work of female calligraphers in early Christianity when he comments about the woman who helped Origen as a scribe (*Ecclesiastical History* 6.23). See also Kim Haines-Eitzen, "Girls Trained in Beautiful Writing": Female Scribes in Roman Antiquity and Early Christianity," *Journal of Early Christian Studies* 6 (Winter 1998): 634-40. Haines-Eitzen summarizes the evidence from inscriptions indicating the presence of female scribes and their skillful, beautiful work in the urban areas during the Roman period. Some were trained in (Gk.) *kalligraphia*; see LSJ, 867: "beautiful writing." In the ancient world, the beauty of a manuscript served to attract people to the document.

Chapter 12: Church Elders Then and Now

1. Lynn R. LiDonnici, "The Images of Artemis Ephesia and Greco-Roman Worship: A Reconsideration," *HTR* 85 (Oct., 1992): 394: The large

majority of the one thousand public and private inscriptions from Ephesus have to do with health care, citizenship decrees, and extensions of credit.

2.   Michael Grant, *Alexander to Cleopatra: The Hellenistic World* (New York: Charles Scribner's Sons, 1982), 137: The university city of Ephesus joined Pergamum and Cos as centers of medical education in the Greco-Roman world of Paul's day. See also Rostovzeff, *The Social and Economic History of the Roman Empire*, 591, note. 34: Based on the presence of the Museum and other evidence, Rostovzeff suggests that Ephesians knew a relatively high level of education.

3.   Pomeroy, *Goddesses, Whores, Wives, and Slaves,* 84. Pomeroy refers to a study of ancient cemeteries, which suggests that female deaths increased during the childbearing years.

4.   Pausanias, *Description of Greece.* 4.30.5: "Artemis feared in childbirth". See also Pomeroy, *Goddesses, Whores, Wives, and Slaves,* 84: "The robes of women who died in childbirth were dedicated to Artemis at Brauron, since she was the patronness of the life cycle of women – and there are several Classical relief sculptures apparently of women who died in childbirth."

5.   Valerie French, "Midwives and Maternity Care in the Roman World," in *Rescuing Creusa: New Methodological Approaches to Women in Antiquity,* ed. Marilyn Skinner (*Helios,* New Series 13(2), 1986), 73: "A mid-third century A.D. marriage contract from Oxyrhynchus in Egypt stipulated that the husband should give to the wife forty drachmae for her confinement if she was pregnant at the time of any separation; the sum probably was intended to cover more than the midwife's fee, but a substantial portion no doubt was to be used for her services."

6.   Ibid., 69. Additionally, based on the volume of writings by Soranus of Ephesus (98-138 A.D.), we can conclude that he saw great need throughout the Mediterranean world for better education regarding proper gynecology and birthing practices.

7.   Knibbe, *Ephesos,* 151. The articles that were placed with her body indicate the possessions that came to mind when family and friends thought of her: a bronze mirror, a container for cosmetics, three glass unguentaria (flasks providing perfume to enhance the afterlife experience), two gold finger rings, and two gold ear rings.

8.   Interestingly, all of the synonyms converge in Luke's record of Paul's final meeting with the elders of the Ephesian church (Acts 20:17-38). See the use of "pastor" as verb and noun (Gk. noun = *poimen*) in Acts 20:28

and Ephesians 4:11, overseer (Gk. *episkopos*) in Acts 20:28, 1 Timothy 3:1-7, and elder (Gk. *presbyteros*) in Acts 20:17. *IAph2007* (fifth century A.D.) inscription no. 13.113, *Epitaph of Theopropios*, includes the Greek word *episkopos*: "(Tomb of) Theopropios, bishop. He lives."

9.   See the Introduction, note 8.

10.   LSJ, 1097-8. Liddell, Scott, and Jones provide a one-stop overview of the collection of words that have as their root the word for "honey" (Gk. *meli*). Listed in the lexicon are words that likely carried significant weight in Greek religious history: *Melissae* – bee, priestess of Delphi; *melitoessa* – honey-cake offering to deity; *melisponda* – drink offering made from honey; *melikreton* – honey-milk mixture offered as a libation to deities; *meliedes* – honey-sweet, compare with "melody;" *meliteion* – mead, i.e. honey-wine.

11.   Scheinberg, 19: "The honey-induced prophetic frenzy of the bee maidens in the *Hymn to Hermes* thus belongs to a tradition in which divination depended upon the ritual drinking of a sacred, perhaps intoxicating, liquid which opened the human psyche to messages from the divine world by bringing the god within the seer."

12.   LSJ, 1098: *melissophyllon*, and *meliphyllon* – healing balm or salve; *melitizo* and *melitismos* – honey used for medical purposes, e.g. as the base for a healing plaster. See also Ortha L. Wilner, "Roman Beauty Culture," *The Classical Journal* 27 (Oct., 1931): 28: Facial lotions often had a honey base.

13.   Ibid., 1096. Gk. *mele*: "my friend!"

14.   Ibid., 645: "take care of." Note the close association between the Greek words *epimeleomai* and *mele*.

15.   See the comment regarding 1 Timothy 5:17 by Everett Ferguson, "Authority and Tenure of Elders," *Restoration Quarterly* 18 (1975): 146: "The translations "be over" and "rule" seem particularly unfortunate. The word literally means "to be out front," "to be at the head of," and so "to manage." Thus it is used of a father managing his household (1 Ti. 3:4, 5, 12), but even here in parallel with "caring for." The word was used especially in the sense "to care for" or "give aid to," as it is translated in Romans 12:8. The development in this direction is emphasized by the sense "to be concerned about, to be engaged in," in Titus 3:8, 14."

16.   Jack P. Lewis, *Leadership Questions Confronting the Church* (Nashville: Christian Communications, 1985), 34.

17.   Osburn, *Women in the Church*, 266-67.

18.   Anderson, *An Emergent Theology For Emerging Churches*, 128-34.

19.   Love, Foster, and Harris, *Seeking a Lasting City*, 92. In contrast to the teaching and practice that were extended broadly (Acts 14:23; Titus 1:5), the authors suggest that, "This diversity, not only in practice, but also in emphasis, reveals a vibrant picture of New Testament churches. No single community in the New Testament fully embodies everything it means to be a congregation of God's people. The unity of the church in the New Testament did not involve uniformity of practice." See pages 71-96 for an overview of how they see diversity within the earliest churches.

20.   Ibid., 91.

21.   Trebilco, *The Early Christians in Ephesus from Paul to Ignatius*, 711. Trebilco concludes that earliest Christianity in Ephesus saw different groups of Christians with somewhat different beliefs. He believes some lined up with Paul, others with John.

22.   Helmut Koester, "Ephesos in Early Christian Literature," *Ephesos*, 139.

23.   W. H. C. Frend, *The Rise of Christianity* (Philadelphia: Fortress Press, 1984), 199: Gnostics claimed a secret knowledge acquired "not by perseverance in moral rectitude but by sudden illumination that enabled them to understand the ways of God, the universe, and themselves." See also R. M. Grant, *Gnosticism and Early Christianity*, 2nd ed. (New York: Columbia University Press, 1966). "The Gnostic is a Gnostic because he knows, by revelation, who his true self is." (8) "He knows that he has, and essentially *is*, the divine spark." (107)

24.   Love, Foster, and Harris, *Seeking a Lasting City*, 107.

25.   Beyond the New Testament teachings, consider the historical example of Ignatius' *The Epistle to the Ephesians*. 6.1. Ignatius provides a clear signal that, consistent with 1 Timothy 3:1ff., as of the early second century the office of elder/bishop/pastor was specific to Christian men.

26.   Mark E. Dever, "Baptist Polity and Elders," *Journal for Baptist Theology and Ministry* 3 (Spring 2005): 37.

Chapter 13. Glorious Bride, or Prostitute?

1.   Sunil Iyengar, Tom Bradshaw, Bonnie Nichols, Kelli Rogowski, and Sarah Sullivan, *To Read or Not to Read: A Question of National Consequence*, Research Division Report #47 (Washington, DC: National Endowment for the Arts, 2007), 5. Available at *www.nea.gov*.

2.   Sven Birkerts, *The Gutenberg Elegies: The Fate of Reading in an Electronic Age* (Boston: Faber and Faber, 1994), 17-19.

3.   Spretnak, *The Resurgence of the Real,* 114. Similarly, research practices by at least a minority of college students reflect something of the growing preference for or even dependence on at-your-fingertips information. When a librarian commented to one student that the article he was interested in reading was only available in hard copy in the periodical section, the student indicated that he would just use a different article. He preferred reading only on-line articles. Conversation with Henry Terrill, Librarian, Harding University, August 22, 2008.

4.   Birkerts, 27.

5.   Tom Bradshaw and Bonnie Nichols, *Reading at Risk: A Survey of Literary Reading in America,* Research Division Report #46 (Washington, DC: National Endowment for the Arts, 2004), 3. Available at *www.nea.gov.*

6.   Two generations have passed since two key culture and technology events occurred. 2009 marks the 50th anniversary of the beginning of color television-based storytelling in the form of a weekly serial; the National Broadcasting Company aired the first episode of *Bonanza* on September 12, 1959. Equally important, the first demonstration of the microchip occurred exactly one year earlier.

7.   See Fred Peatross, "Discipleship: From Application of Scripture to Performance of Scripture," *New Wineskins* (May-June 2008): "Listen. I'm a writer – I like the idea of people reading books. But I wonder if there's a bit of conceit in the idea that the welfare of the body of Christ depends on the welfare of the print era?" While Fred Peatross is not dismissing value from Scripture, he also comments elsewhere in his essay that he is not particularly concerned about the decline in Scripture reading (and the education model) in the nation at present. However, his counsel that people need to mimic a mentor (the apprentice model) is as much under siege. Along with a lack of reading, listening at length is also declining for similar reasons. Discipleship based even on oral communication is more at risk in our time. Available at *www.wineskins.com.*

8.   John Mark Hicks and Bobby Valentine, *Kingdom Come: Embracing the Spiritual Legacy of David Lipscomb and James Harding* (Abilene, TX: Leafwood Pub., 2006), 91. Additionally, they cite with appreciation James Harding's memorable statement: "the most important thing in the world is daily, diligent, prayerful study of the divine word." (91)

9.   Calvin Stapert, *A New Song for an Old World: Musical Thought in the Early Church* (Grand Rapids: William B. Eerdmans Pub. Co., 2007), 194-5.

10. Birkerts, 75-6. As he writes, "When the electronic impulse rules, and where the psyche is conditioned to work with data, the experience of deep time is impossible. No deep time, no resonance; no resonance, no wisdom. The only remaining oases are churches (for those who still worship) and the offices of therapists." (76)

11. Patty Amyx, "Simplicity," *21st Century Christian Magazine* 71 (Jan/Feb 2008): 42.

12. Gk. *endoxos*. BDAG, 332: "to be held in high esteem, honored, distinguished, eminent." Concerning Ephesians 5:27, "Of the church, brilliant in purity." Concerning Lk 13:17, "splendid deeds." Gerhard Kittel, *TDNT*, "*endoxos, endoxazomai*," 2:254: "When the Church is described as ενδοξος [*endoxos*], this refers to its honorable estate, i.e. that it has neither spot nor wrinkle...."

13. Gk. *kosmeo*. BDAG, 560: Use in Rev. 21:2 is "a bride adorned for her husband." Hermann Sasse, *TDNT*, "*kosmeo*," 3:867: The word can mean either "put in order" (as the verb form of *kosmos*) or "adorn." Sasse suggests that the only use of the word as "put in order" is found in Matthew 25:7; the other uses in the New Testament reflect "adorn."

14. G. R. Beasley-Murray, *The Book of Revelation, New Century Bible* (London: Marshall, Morgan, and Scott, 1974). Beasley-Murray asks, "Should a bride be termed a wife? In western societies hardly so, for the two words represent different relationships. Some commentators, therefore, would eliminate the second term as having originated in an explanatory gloss in the margin. In Hebrew society, however, betrothal was a more serious affair and more closely related to the married state than it is among western peoples." (318)

15. Oster, "Ephesus as a Religious Center under the Principate," 1722.

16. On October 11, 1954, Eugenio Pacelli (Pius XII) gave the encyclical entitled "Ad Caeli Reginam" that proclaimed the queenship of Mary. See also Appendix D.

17. Oster, "The Ephesian Artemis as an Opponent of Early Christianity," 40: "To those who call upon Artemis she was Savior, Lord, and Queen of the Cosmos. She was a heavenly goddess, whose being and character could only be described in superlatives...."

18. Robert H. Gundry, "The New Jerusalem: People as Place, Not Place For People," *Novum Testamentum* 29 (1987): 256.

19. Ibid., 260.

20. Ibid., 261.

21.   By the time of Domitian (81-96 A.D.), Ephesus bowed to two patrons. See Giancarlo Biguzzi, "Ephesus, Its Artemision, Its Temple to the Flavian Emperors, and Idolatry in Revelation," *Novum Testamentum* 40 (Jul., 1998): 276-290. The last two sets of seven in the Revelation address two distinct idolatries, not one. (276) Under Domitian, Ephesus was "no longer devoted exclusively to Artemis, but to Artemis and the emperor." (288)

22.   Starhawk and Hilary Valentine, *The Twelve Wild Swans: A Journey to the Realm of Magic, Healing, and Action* (San Francisco: HarperSanFrancisco, 2000), 279.

23.   The word translated "financial gain" (NIV; Gk. *porismos*) is found only two times in the New Testament: 1 Timothy 6:5, 6.

24.   See, for example, Hicks and Valentine, *Kingdom Come*, 195-6: "The world has watched as the church has accommodated to cultural values and judged it inauthentic. Institutional factors like *a cappella* music, a sign that says "Church of Christ," and the exclusion of women from any visible presence in the assembly have been judged irrelevant to a meaningful life and discipleship. We do not think these matters insignificant but we do believe that perhaps our critics have a valid point – these "marks" do not come close to making us authentic disciples of Christ."

Appendix B: Religious Feminism, Women's Studies, and Apostolic Teaching – A Brief Survey

1.   F. LaGard Smith has presented an incisive assessment of the issue in *Male Spiritual Leadership*.

2.   Mary Daly, *Beyond God the Father*, 46-7: "Theologians and scholars generally have failed to confront the fact that in the myth of the Fall the medium is the message. Reflection upon its specific content and the cultural residues of this content leads to the conviction that, partially through this instrument, the Judeo-Christian tradition has been aiding and abetting the sicknesses of society. In a real sense the projection of guilt upon women is patriarchy's Fall, the primordial lie. Together with its offspring – the theology of "original sin" – the myth reveals the "Fall" of religion into the role of patriarchy's prostitute."

3.   Ibid., 44-68. "The story of the Fall was an attempt to cope with the confusion experienced by human beings trying to make sense out of the tragedy and absurdity of the human condition. Unfortunately, as an exclusively male effort in a male-dominated society, it succeeded primarily in reflecting the defective social arrangements of the time." (45-46)

4.   Ibid., 71.

5.   Ibid., 71-72.

6.   Mary Daly, *Amazon Grace: Re-calling the Courage to Sin Big*, 115-121.

7.   Ibid. "*Amazon Grace* is a challenge and an invitation hurled out to Daring, Desperate Women everywhere. In this malignant time the rulers of patriarchy multiply divisions endlessly. They impose multiple blindfolds/mindfolds upon women, rendering us unable to see the artificially constructed walls that cut us off from ourselves, each Other, and the natural world." (1)

8.   Ibid. Daly's critique of the oppression and destruction of creation covers a broad range of topics: the oppression of women (43-54); the mass extinction of life (59, 131-32); the global shortage of clean water (59); the torture of animals (120, 126); the pervasive threat of electromagnetic radiation (134-35); war (201-209).

9.   Daly, *Beyond God the Father*, 23.

10.   One especially telling measurement comes from the index of *Amazon Grace*. Mary Daly lists "animal rights," "Animal Rights and John Kerry," "Animals of Lost and Found, Liberated," and "animals, torture and destruction of." However, no listing exists with the subject of children, infants, or babies.

11.   Francesca Gastagnoli, "Self's 10 Most Inspiring Women," *Self* (September 2006): 43-54.

12.   Daly, *Beyond God the Father*, 73.

13.   Schüssler Fiorenza, *Bread Not Stone*, xiii.

14.   Ibid.

15.   Elisabeth Schüssler Fiorenza, *But She Said* (Boston: Beacon Press, 1992), 33.

16.   Schüssler Fiorenza, *Bread Not Stone*, 88.

17.   Cullen Murphy, *The Word According to Eve* (New York: Houghton Mifflin Co., 1998), 223. In summarizing his review of Schüssler Fiorenza's work, he writes, "The subject of Jesus and women, however, is sometimes presented in popular accounts as if some sort of rough consensus had emerged among biblical feminists, when in fact no such consensus exists and indeed a certain amount of division is evident on a number of fronts." (139)

18.   Charlene Spretnak, *States of Grace: The Recovery of Meaning in the Postmodern Age* (San Francisco: HarperSanFrancisco, 1991), 136.

19.   Spretnak, *The Resurgence of the Real*, 79.

20.   Ibid., 183. Interestingly, the idea of Gaia has even penetrated commerce and business, showing up in Sanyo Corporation marketing (see *www.sanyo.com*).

21.   Rosemary Radford Ruether, *Gaia & God: An Ecofeminist Theology of Earth Healing* (San Francisco: HarperSanFrancisco, 1992). Ruether does not believe the biblical message of sin/redemption. Instead, she suggests that "We pass on our ideals to the future not by escaping personal death, but by partly reshaping "nature" to reflect these human ideals." (31) "Our final gesture, as we surrender ourself into the Matrix of life, then can become a prayer of ultimate trust: "Mother, into your hands I commend my spirit." (253)

22.   See, for example, *www.miaminewtimes.com/2004-10-07*: "Annette Jones, pastor at St. John's on the Lake Church and companion to a Lhasa Apso named Shadow, will conduct a pet blessing service for furry, scaly, or feathered friends and the humans they hang out with." See also Jillian S. Jarrett, "Honoring All Creatures Great and Small," *Washington Post* (Oct. 12, 2006).

23.   Frank Furedi, "In Search of Eco-salvation," *Spiked Online* (Sept. 27, 2007).

24.   Ibid.

25.   Murphy, *The Word According to Eve*, 52.

26.   Phyllis Trible, *God and the Rhetoric of Sexuality* (Minneapolis: Augsburg Fortress Press, 1978), 75.

27.   Ibid., 80. More important, this creature is not identified sexually. Grammatical gender ('adam as a masculine word) is not sexual identification. Nor is sexuality assumed here, since it is created later in the fourth episode. In other words, the earth creature is not the male; it is not "the first man."

28.   Ibid., "After God operates on this earth creature, to produce a companion, its identity becomes sexual." (98) "Their creation is simultaneous, not sequential. One does not precede the other, even though the time line of this story introduces the woman first (2:22)." (98) "Accordingly, in this poem the man does not depict himself as either prior to or superior to the woman. His sexual identity depends upon her even as hers depends upon him. For both of them sexuality originates in the one flesh of humanity." (99)

29.   Ibid., 90: "The Hebrew word *'ezer*, rendered here as "companion," has been traditionally translated "helper" – a translation that is totally misleading because the English word helper suggests an assistant, a subordinate, indeed, an inferior, while the Hebrew word *'ezer* carries no such connotation."

30. John Willis, *Genesis*, The Living Word Commentary on the Old Testament, ed. John T. Willis (Austin, TX: R. B. Sweet Co., 1979), 112.

31. Derek Kidner, *Genesis, The Tyndale Old Testament Commentaries*, ed. D.J. Wiseman (Downers Grove, IL: InterVarsity Press, 1967), 65.

32. Richard S. Hess, "Equality With and Without Innocence (Gen. 1-3)," *DBE*, 84.

33. Ibid.

34. Ibid., 94.

35. Osburn, *Women in the Church*, 124. Additionally, he writes that, "the "order of creation" in Gen. 2 does not teach male superiority or female subordination." (120) See also Rick Marrs's in-depth look at the specifics of this conclusion. Rick R. Marrs, "In the Beginning: Male and Female (Gen. 1-3)," *EWEC*, 2:1-36.

36. See, for example, "A STUDY DOCUMENT ON THE ROLE OF WOMEN," Cahaba Valley Church of Christ, January, 1990. "Jesus entered a world that was completely dominated by men. Religious and political power belonged exclusively to men." Available at *www.cahabavalley.org*.

37. Pomeroy, *Goddesses, Whores, Wives, and Slaves*, 75.

38. Ibid., 214-26: "The cult of the Hellenized Ceres [Cybele] was exclusively in the hands of women. Greek priestesses were brought from Naples or Veleia (Elea) to supervise the new cult. These priestesses were granted Roman citizenship and held positions of prestige." (216).

39. Ibid., 219.

40. Ibid., 176.

41. Goff, *Citizen Bacchae: Women's Ritual Practice in Ancient Greece*, 50.

42. Ibid., 51.

43. Wayne A. Meeks, *The First Urban Christians: The Social World of the Apostle Paul*, 2nd ed. (New Haven, CT: Yale University Press, 2003), 25.

44. Ibid., 44.

45. Oxyrhynchus Papyrus 1380, lines 214-16.

46. Catherine Clark Kroeger, "1 Timothy 2:12 – A Classicist's View," in *Women, Authority & the Bible*, ed. Alvera Mickelsen (Downers Grove, IL: InterVarsity Press, 1986), 233.

47. White, *Ephesos*, 58.

48. Thomas, "Greek Heritage in Roman Corinth and Ephesos." "The College of the Kouretes at Ephesos is a religious association that sponsored traditional civic festivals, and is well-documented from the Hellenistic

through the Roman periods." (7) In the Roman period, the College, which was composed of six to nine Kouretes elected annually, was made up of male members of the leading families of Ephesos. (8-9)

49.   S. M. Baugh, "A Foreign World: Ephesus in the First Century," *WC*, 13-38.

50.   As one example of the point forced, Baugh quotes Ross Kraemer in defense of his position, but omits an important part of her conclusions in *Her Share of the Blessings*. He omits: "The evidence we have considered suggests that, under some circumstances, priesthoods and other religious offices are related to the power, prestige, and authority of those who held office." (90)

51.   *SEG* 36, no. 1518.

52.   White, *Ephesos*, 58.

53.   Sterling, *EWEC*, 1:91. He also makes this observation regarding the influence of the Dionysus cult: "The importance of this cult for women is that it afforded them an opportunity to assert themselves outside of a male-dominated context." (89)

54.   Ibid., 92.

55.   Anderson, *An Emergent Theology For Emerging Churches*, 130-4.

56.   Bellville, "Teaching and Usurping Authority, 1 Timothy 2:11-15," *DBE*, 223.

57.   Ferguson, *Women in the Church*, 35-6.

58.   Susan T. Foh, *Women and the Word of God* (Phillipsburg, NJ: Presbyterian & Reformed Pub. Co., 1978), p. 239.

59.   George W. Knight III, *The Role Relationship of Men and Women* (Phillipsburg, PA: Presbyterian and Reformed Pub. Co., 1985), 19.

60.   Margaret Y. MacDonald, "Rereading Paul: Early Interpreters of Paul on Women and Gender," *WCO*, 245-6.

61.   Osburn, *Women in the Church*, 249.

62.   Sarah Sumner, *Men and Women in the Church: Building Consensus on Christian Leadership* (Downer's Grove, IL: InterVarsity Press, 2003), 257. See also Letha Dawson Scanzoni and Nancy A. Hardesty. *All We're Meant to Be: Biblical Feminism for Today*. 3rd ed. Grand Rapids: William B. Eerdmans Pub. Co., 1992. They take a similar path by not commenting on 1 Timothy 2:13.

63.   See Osburn, *Women in the Church*, 266-67, *www.gal328.org* and *www.cbeinternational.org*.

64.   Mary Kassian, *The Feminist Mistake* (Wheaton, IL: Crossway Books, 2005), 277. See also the argument by Groothuis, "Equal in Being, Unequal in Role: Exploring the Logic of Woman's Subordination," *DBE*, 332: "Whether within marriage or within the Trinity, subordination is not functional but ontological when it defines and characterizes a person in all his or her aspects, in perpetuity – when subordination is thereby inherent in the very identity of a person."

Appendix C: Visiting Ephesus and Three of its Religions

1.   Sirri Erinc and Necdet Tuncdilek, "The Agricultural Regions of Turkey," *Geographical Review* 42 (Apr., 1952): 179-203. "An Anatolian bas-relief of several centuries before Christ depicts a Hittite king at prayer holding in his hands a sheaf of wheat and bunch of grapes." (179) Ephesus lay south of one of the largest clusters of vineyards in all of Asia Minor – home to thousands of wine growers. (182)

2.   Thomas, *Ephesos*, 83.

3.   J. Garstang and O. R. Gurney, *The Geography of the Hittite Empire*, British Institute of Archaeology, No. 5 (Ankara, 1959): 83ff. Garstang and Gurney have suggested that Apasas, capital of the Arzawa Empire that is mentioned in Hittite documents, became the city of Ephesus. Their conclusion is that Apasas/Ephesus had grown into a major city at the same time as the Hebrews were occupying Canaan. See also Hermann Genz, "The Early Iron Age in Central Anatolia in Light of Recent Research," *NEA* 63 (Jun., 2000): 111. "Dark age" Anatolia (1200-800 B.C.) knew inhabitants who decided to stay in the region after the fall of the Hittite Empire.

4.   Oster, "Ephesus as a Religious Center under the Principate," 1699-1728. See also Philippe Borgeaud, *Mother of the Gods: From Cybele to the Virgin Mary*, trans. Lysa Hochroth (Baltimore: Johns Hopkins University Press, 2004). Borgeaud suggests that Artemis Ephesia was a "Cybele," a mother goddess. (7-8) Additionally, see LiDonnici, "The Images of Artemis Ephesia and Greco-Roman Worship: A Reconsideration," 389-415. Lynn LiDonnici has suggested that the image of Artemis as a many-breasted deity served to emphasize her role as a nurturing goddess. (409)

5.   Thomas, *Ephesos*, 93-4. Within the 154 representations of Artemis catalogued as of 2004, most are relatively small and would have been inappropriate for a public sanctuary. "A large-scale production of images for private worship must have existed." (94) (see Acts 19:24)

6. Oster, "Ephesus as a Religious Center under the Principate," 1722, 1724. Seven titles from the list found on page 1722 represent translations by the author, based on information from LSJ. The page number of the lexicon for the cited Greek word or an associated word is provided in the following notes.

7. LSJ, 984.

8. Ibid., 2010.

9. Ibid., 790.

10. Ibid., 1629.

11. Ibid., 821.

12. Ibid., 795.

13. Ibid., 1960.

14. Johnson, "Musical Evenings," 70. LSJ, 800.

15. Horsley, "The Inscriptions of Ephesos and the New Testament," 141.

16. LiDonnici, "The Images of Artemis Ephesia and Greco-Roman Worship: A Reconsideration," 394.

17. Horsley, "The Inscriptions of Ephesos and the New Testament," 142. The name of the goddess was also applied to people beyond Ephesus. See, for example, an inscription from central Greece: "Artemisia, wife of Straton." (SEG 29, no. 493)

18. G. H. R. Horsley, "The Mysteries of Artemis Ephesia in Pisidia: A New Inscribed Relief," Anatolian Studies 42 (1992): 121-3.

19. Portefaix, "The Image of Artemis Ephesia – A Symbolic Configuration Related to Her Mysteries?" 614-6.

20. Oster, "Ephesus as a Religious Center under the Principate," 1717-19.

21. Horsley, "The Inscriptions of Ephesos and the New Testament," 143.

22. Ibid. Additionally, Beate Dignas, Economy of the Sacred in Hellenistic and Roman Asia Minor, (174) provides a helpful map that illustrates the extent both north and east of the supposed goddess's estates in the Cayster valley.

23. Dignas, Economy of the Sacred in Hellenistic and Roman Asia Minor, 144.

24. F. Sokolowski, "Fees and Taxes in the Greek Cults," HTR 47 (July, 1954): 162-3: A first century B.C. decree by the people of Ephesus prescribed the following tax to be paid to the temple of Artemis: birth – 1

drachma; illegal birth – 100 drachmas; grants of various honors – 1 denarius; lease – 60 drachmas.

25. Ibid., 163.

26. Oster, "Ephesus as a Religious Center under the Principate," 1718.

27. Ibid.

28. Baugh, "Cult Prostitution in New Testament Ephesus: A Reappraisal," 457.

29. Richard Oster, "Holy Days in Honor of Artemis," *New Documents Illustrating Early Christianity: A Review of the Greek Inscriptions and Papyri published in 1979*, 4:74-82. ed. G. R. Horsley (North Ryde, New South Wales: The Ancient History Documentary Research Centre, Macquarie University, 1987), 77.

30. Irene Ringwood Arnold, "Festivals of Ephesus," *AJA* 76 (Jan., 1972): 18.

31. Metin And, "On the Dramatic Fertility Rituals of Anatolian Turkey," *Asian Folklore Studies* 39 (1980): 85-104.

32. Maria Aurenhammer, "Sculptures of Gods and Heroes From Ephesos," *Ephesos*, 270. The statue also included imagery from other goddess images as well, such as that of Artemis.

33. Ibid., 267-268.

34. Ibid., 268. Additionally, she notes that "Dionysos's popularity is apparent, too, in the wealth of table legs and herm busts featuring dionysiac motifs; many of these adorn the apartments of slope house 2."

35. Ibid., 267.

36. Oster, "Ephesus as a Religious Center under the Principate," 1673-74.

37. Ibid., 1674. Compare this with the account from Plutarch, *Lives, Antony*. 24.3. When Marc Antony entered Ephesus, women dressed like Bacchanals, and men and boys like Satyrs and Pans led the way before him, the people hailing him as Dionysus.

38. Ibid., 1676. See also *IEph* 275 and 3329.

39. David Magie, "Egyptian Deities in Asia Minor in Inscriptions and on Coins," *AJA* 57 (July, 1953): 163-87.

40. Stanislawski, 427-44. "The long prehistoric existence and association of the Great Mother cult and Dionysus have important bearing on the acceptance of the Dionysus cult and wine, and on expanded commercial production." (427).

41. Kraemer, "Ecstasy and Possession: The Attraction of Women to the Cult of Dionysus," *HTR*, 57.

42. Ibid., 60-61. According to Apollodorus, 3.5.2, as a result of not honoring Dionysus, women were driven mad, and on the mountains they devoured their own infants.

43. Kreitzer, "'Crude Language' and 'Shameful Things Done in Secret' (Ephesians 5.4, 12): Allusions to the Cult of Demeter/Cybele in Hierapolis?" 61.

44. Ibid., 63. Kreitzer provides a translation of the scholion on Lucian's *Dialogues of the Courtesans* 7.4, that describes the women-only *Haloa* festival (*Haloai* being the Greek word for vine branches).

45. Joan Burton, "Women's Commensality in the Ancient Greek World," *Greece & Rome* 45 (Oct., 1998): 153.

46. Ibid., 156. She also notes that "mixed *thiasoi* (groups of Dionysiac worshipers) that involved initiation were including males by the fifth century B.C., and the group activities doubtless included eating and drinking rites." (155). See also Turcan, 125.

47. Ibid., 155.

48. Ibid., 151.

49. Kraemer, "Ecstasy and Possession: The Attraction of Women to the Cult of Dionysus," *HTR*, 72.

50. Livy, *History of Rome*, 39.15. See also Kraemer, *Her Share of the Blessings*, 41.

51. Kraemer, "Ecstasy and Possession: The Attraction of Women to the Cult of Dionysus," *HTR*, 72.

52. Kraemer, *Her Share of the Blessings*, 41.

53. *Bacchae*, 150, 241, 865, 930, 1123, 146-9.

54. J. A. Haldane, "Musical Instruments in Greek Worship," *Greece & Rome* 13 (Apr., 1966): 102.

55. See, for example, Goff, *Citizen Bacchae: Women's Ritual Practice in Ancient Greece*, 85: Ancient Greek choruses, a combination of song and dance, appear to have had the primary function of erotic display. Additionally, Doubleday, 119: In the ancient Mesopotamian Ishtar/Astarte cult, the frame drum was used along with dancing as a type of aphrodisiac.

56. Otto, *Dionysus: Myth and Cult*, 142.

57. Ibid, 121. See also Eric Csapo, "Riding the Phallus for Dionysus: Iconology, Ritual, and Gender-Role De/Construction," *Phoenix* 51 (Autumn-Winter 1997): 253-95. "Dionysus is the god of things that spring up,

fountains, young shoots...vines in particular, and the grape." (258) See also Chapter 5, note 16 and Chapter 7, note 11.

58. *Exhortation*, 31: "Wreathed with snakes, they perform the distribution of portions of their victims, shouting the name of Eva, that Eva through whom error entered into the world; and a consecrated snake is the emblem of the Bacchic orgies."

59. Pomeroy, *Goddesses, Whores, Wives, and Slaves*, 222.

60. Turcan, *The Cults of the Roman Empire*, 75-129. Robert Turcan refers to Isis as "our Lady of the Waves" and describes the numerous water-related rituals that were part of her cult, as well as the connection with the Nile. Places of Isis worship have been uncovered that included an elaborate in-house stream bordered by statues of the supposed goddess.

61. Magie, "Egyptian Deities in Asia Minor in Inscriptions and on Coins," 166-7.

62. Turcan, *The Cults of the Roman Empire*, 114-6. The festival was called "Vessel of Isis." Turcan writes that the procession "reached the port where a brand-new boat waited, decorated with Egyptian-style paintings. The high priest then uttered a solemn prayer, purifying the boat's hull with a torch, an egg and some sulphur." (116)

63. Kraemer, *Her Share of the Blessings*, 74.

64. Ibid., 77.

65. Pomeroy, *Goddesses, Whores, Wives, and Slaves*, 219.

66. Oxyrhynchus Papyrus 1380, lines 214-16, as translated by S. Pomeroy (219).

Appendix D: Wiccan and New Age Spiritualism, the "Queen of Heaven," and "Emerging Churches" – A Brief Look at Present-Day Mysticism

1. See, for example, Borysenko, *A Woman's Journey to God*. Joan Borysenko begins her influential book by referring to Artemis, whose name means "bear." She indicates that the bear is a strong archetype for her. She writes that, "The bear walks on a path of her own. She dares to question. And she dares to believe. She fights for her children." (xv)

2. Carol P. Christ, "Why Women Need the Goddess: Phenomenological, Psychological, and Political Reflections," in *The Politics of Women's Spirituality: Essays on the Rise of Spiritual Power Within the Feminist Movement*, 71-86, ed. Charlene Spretnak (New York: Anchor Press, 1982). Carol Christ was among the first to suggest that the exclusively male focus of Chris-

tianity was psychologically harmful to women. She suggested that women needed to meditate on and worship someone other than a male deity. (73)

3.   Philip G. Davis, *Goddess Unmasked: The Rise of Neopagan Feminist Spirituality* (Dallas, TX: Spence Pub. Co., 1998), 343.

4.   Charlotte Allen, "Scholars and the Goddess: Historically Speaking, the "Ancient" Rituals of the Goddess Movement Are Almost Certainly Bunk," *The Atlantic Monthly* 287 (January 2001), 1.

5.   Starhawk and Valentine, *The Twelve Wild Swans*, 240.

6.   Ochshorn, "Goddesses and the Lives of Women," *WGT*, 399.

7.   Cynthia Eller, *Living in the Lap of the Goddess: The Feminist Spirituality Movement in America* (Boston: Beacon Press, 1993), 139.

8.   Emily Erwin Culpepper, "Missing Goddesses, Missing Women: Reflections of a Middle-Aged Amazon," *WGT*, 433.

9.   Allen, 1.

10.   W. M. Ramsey, "The Geographical Conditions Determining History and Religion in Asia Minor," *The Geographical Journal* 20 (Sept. 1902): 273.

11.   The earliest (Greek) text of the hymn was found in a Coptic Orthodox Christmas liturgy. The first two lines announce, "Beneath your compassion, we take refuge, mother of God...." (author's translation)

12.   *IAph2007* inscription no. 15.353, *Invocation*. The inscription includes the Greek word *theotokos* (God-bearer), the word used to describe Mary by the Council of Ephesos (431 A.D.).

13.   Borgeaud, *Mother of the Gods: From Cybele to the Virgin Mary*. Borgeaud sets out to disconnect worship of Cybele from early veneration or worship of Mary. In the process he succeeds in piecing together evidence to show that the two are linked. For example the oldest hymn to Mary borrows imagery from the Cybele cult. (130) In summary he suggests that in the process of religious blending, Cybele "lost her ancient attributes and assumed the loving, protective stance of the Meter Theou, the Mother of God, her close neighbor." (131)

14.   *The Documents of Vatican II*, 86. During the conclusion of the third session of the Second Vatican Council, Nov. 21, 1964, Giovanni Battista Montini (Paul VI) conferred the title "Mother of the Church" on Mary.

15.   On October 11, 1954, Eugenio Pacelli (Pius XII) gave the encyclical *Ad Caeli Reginam* that proclaimed the queenship of Mary. From the Introduction: "From the earliest ages of the catholic church a Christian people, whether in time of triumph or more especially in time of crisis, has addressed prayers of petition and hymns of praise and veneration to the

Queen of Heaven." See *www.vatican.va* for the full text. See also Joanne Howe, *A Change of Habit* (Nashville: Christian Communications, 1986), 114: "As a Roman Catholic, I was taught that devotion to Mary was the way to Christ. She was my intercessor, my hope, my message bearer before the throne of God. As a child, crowning Mary as the Queen of Heaven and earth was a special event, and it was a privilege for any girl to crown Mary as the 'May Queen!'"

16.   Rosalind Brooke and Christopher Brooke, *Popular Religion in the Middle Ages* (London: Thames and Hudson, 1984), 32.

17.   The *Vox Populi Mariae Mediatrici* movement in Catholicism represents this trend in thinking. The January 31, 1985 sermon by Karol Wojtyla (John Paul II) at the Marian shrine in Guayaquil, Ecuador represents the first formal use of the title "Coredemptrix."

18.   See *www.spiralgoddess.com* and *northernway.org*.

19.   The English rendition of the *Salve Regina* ("Hail Holy Queen") prayer is available at *www.usccb.org/liturgy/rosary.shtml*.

20.   Spretnak, *Missing Mary: The Queen of Heaven and Her Re-Emergence in the Modern Church*, 175.

21.   Ibid., 151.

22.   Ibid., 75.

23.   Daly, *Beyond God the Father*, 87. See the *Apostolic Constitution of Giovanni Maria Mastai-Ferretti* (Pius IX) *on the Immaculate Conception* (8 December 1854).

24.   Spretnak, *Missing Mary: The Queen of Heaven and Her Re-Emergence in the Modern Church*, 131.

25.   *L'Osservatore Romano*, Weekly Edition in English (20 September 1995), 7. Available at *www.ewtn.com* (*Eternal Word Television Network*).

26.   *The Documents of Vatican II*, 92.

27.   The original Spanish address is available at *www.vatican.va*.

28.   Juliana of Norwich, *Revelations of Divine Love*, Chapter 57. Note: Juliana is thought to have been a Benedictine nun who lived in medieval England.

29.   Joseph Alois Ratzinger (Benedict XVI), "Pope Urges the Practice of Eucharistic Adoration," *Zenit News* (June 10, 2007): "May the Virgin Mary, Eucharistic Woman, lead us into the secret of true adoration." Available at *www.zenit.org*.

30.   Catholic tradition has embraced the belief that Mary appeared to Juan Diego Cuauhtlatoatzin near Mexico City from December 9 through December 12, 1531.

31.   I am indebted to John and Fernanda Cannon for their understanding of the religious syncretism found in images of Mary, especially those in Latin America. The Cannons served as missionaries in Ecuador.

32.   Kidd, *The Secret Life of Bees*. The oldest sister states that her worship of the Black Madonna represents her mother's Catholicism with the addition of other ingredients. (90)

33.   Ibid., 141.

34.   Ibid.

35.   McLaren, *A Generous Orthodoxy*, 228.

36.   Ibid., 221.

37.   Young, Jacobsen, and Cummings *The Shack*. "Papa's" wrists bear the marks of the cross as well. (95) Historically, the view has been called Patripassianism – the belief that the Father died on the cross with the Son.

38.   Ibid., 177-82. Young has Jesus say that those who love him, his Church, include many who "are not part of any Sunday morning or religious institution." (182)

39.   Ibid., 96. Young suggests that the Father did not have to forsake the Son at the cross.

40.   Ibid. In the novel the main character, Mack, has benefited little from reading Scripture. For him "God's voice had been reduced to paper, and even that paper had to be moderated and deciphered by the proper authorities and intellects." (65-6) Young also uses supposed dialogue by God to put distance between "Sunday School" and the idea of counsel and knowledge that can truly renew us (98).

41.   Mike Perschon, "Desert Youth Worker: Disciplines, Mystics, and the Contemplative Life," *www.youthspecialties.com*.

42.   See Roger Oakland, *Faith Undone* (Silverton, OR: Lighthouse Trails Pub., 2007). Roger Oakland provides a helpful introductory look at the "emerging church" movement's use of mysticism. See also D. A. Carson, *Becoming Conversant With the Emerging Church: Understanding a Movement and Its Implications* (Grand Rapids: Zondervan, 2005). Donald Carson provides a helpful in-depth review. One of the weaknesses of his work is his conclusion regarding the Disciples of Christ (and Churches of Christ) and baptism. (85) He does not see that apostolic teaching describes immer-

son baptism as a seal of possession and an action of God's grace (more than just a symbol).

43.   Fred Peatross, "Discipleship: From Application of Scripture to Performance of Scripture," *New Wineskins* (May-June 2008). Available at *www.wineskins.com*. See chapter 13, note 6 for more about the essay.

44.   Max Lucado, *The Great House of God* (Dallas, TX: Word Pub., 1997), 74: "The disciples disregarded the Word of God. That was their second mistake. Rather than consult the Scriptures, they listened to their fears. Jesus corrects this by appearing to them and conducting a Bible study [Luke 24:25-27]." He also makes the pointed comment, "I would take issue with the person who justifies her drug addiction as a way to draw near to the mystical side of God." (76)

45.   Ibid., 73: "His plan hasn't changed. Jesus still speaks to believers through believers. "The whole body depends on Christ, and all the parts of the body are joined and held together. Each part does its own work to make the whole body grow and be strong with love" (Eph. 4:15)." Additionally, he writes, "God has given each part of the body of Christ an assignment. One way God reveals his will to you is through the church. He speaks to one member of his body through another member." (74)

46.   Brian D. McLaren, *The Secret Message of Jesus: Uncovering the Truth that Could Change Everything* (Nashville: W. Pub. Group, 2006), 110.

47.   Ibid., 111. Brian McLaren writes, "Religious people today may differ on how much water should be used... but my sense is that the amount of water is less important than the amount of commitment and sincerity with which you choose to go public and identify with Jesus...."

48.   McLaren, *A Generous Orthodoxy*, 29.

49.   Ibid., 290-1.

50.   Ibid., 193.

51.   Ibid., 152-3. See also 198: "Isn't truth often best understood in a conversation, a dialectic (or trialectic), or a dynamic tension?"

52.   Ibid., 35. See also his essay entitled "Why I Am Incarnational" in pages 245-66.

53.   Ibid., 255.

54.   Ibid.

55.   Bede Griffith, *Christ in India: Essays Towards a Hindu-Christian Dialogue* (New York: Charles Scribners Sons, 1966), 247.

56.   McLaren, *A Generous Orthodoxy*, 257-8.

57.   Ibid., 262.

Selected Sources

Amyx, Patty. "Simplicity." *21st Century Christian Magazine* 71 (Jan/Feb 2008): 40-3.

Anderson, Ray S. *An Emergent Theology For Emerging Churches.* Downers Grove, IL: InterVarsity Press, 2006.

Arnold, Clinton E. *Powers of Darkness: Principalities & Powers in Paul's Letters.* Downers Grove, IL: InterVarsity Press, 1992.

Barth, Marcus. *Ephesians 4-6.* The Anchor Bible. Garden City, NY: Doubleday & Co., 1974.

Baugh, S. M. "Cult Prostitution in New Testament Ephesus: A Reappraisal." *Journal of the Evangelical Theological Society* 42 (September 1999): 443-60.

Berding, Kenneth. "Polycarp of Smyrna's View of the Authorship of 1 and 2 Timothy." *Vigiliae Christianae* 53 (Nov., 1999): 349-360.

Birkerts, Sven. *The Gutenberg Elegies: The Fate of Reading in an Electronic Age.* Boston: Faber and Faber, 1994.

Borgeaud, Philippe. *Mother of the Gods: From Cybele to the Virgin Mary.* Translated by Lysa Hochroth. Baltimore: Johns Hopkins University Press, 2004.

Borysenko, Joan. *A Woman's Journey to God, Finding the Feminine Path.* New York: Riverhead Books, 1999.

Bradshaw, Tom and Bonnie Nichols. *Reading at Risk: A Survey of Literary Reading in America.* Research Division Report #46. Washington, DC: National Endowment for the Arts, 2004.

Brents, T. W. *The Gospel Plan of Salvation.* Nashville: McQuiddy Printing Co., 1874; reprint ed. Gospel Advocate Co., 1973.

Bultmann, Rudolf. *Jesus Christ and Mythology.* New York: Charles Scribner's Sons, 1958.

Bumbalough, Debbie and Dwina Willis, editors. *Woman to Woman, A Guide to Teaching and Leading Women.* Nashville: Gospel Advocate Co., 2007.

Carson, D. A. *Becoming Conversant With the Emerging Church: Understanding a Movement and Its Implications.* Grand Rapids: Zondervan, 2005.

Clawson, Julie. "Welcoming the Awakened Woman." *Next-Wave Ezine* (Oct., 2007). Available at *www.the-next-wave.org.*

Clement of Alexandria. Loeb Classical Library. Translated by G. W. Butterworth. Cambridge: Harvard University Press, 1960.

Cottrell, Jack. "The Gender of Jesus and the Incarnation: A Case Study in Feminist Hermeneutics." *Stone-Campbell Journal* 3 (Fall 2000): 171-94.

_____. *Headship, Submission & the Bible: Gender Roles in the Home.* Joplin, MO: College Press Pub. Co., 2008.

Dahl, Nils Alstrup, David Hellholm, Vemund Blomkvist, and Tord Fornberg. *Studies in Ephesians: Introductory Questions, Text- & Edition-Critical Issues, Interpretation of Texts and Themes.* Wissenschaftliche Untersuchungen zum Neuen Testamentum; 131. Tübingen: Mohr Siebeck, 2000.

Daly, Mary. *Amazon Grace: Re-calling the Courage to Sin Big.* New York: Palgrave Macmillan, 2006.

_____. *Beyond God the Father: Toward a Philosophy of Women's Liberation.* Boston: Beacon Press, 1973.

Davis, Philip G. *Goddess Unmasked: The Rise of Neopagan Feminist Spirituality.* Dallas, TX: Spence Pub., 1998.

Dever, Mark E. "Baptist Polity and Elders." *Journal for Baptist Theology and Ministry* 3 (Spring 2005): 5-37.

Dignas, Beate. *Economy of the Sacred in Hellenistic and Roman Asia Minor.* New York: Oxford University Press, 2002.

Dudrey, Russ. "Submit Yourselves to One Another": A Socio-Historical Look at the Household Code of Ephesians 5:15-6:9." *Restoration Quarterly* 41 (First Quarter, 1999): 27-44.

Eller, Cynthia. *Living in the Lap of the Goddess: The Feminist Spirituality Movement in America.* Boston: Beacon Press, 1993.

Ferguson, Everett. "Authority and Tenure of Elders." *Restoration Quarterly* 18 (1975): 142-50.

_____. *Backgrounds of Early Christianity.* 3rd ed. Grand Rapids: William B. Eerdmans Pub. Co., 2003.

_____. "Lifting Our Voices." *Gospel Advocate* (Feb., 2000): 12-13.

_____. *Women in the Church.* Chickasha, OK: Yeomen Press, 2003.

Fitzgerald, John T., Thomas H. Olbricht, and L. Michael White, editors. *Early Christianity and Classical Culture, Comparative Studies in Honor of Abraham J. Malherbe.* Supplements to Novum Testamentum; 110. New York: E. J. Brill, 2003.

Foh, Susan T. *Women and the Word of God*. Phillipsburg, NJ: Presbyterian & Reformed Pub. Co., 1978.

French, Valerie. "Midwives and Maternity Care in the Roman World." In *Rescuing Creusa: New Methodological Approaches to Women in Antiquity*, 69-84. Edited by Marilyn Skinner. *Helios*, New Series 13(2), 1986.

Goff, Barbara. *Citizen Bacchae: Women's Ritual Practice in Ancient Greece*. Berkeley, CA: University of California Press, 2004.

Guthrie, Stephen R. "Singing, in the Body and in the Spirit." *Journal of the Evangelical Theological Society* 46 (December 2003): 633-46.

Guy, Cynthia Dianne. *What About the Women? A Study of New Testament Scriptures Concerning Women*. Nashville: Gospel Advocate Co., 2005.

Haines-Eitzen, Kim. "Girls Trained in Beautiful Writing": Female Scribes in Roman Antiquity and Early Christianity." *Journal of Early Christian Studies* 6 (Winter 1998): 629-646.

Hicks, John Mark and Bobby Valentine. *Kingdom Come: Embracing the Spiritual Legacy of David Lipscomb and James Harding*. Abilene, TX: Leafwood Pub., 2006.

Hoehner, Harold W. *Ephesians, An Exegetical Commentary*. Grand Rapids: Baker Academic, 2002.

Horsley, G. H. R. "The Inscriptions of Ephesos and the New Testament." *Novum Testamentum* 34 (Apr., 1992): 105-68.

Iyengar, Sunil, Tom Bradshaw, Bonnie Nichols, Kelli Rogowski, and Sarah Sullivan. *To Read or Not to Read: A Question of National Consequence*. Research Division Report #47. Washington, DC: National Endowment for the Arts, 2007.

Jividen, Jimmy. *Worship in Song*. Fort Worth, TX: Star Bible Pub., 1987.

Johnson, William A. "Musical Evenings in the Early Empire: New Evidence From a Greek Papyrus with Musical Notation." *The Journal of Hellenic Studies* 120 (2000): 57-85.

Jones, C. P. "Stigma: Tattooing and Branding in Graeco-Roman Antiquity." *The Journal of Roman Studies* 77 (1987): 139-55.

Kassian, Mary. *The Feminist Mistake*. Wheaton, IL: Crossway Books, 2005.

Kelly, J. N. D. *A Commentary on the Pastoral Epistles; I Timothy, II Timothy, Titus*. Harper's New Testament Commentaries. New York: Harper & Row, 1963.

Kidd, Sue Monk. *The Dance of the Dissident Daughter: A Woman's Journey From Christian Tradition to the Sacred Feminine.* San Francisco: HarperSanFrancisco, 1996.

_____. *The Secret Life of Bees.* New York: Viking, 2002.

Kimball, Dan. *The Emerging Church.* Grand Rapids: Zondervan, 2003.

King, Karen L., editor. *Women and Goddess Traditions in Antiquity and Today.* Minneapolis: Fortress Press, 1997.

Kinnaman, David and Gabe Lyons. *UnChristian: What a New Generation Really Thinks About Christianity – and Why it Matters.* Grand Rapids: Baker Books, 2007.

Knight, George W. III. *The Role Relationship of Men and Women.* Phillipsburg, PA: Presbyterian and Reformed Pub. Co., 1985.

Koester, Helmut, editor. *Ephesos, Metropolis of Asia, An Interdisciplinary Approach to its Archaeology, Religion, and Culture.* Cambridge: Harvard University Press, 2004.

Köstenberger, Andreas J. and Thomas R. Schreiner, editors. *Women in the Church: An Analysis and Application of 1 Timothy 2:9-15.* 2nd ed. Grand Rapids: Baker Academic, 2005.

Kraemer, Ross S. "Ecstasy and Possession: The Attraction of Women to the Cult of Dionysus." *The Harvard Theological Review* 72 (Jan., 1979): 55-80.

_____. *Her Share of the Blessings: Women's Religions Among Pagans, Jews, and Christians in the Greco-Roman World.* New York: Oxford University Press, 1992.

Kraemer, Ross Shepard and Mary Rose D'Angelo, editors. *Women and Christian Origins.* New York: Oxford University Press, 1999.

Kreitzer, Larry J. "'Crude Language' and 'Shameful Things Done in Secret' (Ephesians 5.4, 12): Allusions to the Cult of Demeter/Cybele in Hierapolis?" *Journal for the Study of the New Testament* 71 (September 1998): 51-77.

Lena, Marguerite. "A Creative Difference: Educating Women." In *Women in Christ, Toward a New Feminism,* 312-23. Edited by Michelle M. Schumacher. Grand Rapids: William B. Eerdmans Pub. Co., 2004.

Lewis, Jack P. *Leadership Questions Confronting the Church.* Nashville: Christian Communications, 1985.

_____. "New Testament Authority for Music in Worship." In *The Instrumental Music Issue,* 14-59. Edited by Bill Flatt. Nashville: Gospel Advocate Co., 1987.

LiDonnici, Lynn R. "The Images of Artemis Ephesia and Greco-Roman Worship: A Reconsideration." *The Harvard Theological Review* 85 (Oct., 1992): 389-415.

Lightfoot, Neil R. "Exegesis of Ephesians 5:19 and Colossians 3:16." *Abilene Christian University Lectures, 1988.*

_____. *How We Got the Bible,* 3rd ed. New York: Fine Communications, 2003.

_____. *The Role of Women: New Testament Perspectives.* Memphis, TN: Student Association Press, 1978.

Lipscomb, David, Elisha Granville Sewell, and M. C. Kurfees. *Questions Answered, Being a Compilation of Queries with Answers by D. Lipscomb and E. G. Sewell, Covering a Period of Forty Years of Their Joint Editorial Labors on the Gospel Advocate.* Nashville: Gospel Advocate Co., 1921; reprint ed., Gospel Advocate Co., 1974.

Llewelyn, S. R. "Baptism and Salvation." In *New Documents Illustrating Early Christianity: A Review of the Greek Inscriptions and Papyri Published 1984-85,* 8:176-79. Edited by S. R. Llewelyn. Grand Rapids: William B. Eerdmans Pub. Co., 1998.

Love, Mark, Douglas A. Foster, and Randall J. Harris. *Seeking a Lasting City: The Church's Journey in the Story of God.* Abilene, TX: ACU Press, 2005.

Lucado, Max. *The Great House of God.* Dallas, TX: Word Pub., 1997.

Magie, David. "Egyptian Deities in Asia Minor in Inscriptions and on Coins." *American Journal of Archaeology* 57 (July, 1953): 163-87.

_____. *Roman Rule in Asia Minor.* 2 vols. Princeton, NJ: Princeton University Press, 1950.

McLaren, Brian D. *A Generous Orthodoxy.* Grand Rapids: Zondervan, 2004.

_____. *The Secret Message of Jesus: Uncovering the Truth that Could Change Everything.* Nashville: W. Pub. Group, 2006.

Moo, Douglas. "What Does it Mean Not to Teach or Have Authority Over Men? (1 Timothy 2:11-15)." In *Recovering Biblical Manhood and Womanhood,* 176-92. Edited by John Piper and Wayne Grudem. Wheaton, IL: Crossway Books, 1991.

Moritz, Thorsten. *A Profound Mystery: The Use of the Old Testament in Ephesians.* Supplements to Novum Testamentum; 85. New York: E. J. Brill, 1996.

Murphy, Cullen. *The Word According to Eve.* New York: Houghton Mifflin Company, 1998.

Nilsson, Martin P. "The Bacchic Mysteries of the Roman Age." *The Harvard Theological Review* 46 (Oct., 1953): 175-202.

Osburn, Carroll D., editor. *Essays on Women in Earliest Christianity.* 2 vols. Joplin, MO: College Press Pub. Co., 1993-95.

_____. *Women in the Church: Reclaiming the Ideal.* Abilene, TX: ACU Press, 2001.

Oster, Richard. "The Ephesian Artemis as an Opponent of Early Christianity." *Jahrbuch für Antike und Christentum* 19 (1976): 24-44.

_____. "The Ephesian Artemis "Whom all Asia and the World Worship" (Acts 19:27): Respresentative Epigraphical Testimony to 'ΑΡΤΕΜΙΣ ΕΦΕΣΙΑ Outside Ephesos." In *Transmission and Reception: New Testament Text-Critical and Exegetical Studies,* 212-31. Texts and Studies Third Series 4. Edited by J. W. Childers and D. C. Parker. Piscataway, NJ: Gorgias Press, 2006.

_____. "Ephesus as a Religious Center under the Principate, I. Paganism before Constantine." In *Aufstieg und Niedergang der römischen Welt,* II.18.3: 1661-1728. Berlin: Walter de Gruyter, 1980.

_____. "Holy Days in Honor of Artemis." In *New Documents Illustrating Early Christianity: A Review of the Greek Inscriptions and Papyri published in 1979,* 4:74-82. Edited by G. H. R. Horsley. North Ryde, New South Wales: The Ancient History Documentary Research Centre, Macquarie University, 1987.

Otto, Walter F. *Dionysus: Myth and Cult.* Translated by Robert B. Palmer. Bloomington, IN: Indiana University Press, 1965.

Peatross, Fred. "Discipleship: From Application of Scripture to Performance of Scripture." *New Wineskins* (May-June 2008).

Pierce, Ronald W., Rebecca Merrill Groothuis, and Gordon D. Fee, editors. *Discovering Biblical Equality: Complementarity Without Hierarchy.* Downers Grove, IL: InterVarsity Press, 2005.

Pomeroy, Sarah B. *Goddesses, Whores, Wives, and Slaves.* New York: Schocken Books, 1995.

Portefaix, Lilian. "The Image of Artemis Ephesia – A Symbolic Configuration Related to Her Mysteries?" in *100 Jahre Österreichische Forschungen in Ephesos. Akten des Symposions, Wien, 1995,* 611-5. Edited by H. Friesinger and F. Krinzinger. Vienna: Verlag der Österreichischen Akademie der Wissenchaften, 1999.

Prior, Kenneth F. W. *The Gospel in a Pagan Society.* Downers Grove, IL: InterVarsity Press, 1975.

Reynolds, Joyce, Charlotte Roueché, and Gabriel Bodard. *Inscriptions of Aphrodisias.* 2007. Available at *http://insaph.kcl.ac.uk/iaph2007.*

Robinson, J. Armitage. *St. Paul's Epistle to the Ephesians.* 2nd ed. London: James Clarke & Co., 1904.

Rogers, Cleon L. "The Dionysian Background of Ephesians 5:18." *Bibliotheca Sacra* 136 (1979): 249-57.

Rostovzeff, Michael I. *The Social and Economic History of the Roman Empire.* 2nd ed. Revised by P.M. Fraser. Oxford: Clarendon Press, 1998.

Scanzoni, Letha Dawson and Nancy A. Hardesty. *All We're Meant to Be: Biblical Feminism for Today.* 3rd ed. Grand Rapids: William B. Eerdmans Pub. Co., 1992.

Schüssler Fiorenza, Elisabeth. *Bread Not Stone.* Boston: Beacon Press, 1984.

Seim, Turid Karlsen. *The Double Message: Patterns of Gender in Luke-Acts.* Edinburgh: T & T Clark, 1994.

Silvey, Billie, editor. *Trusting Women.* Orange, CA: New Leaf Books, 2002.

Smith, F. LaGard. *Male Spiritual Leadership.* Nashville: 21st Century Christian, 1998.

Spencer, Aida Besançon, Donna F. G. Hailson, Catherine Clark Kroeger, and William David Spencer. *The Goddess Revival.* Grand Rapids: Baker Books, 1995.

Spretnak, Charlene. *Missing Mary: The Queen of Heaven and Her Re-Emergence in the Modern Church.* New York: Palgrave Macmillan, 2004.

_____. *States of Grace: The Recovery of Meaning in the Postmodern Age.* San Francisco: HarperSanFrancisco, 1991.

Stapert, Calvin. *A New Song for an Old World: Musical Thought in the Early Church.* Grand Rapids: William B. Eerdmans Pub. Co., 2007.

Starhawk and Hilary Valentine. *The Twelve Wild Swans: A Journey to the Realm of Magic, Healing, and Action.* San Francisco: HarperSanFrancisco, 2000.

Sumner, Sarah. *Men and Women in the Church: Building Consensus on Christian Leadership.* Downer's Grove, IL: InterVarsity Press, 2003.

Tippens, Daryl L. *That's Why We Sing: Reclaiming the Wonder of Congregational Singing.* Abilene, TX: Leafwood Pub., 2007.

Trebilco, Paul. *The Early Christians in Ephesus from Paul to Ignatius.* Wissenschaftliche Untersuchungen zum Neuen Testamentum; 166. Tübingen: Mohr Siebeck, 2004.

Trible, Phyllis. *God and the Rhetoric of Sexuality.* Minneapolis: Augsburg Fortress Press, 1978.

Turcan, Robert. *The Cults of the Roman Empire.* Translated by Antonia Nevill. Cambridge: Blackwell Pub., 1996.

Weed, Michael R. *The Letters of Paul to the Ephesians, the Colossians, and Philemon.* The Living Word Commentary. Edited by Everett Ferguson. Austin, TX: R. B. Sweet Co., 1971.

Wharton, Edward C. *The Church of Christ.* West Monroe, LA: Howard Book House, 1987.

White, L. Michael. *From Jesus to Christianity: How Four Generations of Visionaries and Storytellers Created the New Testament and Christian Faith.* San Francisco: Harper & Row, 2004.

Woodson, William. "Music in the Early Church." *The Spiritual Sword* 21 (July 1990): 7-10.

Young, Wm. Paul, Wayne Jacobsen, and Brad Cummings. *The Shack.* Los Angeles: Windblown Media, 2007.

Endorsements for *Deceiving Winds*

Well researched and relevant, this study is about connections between the intellectual and spiritual obsessions of antiquity and those of postmoderns. Solomon's dictum comes to mind: there is nothing new under the sun. Ancient mysticism reappears today in a new package, and yet its deceptiveness remains: it is an alternative to bankrupt man-made expressions of faith, but never to a genuine pursuit of Truth. Archaeological and sociological evidence from the Ephesus of 20 centuries ago gives proof of the threats posed to christians then by mystical paths emphasizing the feminine. Morton then convincingly gives examples of contemporary manifestations of the "same winds."

Terry Edwards
Freed Hardeman University

Bruce Morton has been a member of the congregation for which I preached well over a decade. His thoughtful and challenging observations and thinking over those years have been helpful to me and many others who care about the direction of the Lord's church in years to come. This volume which has been produced after years of study, research and presentation is typical of Bruce's careful approach to Biblical topics. My conviction is that this volume will prove to be invaluable in a critical area of study and discussion as we go forward in time. I commend it to concerned and careful students of God's Word.

Cecil A. Hutson
Elder, East Fifth Street church of Christ
Katy, Texas

Bruce Morton has done our brotherhood a great service in writing *Deceiving Winds*. His research is thorough, his writing is plain, and his conclusions are convincing. His respect for Scripture is the hallmark of the book and every believer will benefit from a careful reading of it.

Jay Lockhart
Whitehouse Church of Christ
Whitehouse, Texas

In a time when much of the New Testament is being dismissed as "just cultural," Bruce Morton challenges us to take another look at the striking parallels between our times and those of the first century Ephesians. *Deceiving Winds* is a well-researched exploration of the impact that the worship of Artemis and Dionysus had on the recipients of Paul's letters to the Ephesians and Timothy. Morton applies the insights from his historical research to such contemporary topics as postmodernism, the emerging church, feminism, and congregational leadership. The content of this book thoughtfully addresses the current context, and the information-rich reference section will guide the reader in continuing the important discussions that Morton engages in *Deceiving Winds*.

Bruce McLarty
Vice President of Spiritual Life, Harding University

Bruce Morton's research and application of the pagan religious background of the Artemis-Dionysus cult-worship in Asia Minor, and in particular at Ephesus, opens up the purpose for Paul's emphasis on specific themes in Ephesians and 1 & 2 Timothy. Such themes as Christ's cosmic sovereignty in behalf of the church, the spirit powers - both real and imaginary - against which those ancient Christians wrestled, sexual immorality, debauchery and feminine submission, emphasis on God's true riches and financial banking terms, and the mention of wine in the context of church music. Morton's accuracy of application to the same wrestlings in the modern church is stunningly revealing and convincing. A masterpiece of Scripture exposition and application.

Edward C. Wharton
Sunset International Bible Institute.

I have read much of this fine book, and am re-reading much of what I have read: It is that good! Several impressions arise as I continue to study this new, significant work. First, it is well researched and written for the popular level reader--not a demerit by any means. Second, the writer is most familiar with the text of the New Testament and the various sources of study for the culture and time of his focus--ancient Ephesus in multiple aspects. Third, these two emphases--New Testament text and ancient culture of Ephesus-- are combined to express relevant comparisons and comments on the relation of same to situations faced today. Penetrating insights of ancient and contemporary significance recur time and again as the text unfolds. Knowing something of the writer's background as a former student, I expected no less, but it is pleasant to recognize he has set a high standard for his work and attained it. There is a breaking of new ground in various ways, but when each of these focus areas has been read carefully one sees the merit of the section being studied. There may not always be agreement, but there is always food for careful thought. Finally, it is no small accomplishment to have conceived, researched, and written this fine book. He is to be commended for accomplishing a daunting task. A good book, one to be read somewhat slowly, and mulled over often. I commend it heartily.

William Woodson
Late Professor of Bible, Lipscomb University

"I believe this is a unique and useful tool for Bible study, as it focuses on the various Pauline epistles addressed to those in the area of Ephesus. I am impressed with the depth of knowledge of this background, and with the way it is used to illuminate Paul's teaching. I like how *Deceiving Winds* has drawn attention to Paul's emphasis on the Fatherhood of God, in contrast with the society drenched with speech about a supposed mother goddess.

Bruce Morton has used his research to undermine the false claims of feminism, and to critique the emerging church movement. His knowledge of modern culture currents is impressive. Also, his general conclusions about women's roles are Biblical, I believe.

I think it (*Deceiving Winds*) deserves to be 'out there.'"

Jack W. Cottrell
Professor of Theology, Cincinnati Christian University